Mothering Queerly,
Queering Motherhood

Mothering Queerly, Queering Motherhood

Resisting Monomaternalism in Adoptive, Lesbian, Blended, and Polygamous Families

Shelley M. Park

Published by State University of New York Press, Albany

For information, contact State University of New York Press, Albany, NY
www.sunypress.edu

Production by Diane Ganeles
Marketing by Anne M. Valentine

Library of Congress Cataloging-in-Publication Data

Park, Shelley M., 1961–
    Mothering queerly, queering motherhood : resisting monomaternalism in adoptive, lesbian, blended, and polygamous families / Shelley M. Park.
        p. cm.
    Includes bibliographical references and index.
    ISBN 978-1-4384-4717-9 (hc : alk. paper)–978-1-4384-4716-2 (pb : alk. paper)
    1. Motherhood. 2. Lesbian mothers. 3. Adoptive parents. 4. Interracial adoption. 5. Families. 6. Queer theory. I. Title.

    HQ759.P266 2013
    306.874'3—dc23   2012027591

10 9 8 7 6 5 4 3 2 1

To my daughters, Tomeka and Dakota,
and all of their other mothers,
Trish, Claudia, Anne, Cathy, Karen, and Grandma Kate,
with much love and gratitude for all that you have taught me

⁊≈

Contents

Contents

Acknowledgments

I wrote this book between 2009 and 2012, but in many ways the project started long before this. Since becoming a mother, I have been immersed in thinking about motherhood and for fifteen years I have been writing about it. Some of the ideas contained here have their roots in earlier work presented or published elsewhere. Chapter 2 originates from an essay earlier published as "The Adoptive Maternal Body: A Queer Paradigm for Mothering?" in Park (2006). This article marked my first turn toward using queer theory to think about mothering and the chapter continues to benefit from the astute philosophical insights and friendly editorial assistance of Rebecca Kukla on that earlier version. Chapter 3 represents the evolution in my thinking about transracial adoption over two decades. I thank Maureen Reddy for her feedback on my earliest (although I now think somewhat naïve) published attempts to think about resisting racism in mothering a child of color (see Park 1996) and for encouraging my use of personal narrative in theorizing my experiences of mothering. Chapter 3 also benefits from my cross-disciplinary collaboration with Cheryl Green on legal and scientific interpretations of the best interests of transracially adopted children (see Park and Green 2000). As an African American mother, a social worker and, most importantly, as my friend, Cheryl taught me how to think about adoption from the perspective of black mothers and black social workers. I miss her compassionate, witty, and unflinchingly honest presence in this world, as do many others. Material in Chapter 4 was previously published as "Real (M)othering: The Metaphysics of Maternity in Children's Literature" in *Adoption Matters* (see Park 2005). This essay was one of my early attempts to bring cultural studies to bear on issues of mothering and also my first substantial written attempt to grapple with analyzing the troublesome notion of "real" mother as this plays itself out in various maternal theories and practices. Sally Haslanger, one of the book's editors, gently cautioned me against playing too fast and loose with notions of constructed reality; although the readings of children's literature contained here have taken a rather queerer turn than in the original essay, the chapter continues to benefit from Sally's earlier cautions and guidance. The first half of Chapter 5 draws, in part, on my thinking about queer domestic time and space as explored in the essay "Is Queer Parenting Possible?" published in *Who's Your Daddy? And Other Writings on Queer Parenting* (Park 2009). The second half of Chapter 5, on mothers who use technologies in ways that both replicate and resist ideals of good mothering, draws from the previously published "Cyborg Mothering" in *Mothers Who Deliver: Feminist Interventions in Public and Interpersonal Discourse* (Park 2010). Together these articles marked a turn in my thinking toward queer ways of "doing" family and inhabiting the places we call "home." I am grateful to the editors for providing venues in which I could begin to work out these ideas. Thanks also to the various publishing houses for granting me the right to use portions of my earlier works here.

Along the way, various portions of this work have also been presented at numerous conferences including the annual meetings of the Florida Philosophical Association, the National Women's Studies Association, the Popular Culture Association, the Association for Research on Mothering (now the Motherhood Initiative for Research and Community Involvement), the Society for Women in Philosophy, and the biennial Feminist Ethics and Social Theory conference, among others. I am grateful for the feedback and encouragement I have received from various participants at these conferences. Thank you also to the University of Central Florida for granting me a sabbatical leave in spring 2009 that enabled me to complete the first draft of my book manuscript and to the anonymous reviewers at SUNY Press who encouraged me to reframe the project—originally written around the theme of "real" mothering—as a book on queer mothering. Large portions of this book have been rewritten since its original submission and it is a much better project for their assistance and advice.

I am especially thankful to my partner and colleague, Claudia Schippert, for the expertise in queer theory and the careful editorial eye she has brought to reading this manuscript, as well as for the many books and essays she has brought to my reading table over the past several years. It is always a pleasure to read and discuss books and to critically analyze films and other visual texts with her; several of the scholarly works and cultural artifacts discussed in these pages were discussed with her first and many of the ideas forwarded here would not have germinated without her ongoing intellectual companionship. I am also grateful for Claudia's ongoing love, patience, and assistance in caring for my/our daughters and for me as we have negotiated the real-life challenges of mothering and of "living apart together."

I have been fortunate to benefit from the practical wisdom, example, and challenge of many other mothers as I have raised my children, including friends, acquaintances, and siblings. I am particularly grateful to those who have been other mothers to my/our children. In addition to my partner Claudia, this list includes my elder daughter's birth mother, Trish; my younger daughter's friends' mothers, Karen and Cathy; my ex-husband's partner, Anne; and my daughters' godmother, Kate.

To my own mother, Elizabeth, thank you for loving me even when I was difficult and for teaching me to follow my own path even when it departed from your own. I have missed having you in my life as I have raised my own children, but am immensely grateful to have had you for my mother, even if our time together was cut short. To my father, Ewart, thank you for your unwavering faith—even if occasionally, misplaced—in my abilities to do the right thing and for accepting, and not merely tolerating, the rather queer turns my life took as you aged. Although fathers are not the subject of this book, I am fortunate to have had you in my life.

Last, but certainly not least, thank you to my daughters, Tomeka and Dakota, for being my teachers as I have learned (and am still learning) how to be your mother and for allowing me to share our story. This book would not have been possible without your presence in my life. I love you deeply. For your love and your challenge, I will always be grateful.

Introduction

Mothering Queerly, Queering Motherhood

What does it mean to mother queerly? And how might such practices, if taken seriously, queer the study of motherhood? As someone who mothers outside of heteronormative contexts, I have been struck by how infrequently the scholarship of motherhood questions the heteronormative boundaries of kinship and maternal practice. Too often, studies of motherhood, including feminist studies of motherhood, require the reader to leave her queerness behind. At the same time, in seeking to find a scholarly home within queer theory, I frequently have to bracket my interest in mothering. Insofar as mothers are "breeders" and breeders are the presumed antithesis of queer, the notion of queer mothering is rendered oxymoronic. This volume emerges from a desire to bring feminist theories of motherhood and queer theory into closer conversation. I do so by exploring motherhood and mothering within families created through adoption, lesbian parenting, divorce-extended and marriage-extended kinship networks, or some combination of these. Without denying the differences between and within such forms of kinship, my focus is on what these families have in common, namely the presence of two or more mothers. The polymaternal family, I suggest, is a queer family structure that requires the queering of intimacy in triangulated—or even more complex—relations of mothers and child(ren).

It is my own experiences of mothering within queer (as well as normative) and marginal (as well as privileged) spaces that give rise to this project. Two decades ago, as a married woman, my husband and

1

I (both white) adopted a biracial baby girl in a semi-open adoption. Shortly thereafter, I gave birth to a second daughter. Approximately a decade later, my husband and I separated and I entered a long-term same-sex relationship. As my daughter's father also entered a relationship with another woman, the number of women mothering our children rapidly proliferated. These circumstances, coupled with some unorthodox custodial and living arrangements, a relationship with my elder daughter that became strained during her teenage years, and a relationship with her birth mother that suffered strains of its own during this time, have made it necessary to think about how to negotiate complex relations of intimacy departing significantly from norms of mother–child relationships within the "traditional" nuclear family.

In recounting their experiences within a nontraditional family, my daughters' perspectives frequently have differed from my own and from each other's. My elder daughter has struggled throughout her life with the question of who is her "real" mother. At times, she has insisted that her birth mother is her real mother; at other times, she has rejected her birth mother in favor of me as her real mother. Except in rare instances where she has found joy in the game of accumulating as many mothers as possible (including whoever might walk in the door), Tomeka has resisted queering her familial status. She bemoans being from a "broken" home and is frequently melancholic about the traditional, nuclear family that was lost to her once when she was adopted and then again when my husband and I separated and subsequently divorced. My younger daughter has been less resistant to multiplying her mothers, indeed voluntarily adding two neighborhood mothers as (in her words) her "other mothers." Dakota also has been more flexible than her sister about inhabiting a queer family—a family that provides her with a badge of uniqueness among her largely privileged and traditional peers. Like her sister, however, she will resist the authority of an adult female figure with whom she does not wish to negotiate by insisting that person is "not her [real] mother." As her legally recognized, biologically related parent, I am the only one to consistently escape this rhetoric. Although sometimes cast as "annoying," I am never cast as "unreal," as anything other than her mother.

In many ways, my interest in queer mothering has its origins in the claims about "real" mothers made by my children, as well as other family members, neighbors, friends, members of various professions (social workers, doctors, teachers, and lawyers), and even strangers I have encountered. As a mother, I have been frustrated, angered, dismayed, and dumbfounded by both assertions of and denials of my status as a "real" mother. However, as a feminist philosopher and queer theorist, I also have been fascinated with the complex webs of epistemological, ethical, and political norms embedded in metaphysical claims about reality. Claims about reality frequently serve to render certain phenomena central to our field of vision while relegating other phenomena to the background, to uphold certain values to the exclusion of others, to illuminate or obscure certain relations of power. As Marilyn Frye (1983) so eloquently reminds us in *The Politics of Reality*, the etymology of the word "real" traces to that which is "regal" or "royal"; thus "reality is that which pertains to the one in power." "The ideal king reigns over everything [his] eye can see. . . . What he cannot see is not royal, not real." Noting that the king sees only "what is proper to him," Frye reminds us that "[t]o be visible is to be visible to the king" (155).

What is at stake in claims about who is or is not a "real" mother? What is it that power is unable or unwilling to see? And what would happen if we made it more readily visible? In this book, I argue that what is at stake in our claims about "real" mothers is the notion that children must have *one and only one* mother. Heteronormative power cannot countenance polymaternal families and practices of childrearing. By making such practices visible, perhaps we can begin to queer motherhood.

"Real" Mothers and Monomaternalism

I refer to the ideological assumption that a child can have only one real mother as the assumption of *monomaternalism*. The ideology of monomaternalism stems from a combination of beliefs about the socially normative and the biologically imperative. Claims about what is real are frequently claims about social norms. As gender theorists have noted, claims about "real men" and "real women" are not empirical claims (although often postulated as such) but are, rather, injunctions mandating that we perform gender in socially circumscribed ways. As such, claims about real men and women are intended to keep us in line with gendered binaries and to bring those who might deviate from proscribed norms of masculinity and femininity back into line with normative ideals. Assertions about who is or is not a "real" mother often carry normative weight similarly intended to discipline those who deviate from norms of femininity. Consider, for example, Danzy Senna's (1995) reflections on her childhood relationship with her mother in an essay aptly entitled "To be Real." Here Senna recounts asking her mother "Why can't you be a real mother?" and elaborates the tension between her mother's performance of adult femininity and social norms of mothering as follows:

> In my mind, real mothers wore crisp floral dresses and dia-mond engagement rings; my mother wore blue jeans and a Russian wedding ring given to her from a high school boyfriend. (She had lost the ring my father gave to her.) Real mothers got married in white frills before a church; my mother wed my father in a silver lame mini-dress which she later donated to us kids for Barbie doll clothes. Real mothers painted their nails and colored their hair; my mother used henna. And while real mothers polished the house with lemon-scented Pledge, our house had dog hair stuck to everything. (8)

Claims about real mothers, such as this one, are roughly trans-latable as claims about *good* mothers. Such claims are frequently (although not always consciously) racialized and class-coded claims. Consider Senna's implicit childhood assumptions about how real moth-ers should perform the role of domesticated femininity. Her childhood complaints about her mother include criticisms of her mother's lack of Western-ness (she wears a Russian wedding band instead of a diamond engagement ring; she uses henna rather than hair dye) and her lack of class (she got married in a trashy dress, she wears jeans, and both her nails and house are unpolished). As this makes clear, part of what is at stake in claims about real mothers is white privilege and class privilege as these intersect with norms of femininity.[1]

A failure to recognize the ways in which various interlocking systems of privilege and oppression shape our claims about who has the right to claim the social and legal status of mother stems, in part, from biocentric theories of motherhood. All too often, claims about "real mothers" equate maternal reality with participation in a particular set of biological processes such as pregnancy, birthing, and lactation. Because of participation in these biological processes, a mother is fre-quently thought to possess a special bond with a child such that loving and caring for that child is natural, a matter of "maternal instinct." Conservatives frequently voice such claims; occasionally feminists do as well. In her memoir of motherhood, *Baby Love,* for example, Rebecca Walker (2007) argues, "the love you have for your non-biological child isn't the same as the love you have for your own flesh and blood" (69). Reflecting on her relationship with her stepmother (who claims Rebecca as "one of her children," raised as "her own") and her relationship with her biological mother (with whom the adult Rebecca has a fraught relationship at best), Walker finds herself nonetheless agreeing with a "study that finds that children living with a stepmother receive a good deal less food, health care, and education than they would if they lived with their biological mother" (73). Similarly, reflecting on her relationship with her stepson (the son of her previous lover) and her relationship with the child she now carries in her own womb, Walker claims that she "would do anything for [her] first son, within reason," but that she "would do anything at all for [her] second child, without a doubt" (73). Walker dedicates her book to her newborn infant, "Tenzin, who made it [motherhood] real."

Unfortunately, Walker's privileging of biological motherhood is not uncommon. Within blended families (such as Walker inhabited both as a child and later as an adult), the nonbiological or "step" mother is frequently reduced to a secondary status due to a lack of blood ties (combined, perhaps, with a lack of seniority). Lesbian co-mothers often encounter a similar phenomenon, wherein the status of their relationship to the child borne of their partner is queried and they find themselves named (sometimes by their own partners or ex-partners) as something other than mother. Likewise, the status of adoptive mothers as "real" mothers frequently is queried by those (including one's own children) who insist that a real mother is a biological mother. My adopted daughter frequently echoes Rebecca Walker's sentiments, insisting her "real" mother is her biological mother (despite their inconsistent relationship) and that I love her less than her sister, my biological daughter. Tomeka's commitment to biological essentialism has, moreover, been solidified—like Walker's own—by becoming pregnant with her own child (a child for whom, she claims, "she would do anything"). There is, of course, a circular logic here: Antecedently convinced of biological essentialism, the romanticization of the biological mother–child bond shapes one's phenomenological experiences of biological motherhood; those experiences then become "proof" of the essentialist hypothesis, making it a difficult hypothesis to dislodge.

When we equate "real mother" with "biological mother," we render polymaternal families invisible by representing them as monomaternal ("normal") families, wherein children have one and only one "real" mother. At the same time, we may do psychic harm to children who do not live with their biological mothers, causing children who are adopted or raised by another mother to wonder why their real mother failed to exhibit maternal instinct. If the instinctual drive to care for one's own offspring is as strong as biologically essentialist accounts of motherhood contend, then it is a mystery why any woman might relinquish her child into another woman's care. A failure to interrogate biological essentialism typically leads to the conclusion that either the child must have been unlovable or the biological mother must have been monstrous. Notably, Rebecca Walker struggles with precisely this dilemma. Feeling that her biological mother has hurt her "over the years with neglect, withholding, and . . . ambivalence," Walker asks for an apology. When her mother refuses to provide the requested apology (saying she has "apologized enough"), Walker terminates contact with her (monstrous) mother on the grounds that "she is too emotionally dangerous to me and my unborn son." When her mother agrees to termination of contact, writing that their relationship has been "inconsequential for years" and that, after thirty years, she is "no longer interested in the job" of being Rebecca's mother, Walker shifts into wondering why she (the daughter) is unlovable: "Am I that awful," she asks, "that I should no longer have a mother?" (155–56).

Although children may wonder about their own self-worth in cases of familial unrest, the general public rarely does. In most cases of tension between mothers and their children, therefore, the "monstrous mother" hypothesis is the one that prevails. Because of the romanticization of biological motherhood—combined with a belief in childhood innocence, biological mothers who do not share or cannot live up to these romantic ideals of motherhood, may be deemed "unfit." Indeed, the only exceptions to the normative equation of "real" mother with biological mother occur when biological mothers are publicly adjudicated as neglectful or abusive. In these cases (frequently characterized by racialized and class-coded portrayals of maternal fitness), a secondary mother will be promoted to the status of "real" mother. That her promotion to this status hinges on the first mother's simultaneous demotion, however, once again demonstrates the ideological force of the notion that children must have one and only one mother.

The ideology of monomaternalism, like the ideology of monogamy, promotes practices that uphold the heteropatriarchal, nuclear family. Those who advocate ethical, cultural, and legal norms of "one mother per person"—much like those who advocate ethical, cultural, and legal norms of "one mate per person"—frequently defend their values as determined by biological dictates. Indeed, sociobiological explanations for monogamy typically emphasize the importance of long-term, monogamous, heterosexual pairings as an advantage for successful rearing of the young in the animal kingdom (see, e.g., Kleiman 1977; Young and Wang 2004). However, there is ample evidence in nature for a variety of patterns of raising the young, just as there is ample diversity in mating rituals to be found in both human and non-human nature. We tend not to notice this diversity because of our proclivity to view both human and non-human behavior through a heterosexual lens (Halberstam 2011, 40). By replacing that lens with one that is queer, perhaps we can begin to dislodge monomaternalism and queer our heteronormative notions of kinship.

Monomaternalism, as an ideological doctrine, resides at the intersection of patriarchy (with its insistence that women bear responsibility for biological and social reproduction), heteronormativity (with its insistence that a woman must pair with a man, rather than other women, in order to raise children successfully), capitalism (in its conception of children as private property), and Eurocentrism (in its erasure of polymaternalism in other cultures and historical periods). Monomaternalism is normative in the contemporary, industrialized world—as well as in some postcolonial cultures that have adopted these contemporary Eurocentric values. Indeed, the assumption is so taken for granted that it has received slight attention even from feminist theorists. Part of my goal in this book is to highlight the negative consequences of monomaternal policies and practices for women and children and to suggest ways in which adoptive, blended, lesbian, and other queer families can be sites of resistance to monomaternalism.

Among the negative consequences of monomaternalism are the following:

- Competition among women for maternal status

- The erasure of many women's childbearing and childrearing labors.

- The treatment of children as private property.

- The separation of children from mothers (and mothers from children)

- The maternal grief and guilt often suffered both by those who relinquish custody of their children and those who come to bear full responsibility for them.

- A lack of attention to the ways in which women might—
  and sometimes do—mother cooperatively.

- A lack of imagination concerning ways in which laws, policies, and practices could be transformed to better serve
  both women and children.

Public policies deserving critical examination include monomaternalistic policies governing adoption practices, specifically, and those
governing custody and guardianship, more generally. It is the assumption that children must have one and only one mother that prevents
us, for example, from acknowledging multiple mothers (say both a birth
mother and an adoptive mother or both lesbian parents or even a birth
mother plus two lesbian adopters) on a child's birth certificate; monomaternalism likewise has been an impediment to opening adoption
records and to allowing same-sex couples or other polymaternal forms
of family to adopt. More generally, the assumption that monomaternalism is in the best interests of children prevents us from developing
child welfare policies and custody laws that preserve the bonds between
children and multiple caregivers and allow for what Eva Feder Kittay
(1999) terms "distributed mothering." If a divorced heterosexual couple
can share custody of a child (and the legal rights and responsibilities
and institutional supports associated with this), then why can't two
or more mothers? The policy ramifications of shifting from monomaternalism to polymaternalism are far-reaching, effecting current laws
governing visitation rights, guardianship and custody, child protection
policies, family preservation policies, social welfare policies, tax incentives, census bureau definitions of family, school policies, hospital policies, employer benefit policies, and (in the case of diasporic families
created through transnational adoption or by some other means) even
foreign policy. I touch on some of these policy concerns in various
chapters, but my primary focus here is on the importance of developing
practices of solidarity between mothers and children and among mothers themselves in complex, polymaternal kinship systems. There is no
doubt that cooperative mothering would be facilitated by transformed
public policies. However, as queer theory has taught us, kinship need
not (and should not) be dependent on state recognition.

Indeed, the desire for recognition and approval of non-normative
family forms may (and frequently does) lead to assimilation to normative expectations, thus neutralizing the radical politics adoptive, lesbian, blended, and polygamous families potentially embody. For example,

much as the resistance to heteronormativity embodied in lesbian mothering is recuperated by the assimilationist politics of gay marriage and
replications of the domestic spaces and practices of nuclear families, the
queerness of adoptive mothering is recuperated into dominant ideologies of mothering when adoptive kinship is closeted by sealed public
records and practices of "as-if-genealogical" mothering (Modell 1994).
Moreover, the resistance to racism and colonialism potentially embodied
in transracially adoptive kinship systems frequently is neutralized by
Eurocentric standards of maternal fitness that keep mothers of color
and white mothers divided along and differentially empowered by ideological fault lines. Resistance to what Kathleen Franke (2004) aptly
terms "domestinormative" kinship structures is potentially embodied in
divorce-extended and other families who inhabit queer familial space and
time. And yet this resistance may be, and often is, undercut by custodial
practices that insist children have a "primary" (nuclear) family home. In
these and myriad other ways, the potential of polymaternal families to
resist dominant cultural perspectives on and practices of family-making
is too often recuperated into normative kinship by mothers and others
who—wittingly or unwittingly—refashion their families in ways that
mirror traditional ideals of family and home. As I also discuss here, the
ways in which lesbian, adoptive, and extended/blended families might
teach their children to disidentify with dominant cultural ideologies
may be undermined by maternal disciplining, training, and abjection
of children who fail to conform to familial and/or social conventions.

Polymaternalism and the Queering of Intimacy

One of the ways in which queer forms of life are recuperated into
normative spaces is through reframing queer practices as practices of intimacy. As Berlant and Warner (1998) note, when "complex
cluster[s] of sexual practices" are confused with "the love plot of intimacy and familialism," "[c]ommunity is imagined through scenes of
intimacy, coupling, and kinship," and historical relations to the future
are "restricted to generational narrative and reproduction, [a] whole
field of social relations becomes intelligible as heterosexuality, and this
privatized sexual culture bestows on its sexual practices a tacit sense
of rightness and normality" (554). Moreover, reducing queer lives to
forms of same-sex intimacy threatens to uphold neoliberalism's privatization of public concerns thus obscuring the sexism, classism, and
racism—as well as the heterosexism—of practices of familial intimacy

(Eng 2010; Griffin 2007). For these reasons, many queer scholars have resisted portrayals of non-normative sexual practices and the communities emerging from and facilitating such sexual practices as kinship relations based on intimacy.

In situating polymaternal families as potentially queer communities of kinship, I wish to explore the relations between the queer and the intimate from a different angle. What if, instead of domesticating the queer by cloaking it in the rhetoric of intimacy, we were to make intimacy strange by revealing it to be (at least sometimes) queer? My claim here is that polymaternal families (like polyamorous relations) might queer intimacy in both its psychological and its material dimensions. Psychologically, such families (minimally) triangulate the mother–child relationship, thus propelling us away from a romanticized version of mother–child love as a dyadic relationship of mutual recognition. Materially, polymaternal families queer intimacy by destabilizing the domestic space and time in which intimacy is lived, thus propelling us away from a notion of home as a safe haven from the challenges of public life.

For Freud, sexuality and identity are the result of a triangulation between a child and its mother and father. Although the dyadic mother–child bond is assumed to be the earliest and primary bond, the triangular Oedipal drama breaks the bond between child and mother, redirecting a child's attention toward the father as the all powerful figure and resignifying the previously all powerful mother as deficient by virtue of her discovered lack of a penis. As many feminist scholars have noted, the Freudian story of a child's maturation is deeply misogynist in its assumption that sexual differentiation is marked by the presence or absence of masculinity and its corollary assumption that a girl's sexual maturation is necessarily more vexed than a boy's sexual maturation because of her lack of desired male genitalia. In response, feminist psychoanalytic theorists have modified Freudian theory in various ways, attempting to rewrite the Oedipal drama in ways that rid it of sexist bias, thereby depathologizing girls and women and allowing for a celebration of the mother–child bond.

With few exceptions, however, feminist psychoanalytic accounts fail to contemplate a family structure wherein the mother–child dyad is broken not by the presence of a father, but is instead triangulated by a second mother. If we resignify the family in less heterosexist, less monomaternalist terms, it becomes obvious that the Oedipal story will not suffice to explain a child's developmental process or psychic structures. The child of two (or more) mothers—like the child in a heteronormative nuclear family—has to accommodate itself to the fact that it cannot identify (solely) with one parent. But unlike the child in a heteronormative family, the child's recognition of differences between parents in a polymaternal family cannot be reduced to recognition of sexual difference or sexual hierarchy. Instead, such a child's psychic development may well respond to other salient differences. Primary among these is the difference between biological mothers and others. Equally salient in some cases, however, will be differences such as race, class, ability, and age. When a child does not have psychic room for two mothers and insists on prioritizing one mother as the "real" mother, a psychoanalytic account of this will need to take into account the ways in which social norms of good mothering privilege the normative female body as biologically fertile, as white, as middle class, and so forth. A queer analysis of mothering will need to attend to the ways in which these and other received norms of femininity help to structure a child's affective psychology and sense of self.

To queer our notions of mothering, however, we cannot attend merely to the ways in which the presence of multiple mothers affects the child. A purely child-centered approach to mothering too easily recuperates polymaternalism into heteronormative family structures and affective relations wherein the mother–child dyad remains primary and becomes the site of contestation between mothers. A queer account of mothering needs to explore the third arm of the mother–mother–child triangle, namely the affective relationship between the mothers themselves.

In understanding why accounts of motherhood so rarely focus on the relationship between mothers, Eve Sedgwick's (1985) analysis of male homoeroticism is instructive. In *Between Men*, Sedgwick argues that male homoerotic relationships are typically configured as relationships of rivalry that are triangulated around a woman. Much as our culture insists on framing male–male desire as male rivalry triangulated around a woman (thus reframing queer desire as heterosexual desire), we frequently render female–female desire intelligible by triangulating it around a child (thus reframing queer desire as reproductive desire). For example, we assume that a daughter cannot truly understand her mother until she becomes a mother herself; we assume that all mothers have an empathetic bond by virtue of their relationship to children, and perhaps even that all women share a common bond by virtue of their mere reproductive potential. In cases of polymaternal families, moreover, female bonding over children is frequently signified (like male homoeroticism) as a site of rivalry. Grandmothers are viewed as "interfering" in a new mother–child relationship; adoptive mothers are fearful that a child's birth mother will return to reclaim their child; stepmothers are depicted as intruding on a biological mother's territory. Much as both men and women are oppressed by a cultural system wherein male–male desire becomes intelligible by routing it through putative male desire for a woman, both women and children are harmed by a cultural system wherein relationships between women are rendered intelligible by routing female–female desire through putative desire for a child.

To queer mothering is, in one sense, to understand lesbian mothering as a prototype for other forms of mothering (rather than viewing it as an odd or deviant form of mothering). What would happen if we viewed (and lived) mother–mother relationships as (at least) equal in importance to the affective bonds between mothers and children? What would happen if maternal love was configured not only (or even primarily) as a putatively unconditional bond between a woman and her offspring, but also as an affectionate—and perhaps even erotic—relationship between mothers?

Although lesbian mothering highlights loving relationships between mothers, adoptive mothering, foster mothering, and stepmothering highlight forms of kinship that resist the logic of the nuclear family. As Judith (Jack) Halberstam (2005) suggests, queerness may be less a matter of sexual identity than it is an outcome of strange temporalities and spatial configurations. Adoptive families and blended families frequently become queer (whether that is their conscious intention or not) because of the ways in which they live outside of normative familial time and space. Adoptive mothers and stepmothers exemplify a form of motherhood that is not ruled by a biological clock and whose story of motherhood may not begin with mothering an infant. Moreover, they inhabit domestic spaces that lack picket (or other) fences to define their boundaries. Unlike the nuclear (homonormative) lesbian family, adoptive and blended families reveal the family to be a permeable and malleable structure spread across multiple households and, not infrequently, across more than one city, nation, or even continent (as in the case of transnational adoption). In such cases, lived intimacy—between mothers and children and between the mothers themselves—cannot be based on geographical proximity or the practices of everyday domesticity, but must find other modes of embodiment. One such mode of

embodiment considered here is cyborg mothering or the use of communication technologies to enable intimacy at a material distance.

What might transpire if we viewed adoptive mothering and stepmothering as a lens through which to view mothering more generally?
What happens if we treat such polymaternal families not as deviations
from the familial norm, but instead as revealing facets of maternal
practice simply hidden in normative families? How might our theories
of maternal practice change if we no longer envisioned home as a stable
and coherent material place? Families that are spread across multiple
geographical spaces, I suggest, trouble the alleged boundary between
private and public spaces, encouraging us to rethink (or reimagine)
the distinction between home and elsewhere. Living intimacy within
the complex configurations of time and space inhabited by mothers
and children in adoptive and blended families requires abandoning
the notion of home as a fixed and static location wherein one always
feels safe, protected, or even comfortable. Thus, to move adoptive and
blended families to the center of our theorizing about motherhood
specifically and kinship generally is to move toward a notion of families as coalitional entities requiring practices of solidarity among and
between the various inhabitants of diasporic homes.

Good (Queer) Mothers and Bad (Queer) Mothers

Contested norms of good mothering provide an ideological terrain that
too often prevents practices of solidarity between mothers—whether
those mothers are members of different families or belong to the same
family. The adoptive mother may stereotype the birth mother as incapable, neglectful, or abusive. The first mother may characterize the
stepmother as too harsh in her discipline. The daughter-in-law may
reject the advice of her mother-in-law as intrusive and unwelcome. The
righteousness (and self-righteousness) we bring to our own practices of
mothering makes it difficult for us, as mothers, to embrace practices
of mothering different from our own and, related to this, makes it
difficult to share responsibility with the other women who do play or
who would like to play a maternal role in our children's lives. Instead
of acting in solidarity with other mothers, we too often criticize, judge,
and feel criticized and judged by one another. The good mother/bad
mother dichotomy, in other words, works to uphold the ideology of
monomaternalism by giving us a personal stake in claiming to be a

child's "real" mother and thus the only mother who counts. Attempting to control the interactions of other mothers with our children, we lay claim to a centrality in our children's lives, establishing by word and deed a hierarchy of command that our children's other mothers (stepmothers, foster mothers, birth mothers, nannies, neighbors, relatives, friends, and lovers) dare not transgress.

Much as the good mother/bad mother dichotomy upholds the ideology and practices of monomaternalism, the good queer/bad queer dichotomy upholds the ideology and practices of heteronormativity. As many queer theorists have noted in the past decade, an implicit distinction between good queers and bad queers has been operative in the struggles to obtain marriage and adoption rights for (some) gays and lesbians, struggles that have eclipsed the more radical queer politics of AIDS activism, struggles for economic redistribution, and struggles for a wide-ranging sexual freedom. Lisa Duggan (2003) identified the trend toward recognizing the citizenship and consumer rights of those gays and lesbians who most closely mimic heteronormative standards of gender identity (namely, those who espouse a commitment to monogamy and childrearing within nuclear domestinormative middle-class families) as evidence of a "new homonormativity . . . a politics that does not contest dominant heteronormative assumptions and institutions but upholds and sustains them" (50). As Duggan asserts, homonormativity has fragmented the queer community into hierarchies of worthiness that seek recognition of those who mimic gender-normative social roles while marginalizing those who challenge monogamy as well as those who resist a binary gender or sex system.

One example of the ways in which homonormativity has fragmented the queer community is found in the response of same-sex marriage advocates to what has become widely known as the "slippery slope" argument. According to this argument, any move away from the Defense of Marriage Act (DOMA), which defines marriage as a bond between "one man and one woman" would open the floodgates to approving of a wide variety of marital relationships including polygamy, as well as same-sex marriage. According to the Human Rights Campaign (the primary U.S. advocate for same-sex marriage and also a fierce advocate for "ending abuses against women and girls in polygamous fundamentalist Mormon communities in the U.S."), the link between same-sex marriage and polygamy is "offensive" (Saunders 2010). Same-sex marriage and polygamy are fundamentally distinct, the campaign argues, claiming "two people is the defining element in our system of government on contractual marriage" (Saunders 2006). In response to polygamists who claim to lead happy, harmonious lives, same-sex marriage advocates argue that the practice is, nonetheless, "poison for cultures at large," arguing that the institution is intrinsically oppressive to women and bad for children, citing as evidence for this "polygamy's most famous son: Osama bin Laden, whose father sired 54 children with 22 wives" (Saunders 2006).

As these comments suggest, at the same time as adoption, divorce and remarriage and (monogamous) same-sex relationships have become a "normal" part of our social fabric in recent decades, polygamy as a form of kinship remains largely exoticized and vilified as the queer (and apparently terrorist-producing) "other." Thus, it is not surprising that both feminist theorists of motherhood and queer theorists and activists have largely ignored polygamy—except insofar as it is used to highlight an oppressive practice against which the gender freedoms sought by feminists and queers can be upheld. The common assumption is that polygamous families are inevitably heteropatriarchal and thus could be neither feminist nor queer. This assumption, however, like the assumption that mothering (breeding) itself is inevitably complicit with heteronormativity, has prevented strategic alliances among a variety of persons interested in creating non-normative kinship relations, as well as between these persons and those interested in a variety of non-normative erotic relations. Indeed, polygamous kinship highlights, perhaps better than any other form of kinship, a meeting place for feminists seeking to resist normative (monomaternalist) forms of motherhood and queers seeking to resist normative (monogamous) forms of intimacy. With these considerations in mind, I have chosen here to examine polygamous families as part of a larger spectrum of polymaternal families, alongside adoptive families, stepfamilies, and same-sex families. My hope is that by doing so, I might blur the distinction between "good" queers and "bad" queers that undermines a truly queer political theory and movement.

In developing an account of queer mothering here, I wish to resist both the good mother/bad mother dichotomy as well as the good queer/bad queer dichotomy. In identifying practices of queer solidarity between mothers (as well as noting failures of such solidarity), I hope to contest the multiple hierarchies of worthiness that pit mothers against one another, queers against one another and queer mothers against one another. To this end, I examine a variety of maternal bodies and practices that are frequently abjected as unintelligible. These bodies and

practices include the "mad" and "bad" mothers who commit infanticide
and filicide, the drug-addicted black or brown mother and the unwed
teen mother (all of whom can be seen as resisting social norms), as
well as the "controlling" mother (who forces social norms on her children) and the "submissive" mother (who, in not questioning the norms
imposed by her husband or other patriarch, may be seen as neglecting
her maternal responsibilities). If we are to overcome our tendency to
abject these and other cases of allegedly "bad" mothering, I suggest,
we must strive to recognize the Other as a potentially analogous being
who, although not a mirror image of ourselves, is not our opposite
either. To avoid the good mother/bad mother dichotomy, we will need to
re-cognize ourselves in ways that allow us to accept and care for those
parts of ourselves that we may find strange, alienating, or shameful.
By allowing the lines between our (good) selves and the (bad) Other
to blur, we queer both our notions of self and other thus laying the
groundwork for solidarity between and among diverse mothers.

Queering Queer Theory

The theoretical grounding for this book draws from a combination of
feminist philosophy, post-structuralist theory, critical race theory, postcolonial theory, cultural studies, and queer theory. It is my training as
a feminist philosopher that leads me to interpret statements about real
mothers as having meanings located at the intersections between questions about reality (ontology, epistemology, metaphysics) and questions
about values (ethics and politics). A fundamental assumption of this
book is that our theories about reality are never value-neutral. Post-
structuralist thinking shapes the ways in which I approach some of the
central dichotomies in this book. It is with a deconstructive sensibility
that I approach the binary thinking underlying discourses of "real"
mothering: dichotomies between biological and social mothers, good
mothers and bad mothers, materially present and materially absent
mothers, and so on. A similar deconstructive sensibility also informs my
desire to blur the boundaries between heteronormative and homonormative forms of mothering, and to contest the dichotomous opposition
between "breeders" and "queers" that may make the notion of "mothering queerly" advanced in this work sound oxymoronic to some. Critical
race and postcolonial theories inform my thinking about the race- and
class-inflected politics of mothering. They also have assisted me in

thinking about families that are geographically dispersed, whereas cultural studies has shaped my thinking about the possibilities of cyborg mothering as a queer, postmodern phenomenon. Both cultural studies and queer theory have enabled me to rethink maternal embodiment and our traditional notions of domestic or familial space and time. Feminist psychoanalytic theory and queer theory inform my thinking about the development of adolescent subjectivity and the processes of abjection that haunt the boundaries of the self, for both mothers and their rebellious teens. Queer theoretical approaches to love and family, together with feminist theories of dependency work and critiques of romanticized motherhood, figure prominently in my attempts to theorize mothering outside of the confines of the heteropatriarchal, nuclear family. Although queer theory takes center stage here, I am particularly indebted to those scholars who work at the intersections of queer, feminist, and postcolonial theories. My reflections in the following chapters have been heavily influenced by the work of disciplinary border-crossers such as Michel Foucault, Sara Ahmed, David Eng, Maria Lugones, and Jasbir Puar, among others. Although none of these scholars study motherhood, their work has been an ongoing source of pleasure and insight that has consistently provoked me to rethink many of my own assumptions on normative and non-normative identities, practices, and perspectives as these relate to mothering.

I have framed this project as an attempt to queer motherhood—including motherhood studies. In applying the term "queer" to mothering and families, however, I also participate in the project of queering queer studies itself. The family is a point at which the axes of feminism, postcolonialism and queer theory frequently diverge. During the 1970s and 1980s, feminists critiqued the family as a site of patriarchal oppression. In response, women of color and critical race theorists pointed out that families of color were a critically important site of resistance to racism and colonization. As feminism began developing more intersectional analyses of gender as inflected by race, class, nation (and other variables), more nuanced analyses of the family slowly began to emerge, resulting in what is now a prolific field of motherhood studies that provides one important (albeit still underdeveloped) point of contact for postcolonial and feminist theorists.

Early lesbian and gay studies, like early feminist scholarship, voiced misgivings about the family. For many lesbians and gays, the family was experienced as a site of closeting or rejection—although, again, the experiences of people of color complicated this vision of the family. Later lesbian, gay, bisexual, and transgendered (lgbt) scholarship began developing more positive portrayals of the family, featuring lesbian- and gay-headed households. These accounts of lgbt families have provided a point of intersection between contemporary gay and lesbian studies and feminist studies of motherhood. Such intersectional studies continue, however, to be largely (although not exclusively) dominated by portraits of white, middle-class, nuclear families—giving rise, in part, to queer theory's denunciation of the "homonormative" family as upholding heteronormative ideals.

In providing analyses of discursive forms of sex, gender, and sexuality and the implications of these for queer subjectivities, queer theory has largely ignored the family altogether—except as an institution through which "abnormal" sexuality is regulated by the state. Moreover, insofar as queer theory *has* positively addressed issues of family, the focus has been on intragenerational forms of kinship based on friendship (in the Foucauldian sense), communities of those engaged in non-normative sexual practices (e.g., BDSM [bondage, discipline, dominance, submission, sadism, masochism] communities and polyamorous intimacies) and communities of persons who embody non-normative forms of gender (e.g., drag culture, and the social and political alliances among transgendered, transsexual, and/or intersexed persons). These and other queer kinship relations are frequently premised on the rejection of children insofar as queerness is viewed as incompatible with breeding as a matter of both theory and practice. Theoretically, queerness resists narratives of reprosexuality; practically speaking, queerness resists the alterations to lifestyle that childrearing (allegedly) requires. One cannot, it is presumed, rear children without succumbing to homonormative and domestinormative practices, schedules, routines, and concerns.

I agree that queerness involves (minimally) an uncoupling of sex and reproduction. Procreation is not the *telos* of sex; heterosexual coupledom is not mandated by biological dictates, nor should it be mandated by cultural or legal norms. Nor do I believe that child-free lives are less meaningful, satisfying, or fulfilling than those featuring children. However, the idea that queerness *demands* the absence of children in one's life (and hence the idea that mothering queerly is an *im*possibility) arises, I think, from several interlocking, but questionable, assumptions. One assumption is that dependency work inevitably structures one's life in normative ways. As anyone who has cared for a child, an aging parent, or an ill partner or friend knows, caregiving work (which still falls disproportionately on the shoulders of women) often is physically and emotionally demanding. And it can, to be sure, deprive one of the time and energy to engage in other pleasurable pursuits. It is highly unlikely, however—given the historical emergence of queer theory and queer activism from the AIDS crisis—that queer scholars would claim that all forms of caregiving inevitably render one homonormative. Why, then, presume that caring for *children* specifically threatens queerness?

Underlying the presumption that in childrearing we cease to be queer may be an implicit notion of childhood innocence as incompatible with adult perversities. As Lee Edelman's (2004) work reveals, however, the ideal of childhood innocence is a conservative one; furthermore, as Kathryn Stockton's (2009) work on queering childhood reveals, the idea of childhood innocence is a myth. Arguing that children "grow sideways" (rather than "up") and require intensive training in order to "mature" into heteronormative citizens, Stockton proposes that childhood is an essentially queer experience. Indeed, as any mother knows, infants and toddlers are shameless about playing with their sexual organs and even their own excrement; teens and young adults, although sometimes shamed by their peers, frequently continue to rebel against most forms of adult prohibition. If children are, as Halberstam (2011) suggests, "always already anarchic and rebellious, out of order and out of time" (27), they would appear to be right "at home" with queer-identified adults. Indeed, in my experience, children are quite happy to accompany their parents (or friends' parents) to drag shows and other counter-public spaces.

The fact remains that few parents do, however, identify as queer. Moreover, even those who do so identify may want, as Michael Warner (1999) suggests, to be (or to pass as) "normal." This leads us to the third assumption underpinning the suspicion that childrearing threatens queerness, namely, the presumption that childrearing inevitably takes place within nuclear families that seek to replicate culturally (hetero- or homo-) normative practices and identities. It is this assumption that is the focus of the present work. Although I agree that most mothers (and I am no exception) internalize normative practices of mothering that abject the disorderly conduct of their children—partly out of the shame that attends being seen as a "bad" mother and partly out of a concern for children's future well-being, I wish to argue for the *possibility* of a form of mothering that resists such tendencies. Such resistance is, I think, facilitated by childrearing and homemaking practices that are "shared and improvised," and view mothering as an act "of culture rather than nature, an act of construction rather than reproduction" (Halberstam 2011, 45).

A central argument of this book is that caring for children has been queered by a proliferation of nonbiological polymaternal families of choice who resist (although they may not entirely transcend) normative familial configurations and normative domestic patterns. I do not claim that mothering is essentially a queer activity (to be sure, it is not). Nor do I claim that non-normative forms of mothering are always chosen or practiced as intentional incarnations of queer subjectivities. (Often they are not, although this doesn't preempt providing queer readings of such practices, much as literary theory has frequently queered literary texts whose authors may not have "intended" such readings.) My goal is simply to create a space in which to make room for the possibility of mothering queerly by investigating how mothering—as both practiced and theorized—may be importantly transformed by two (or more) mother families. In adoptive, lesbian, extended-blended, and polygamous families, narratives of reprosexuality frequently are (albeit not always) displaced by narratives of chosen kinship—choices that may include homosocial and even homoerotic relationships between women. In such families, moreover, practices of distributed mothering make it possible to inhabit intergenerational kinship networks while continuing to enjoy adult pursuits and intimacies (including, but not limited to, non-normative sexual pursuits and intimacies) outside of the family. By providing alternative models of kinship featuring female homosociality and resistance to gendered norms of self-sacrifical mothering, polymaternal families allow for (although they do not guarantee) the formation of queer subjectivities in both mothers and children.

In using feminist and postcolonial theory to interrogate the limits of queer theory, I work alongside a trend of queering queer studies that emerges primarily from queers of color.[2] Using a strategy José Muñoz (1999) terms "disidentification," many queers of color argue against wholesale dismissals of family—even those with heteropatriarchal tendencies—adopting instead the tactics of working "on, with, and against" kinship structures that simultaneously nourish, contain, and exclude complex, even contradictory, identities (12). In *Queer Latinidad*, for example, Juana Maria Rodriguez (2003) claims that "the spaces of *familia* . . . have taught me almost everything I now know about queer, about desire, about bodies on the margins and dance floors creating momentary centers" (155). A similar claim pervades E. Patrick Johnson's (2005) formulation of "quare studies" as a queer of color alternative to queer studies. Claiming that "(almost) everything I learned about queer studies, I learned from my grandmother," Johnson coins the term "quare studies" (borrowing from his grandmother's African American vernacular) to make room for (among other things) discussions of family, home, and church that neither uncritically embrace these sites of black refuge nor simply dismiss them. Although Rodriguez, Johnson, and I have different motivations for rubbing up against the boundaries of queer theory, there is a parallel between their attempts to develop models of queer subjectivity that acknowledge the importance of ancestry (especially mothers and grandmothers) and my own attempt to make room in queer theory for the intergenerational bonds between mothers and children.

The question remains whether we can rub motherhood up against queer theory without eroding queer theory in ways that make it lose its critical edge. There are those who will, no doubt, object that the family forms I consider here cannot be described as queer without stretching the term *queer* beyond the bounds of its elasticity. Aren't adoptive families (as an example of non-reprosexual families) and divorce-extended families (as an example of complicated, two-mother families) frequently heteronormative? Aren't lesbian families (whether created through adoption or through the use of in vitro fertilization or surrogates) frequently homonormative? Worse yet, don't polygamous families (with one husband and many wives) frequently exemplify a hyper-heterosexual, patriarchal family form?[3] The answer to all of these questions is "yes . . . and no." The fact that many adoptive, divorce-extended, lesbian, and polygamous families may be shaped by normative values and practices does not mean that this is an *essential* property of such families. Nor does it mean that these are the *only* values embodied by such families. A central assumption of this project is that just as some folk who identify as queer may sometimes "play it straight," some folk who identify as straight may engage in deviant practices. I speak here of mothering queerly (rather than of queer mothers) in order to avoid the politics of identity and instead focus on specific maternal practices that (wittingly or unwittingly) resist the heteronormative standards of "good" mothering and, in so doing, provide a model for queering motherhood.

Mothering Queerly; Queering Motherhood

The first part of this work explores polymaternal families created through adoption, examining the queer affective geographies of adoptive families, and the consequences of attempting to closet or straighten such queerness by acting "as if" adoptive families are genealogical families. Counterposing my experiences as both an adoptive mother and a birthmother, Chapter 1 sketches my early steps (and missteps) toward recognizing the importance of both forms of motherhood and thus the necessarily queer triangulation of mothering within the adoptive family. Using Sara Ahmed's *Queer Phenomenology: Orientation, Objects, Others* as a theoretical starting point, I explore the ways in which the potential queerness of adoption may be contained and obscured within otherwise straight lives—lives characterized by a mother's (dyadic) orientation toward a child and away from the other woman whose labor made her own motherhood possible. Iris Young's phenomenology of the pregnant body helps to illuminate the potential queerness of pregnancy itself, as an embodiment that blurs the boundaries between self and other and gives rise to moments of disorientation. Taking seriously Ahmed's notion that moments of disorientation are queer moments laden with the potential to learn to see the world from a "slantwise" perspective, Chapter 1 begins to challenge the antithesis between breeders and queers that has been responsible, in large part, for the cleavage between feminist theories of motherhood and queer theory. Insofar as pregnancy impedes one's mobility in the world, it provides the opportunity (however momentary) for reflection on how other non-normative bodies struggle to navigate the world. Pregnancy also reveals reproductive labor as labor, making visible the other maternal subjects whose work stands behind adoption as a consumer process.

In addition to offering a preliminary challenge to the distinction between "breeders" and "queers," Chapter 1 raises questions about the distinction between "good" and "bad" mothers, as well as "good" and "bad" queers. Developing a queer reading of Charlotte Perkins Gilman's "The Yellow Wallpaper" to frame my own experience of postpartum depression, I suggest that the disorientation of such postpartum experiences may be understood as a queer moment providing insight into the monstrous (m)others who lurk behind Gilman's wallpaper and, in our own time, behind stories of child neglect and abuse. Exploring some of the highly publicized cases of maternal infanticide and homicide in the United States at the turn of the century, I sketch the phenomenon of maternal profiling that targets women—especially those who are poor or non-white—as the primary source of child endangerment. This phenomenon, I suggest, is analogous to the racial profiling that targets black and brown bodies as a source of danger to citizens of the United States. Drawing on Elizabeth Rapaport's legal analysis of the distinction between "mad" (good, but crazy) mothers and "bad" white mothers who have become infamous for killing their children, I argue that this distinction between "mad" and "bad" mothers is a racialized, class-coded, and heteronormative distinction bearing similarities to the distinction between "good" and "bad" queers. Applying Jasbir Puar's analysis of the ways in which the figure of the terrorist elicits our affective response through representations of the terrorist as sexually queer, I suggest that the female perpetrators of infanticide and filicide who are sentenced to death (unlike those who escape such a punishment) are "blackened," in part, by our affective responses to their non-normative sexual behavior. Affective responses such as pity for the "mad" mother and hatred for the "bad" mother serve, in Ahmed's terms, to bring some bodies "in line" with us, while aligning us "against" others. As such, cases of infanticide and filicide—as well as other less dramatic cases of "bad" mothering—call for a queer reading of our racialized and class-coded norms of good mothering and the affective responses they elicit.

Chapter 2 takes a closer look at the adoptive maternal body as a potentially queer body from which we might gain a queer (or "slant-wise") perspective on mothering more generally. Without denying important differences between adoptive and biological maternal bodies—or among adoptive bodies themselves—my goal in this chapter is to explore how the (representational) figure of the adoptive body as produced by disciplinary discourses and practices gives rise to the (phenomenological and epistemological) experience of double-consciousness, thus making the adoptive maternal body a site of potential resistance to dominant discourses on mothering, including the ideologies of pronatalism, reprosexuality, repronarrativity, and monomaternalism. Drawing on Foucault's insight that power produces subjects, I begin by examining the techniques of surveillance that produce adoptive mothers as "good" mothers and adoptive families as "good" (i.e., white, middle-class, heteronormative) families, despite their obvious deviance from the biocentric, pronatalist script of mothering. Arguing that techniques of surveillance also produce biological mothers as "good" (and "bad") mothers, I suggest that adoptive mothers differ from biological mothers, in part, by their heightened awareness of being watched. Like light-skinned blacks or closeted queers, adoptive mothers know that we are "passing." It is incumbent on us (in order to pass muster success-fully) to know the script for good mothering well and to audition for the role convincingly. Whereas biological mothers may not—and frequently do not—experience themselves as role-playing, adoptive mothers (as well as stepmothers and other Othered mothers) do.

In the second part of Chapter 2, I turn my attention to the ways in which the ambiguity of the adoptive mother as a "real" maternal body provides opportunities for adoptive mothers to subvert the dom-inant script of mothering. Insofar as the adoptive mother does not (literally) procreate, she is a close relative to Eve Sedgwick's "non-procreative adult" and thus a queer adult body. In resisting genetic reproduction, the adoptive maternal body chooses whether, when, and how to become a mother. These choices may—like the choices of the closeted or homonormative queer—embody domestication by dominant scripts of normative kinship. They may also, however, and sometimes do, openly resist domestication. One way in which they do so, I suggest, is through participating in open adoptions. When adoption is unclos-eted, the practice openly resists two pernicious narratives that Michael Warner (1991) associates with "a breeder identity": "reprosexuality" and "repronarrativity." Open adoptions, like open practices of queer sex, delink reproduction from sexuality and, in so doing, resist the myth that personal fulfillment is to be found in genetic transmission to future generations. Open adoption also queers kinship by challenging the ide-ology of monomaternalism and insisting on the reality and presence of two different mothers in a child's life.

Chapter 3 uses a queer postcolonial framework to examine trans-racial and transnational adoption. Like many others who have adopted transracially, my husband and I pursued adoption as a family-making strategy consistent with political aims of racial integration. The limita-tions of such strategies are apparent, however, if we consider the ways in which closed adoptions separate children of color from their mothers and from larger familial and ethnic communities. Concerns about the removal of children from their families and cultures of origin prompted the National Association of Black Social Workers (NABSW), among oth-ers, to denounce the practice of transracial adoption in the 1970s as a practice of cultural genocide. In Chapter 3, I take these concerns seriously, sketching the historical and legislative contexts wherein neo-liberal ideologies of colorblindness have facilitated ongoing transfers of wealth (including children) from mothers, families, and communities of color to white mothers, families, and communities. Paying special attention to the "orphan" narratives that have framed practices of both transracial and transnational adoption as humanitarian endeavors, I argue that such rhetorical strategies serve to queer the adopted child while rendering birth mothers (and other living kin) invisible to the adoptive parent.

Drawing on David Eng's *The Feeling of Kinship: Queer Liberalism and the Racialization of Intimacy*, Chapter 3 further suggests that neoliberal accounts of colorblindness may give rise to racial melancholia for the transracially adopted child. As the recently emerging accounts of adult adoptees suggest, transracial and transnational adoptions remove the child of color from an intergenerational context wherein racial identity and mourning can be negotiated, while simultaneously demanding that the adopted child consolidate the intimate boundaries of her white family through her affective labor. A poignant illustration of this is to be found in Deann Borshay Liem's documentary, *First Person Plural* (which Eng also analyzes), and her follow-up documentary, *In the Matter of Cha Jung Hee*, both of which address her attempts to negotiate her identity and belonging as the Korean born child of a white adoptive family in the United States. Together with the artwork of Tracey Moffat and the narrative accounts of other adult adoptees, which I also examine here, Borshay Liem's films highlight the negative affective consequences for the adoptee whose history and identity is erased and contained by the narratives of colorblindness that frame discussions of adoption under global capitalism and neocolonialism.

In response to the negative consequences of transracial and transnational adoptions for adopted children and their birth families, NABSW, the United Nations, and others have advocated for policies of family preservation. I close Chapter 3 by querying this goal. Within the context of national and international emphases on the privatization of public concerns, I suggest that we should be suspicious of family preservation policies as the conduit to social and economic justice for mothers, children, and communities of color. Moreover, family preservation is a highly suspect goal within a domestic context that emphasizes marriage and fatherhood promotion as the route to social well-being. Returning to Borshay Liem's documentaries, I suggest that a return to the ideals of the Oedipal (biocentric, heteronormative) family is an inadequate solution to neocolonial practices of destroying families of color. A queer orientation toward kinship suggests the need to instead reimagine the boundaries and nature of kinship.

Chapter 4 examines more closely the child's perspective on adoption. Like Borshay Liem, my adopted daughter has struggled with making "room in her mind for two mothers." Here I explore the affective geography of the child of two mothers through a close reading of the familial narratives embodied in children's literature. Seeking a metaphysics of motherhood that is more inclusive than monomaternalism and more fluid than serial maternalism (wherein one affectionate dyad is substituted for another), I argue for an ontology of motherhood that embodies what Caroline Whitbeck describes as a "self–others relation"—an ontology that will encourage, rather than discourage, a child's attempts to respond to an often complex configuration of familial relationships.

Beginning with the children's books, *Are You My Mother?* and *A Mother for Choco*, I explore the ways in which the nature/nurture dichotomy, as conveyed to children, upholds the ideology of monomaternalism, implying that children in polymaternal families must choose either their "natural" mother or their "social" mother (but not both). In comparison to the biologically essentialist narrative of *Are You My Mother?* and the construction of mothering as solely an act of nurture forwarded by *A Mother for Choco*, the children's stories *Stellaluna* and *Horton Hatches the Egg* provide welcome complexity in their narratives of mothering, querying both sides of the nature/nurture debate. Indeed, both tales have queer elements: *Stellaluna* may be read as a tale about a queer child, whereas *Horton* may be read as a tale of queer diasporic mothering from which emerges a rather queer hybrid subject. The queerness of these stories, however, is undermined by their moralizing about maternal fitness. Ultimately, both *Stellaluna* and *Horton* erect a good mother/bad mother dichotomy that compels the young reader to choose one mother over another. I close Chapter 4 with a reading of *The Velveteen Rabbit*, a story that is not explicitly about mothering or kinship, but that respects the child's agency in defining his or her own reality. Drawing on Maria Lugones' notion of "loving perception" and Sara Ruddick's notion of "attentive love," alongside the advice of the skin-horse in *The Velveteen Rabbit*, I explore the epistemological skills children need in order to bring multiple mothers into being for themselves.

In the second part of this book, I turn my attention toward the queer material geographies of postmodern family forms such as divorce-extended families and other queer kinship networks who, as described by Gil Valentine, "live apart together." Here, as in the previous chapters, my analyses emerge from my own changing life experiences and practices. Chapter 5 uses my experiences as a commuting, quasi-divorced, part-time custodial parent to investigate the ways in which "home" becomes enmeshed in queer geographies of space and time for those who live outside of domestinormativity (i.e., outside of private spaces of intimacy with carefully controlled borders). Drawing on Rosi Braidotti's *Nomadic Subjects* as well as Sara Ahmed's critique of this work, I caution against both appropriating and romanticizing nomadism. For many postmodern subjects (as for most postcolonial subjects), "home" lacks a fixed geographical referent. This lack of fixity may be liberating for some, but traumatic for others—especially for children who (like colonized subjects) may have little choice in determining how their home is configured. Exploring and rejecting different metaphorical understandings of the post-divorce family, including the notions of "broken" homes and "blended" homes, as well as the notion of "nomadic" families, I turn to the notion of "queer assemblages," as developed by Jasbir Puar, as a more accurate and less normatively loaded description of divorce-extended families. In particular, the notion of an assemblage, as originally developed by Deleuze and Guattari in *A Thousand Plateaus*, captures the irreducible multiplicity and fluidity of post-divorce and other queer families who live outside of normative domestic space and define themselves through ongoing processes of territorialization, deterritorialization, and reterritorialization.

In the second part of Chapter 5, I examine a particular assemblage within the postmodern familial assemblage, namely, the cyborg mother as a fusion of organic and nonorganic forces that negotiates and enables intimacy across geographical distance. As a part-time custodial parent, continuity of my mothering practices was maintained, in large part, through inhabiting shared virtual space with my daughters on an ongoing basis. Seeking here to initiate a dialogue between cultural theorists exploring the influence of digital technologies and feminist theorists exploring practices of motherhood, I argue that communication technologies such as cell phones, texting, email, instant messaging, videoconferencing, and social networking extend and modify both the bodies of twenty-first-century teenagers and those of their parents. Thus, "real" mothering has, in the post-industrialized world, become inextricably intertwined with technology. This form of mothering in queer space and time—like other forms of inhabiting queer space and time—should be neither romanticized nor demonized. Making a distinction between what I term *technomothering*, as a potentially oppressive practice, and what I call *cyborg mothering*, as a potentially liberatory practice, I suggest that communication technologies (or what I refer to as "technologies of co-presence") create new familial social spaces, thus expanding our opportunities for daily meaningful contact among intimates who are not in physical proximity to one another. Whether we use such opportunities to engage in queer forms of mothering that transform the meaning and experience of maternal love or instead use these spaces to extend practices of heteropatriarchal mothering is up to us.

Chapters 6 and 7 focus on maternal confrontations with difference. Here, I critically examine notions of home and family and develop an account of love as a practice of solidarity that holds homes and families together. Chapter 6 draws on my experiences of mothering teens within a kinship structure queered by adoption, divorce and repartnerings to confront idealized versions of home and family as places of unity, harmony, and unconditional love. I begin by critically interrogating the notion of "chosen family." As teenagers, my daughters reacted quite differently to the notion of chosen family on which they had been raised. My younger daughter embraced with pride what she deemed the "weirdness" of her (cross-national, multiethnic, interracial, polymaternal) family and its eclectic practices. In contrast, my older daughter distanced herself from most members of her nuclear and extended family, claiming her friends to be her family and declaring the rest of us—biological, adoptive, and step kin alike—to be "random strangers." In the first part of chapter 6, I explore what it means to choose one's family, focusing on the liberal underpinnings of the rhetoric of "chosen families."

In the middle sections of Chapter 6, I turn my attention to the specific struggles engendered by mothering alienated teens. Drawing on Judith Butler's work on abjection and the notion of "disidentification" as developed by José Muñoz, I suggest we might understand the adolescent as a queer subject. Using the psychoanalytic explications of abjection offered by Julia Kristeva in her *Powers of Horror*, I explore the ways in which adolescent subjectivity—like the emerging subjectivity of the young child first entering the symbolic order—may require redrawing boundaries between self and (m)other that result in a child's abjection of her mother(s). This is painful both for the mother who is Othered and for the child who is subjected to practices of abjection by a maternal politics of colonization and/or tolerance. Like Dorothy in

The Wizard of Oz, both adolescent and mother(s) are caught between a desire to escape home and a simultaneous yearning for the comforts of (an idealized) home. Both the pain and the frequency of such struggles and our ambivalence about home suggest that home is misconceived (by social conservatives and feminist and queer theorists alike) as a site of safety, comfort and homogeneity. I conclude this chapter by forwarding the suggestion that home may be the place wherein we are most directly and consistently challenged to remain open to the Other. To value real families (and real family members), as opposed to those constructed by the social imaginary, is, I suggest, a lot like coalition work. One must be willing to take on a long-term commitment to negotiating differences with and understanding the Other.

Chapter 7 explores how coalitional mothering emerges as an ideal and practice in the polygamous families depicted on the HBO series, *Big Love*, the reality television show, *Sister Wives* and the memoir, *Love Times Three*. As a queer familial assemblage, the polygamous family is characterized by multiplicity and the ongoing need to reflectively engage with difference. Adopting but reframing the distinctions between conventional, affectional, and reflective solidarity developed by Jodi Dean in *The Solidarity of Strangers*, I suggest that "doing" family queerly requires ongoing practices of reflective solidarity (which Dean notes is necessary to coalitions among heterogenous publics) as well as affectional solidarity (which Dean suggests is the primary form of solidarity in kinship relations). Love is enlarged beyond parochial and privatized understandings of intimacy by merging care (affection) for particular, concrete others with a reflective commitment to understanding, respecting, valuing, and openly negotiating our differences from them. The demand for shared adherence to principles and norms (conventional solidarity), I argue, is what gives rise to colonial love, as critiqued in earlier chapters by adult adoptees, adolescent children, and others. Without critical reflection and self-reflection, love is indeed blind and, as such, fails to recognize the differences between self and others. A critically reflective love of difference itself, however—in the absence of caring relationships with concrete others—becomes an abstract ideal that is empty.

By means of exploring both interfamilial dynamics and intrafamilial dynamics, the polygamous family may teach us lessons about the potential for transcending practices of abjection both within and among families. Chapter 7 thus opens with an examination of the interfamilial dynamics of the suburban, polygamous families portrayed in *Big Love*,

Sister Wives, and *Love Times Three,* emphasizing the development and transformations, over time, of practices of solidarity between mothers and children and—as importantly—between mothers themselves. Following this, I examine the ways in which sympathetic portrayals of the suburban polygamist family emerge against the backdrop of the villainized polygamous compounds of the American west, threatening to instantiate a distinction between "good" and "bad" polygamists that is closely linked to what Halberstam (2005) has termed "metronormativity" (36). The presumed moral, epistemological, and aesthetic superiority of suburban polygamists parallels the implicit distinction between "good" (urban) and "bad" (rural) queers that operates in queer theory, while simultaneously forwarding the distinction between "good" (homonormative) and "bad" (perverse) queers operative in current arguments for gay marriage. Both the good polygamist/bad polygamist and good queer/bad queer dichotomies intersect with the good mother/bad mother dichotomy examined in earlier chapters.

It is because polygamous families continue to stand outside of the more accepted forms of polymaternal families (and outside of my own experience) that I include an examination of them here alongside adoptive families, lesbian families, and stepfamilies. Polygamous families, like other forms of polymaternal families, I suggest, can teach us important lessons about non-normative embodiments of intimacy. Chapter 7 thus concludes with an examination of the politics of love in its practical, epistemological and phenomenological dimensions, arguing for an understanding of maternal love as a practice of (queer) solidarity. Such a practice of solidarity (with our children and with other mothers who—whether strangers or kin—embody a resistance to the politics of monomaternalism) requires both recognizing others and—as importantly—re-cognizing ourselves, as mothers.

PART I

Triangulating Motherhood

1

Querying a Straight Orientation

Becoming a Mother (Twice, Differently)

It matters how we arrive at the places we do.

—Sarah Ahmed (2006)

I begin this book by examining my beginnings as a mother—once through adoption and then, shortly thereafter, through pregnancy and birth—as my journey toward querying and queering motherhood began with the juxtaposition of these two different routes to "having" children. As I subsequently argue, adoption is a potentially queer form of motherhood. Ironically, however, I did not recognize this fully until I had experienced biological motherhood. More specifically, it was not until after I had experienced an unintended pregnancy that I came to see adoptive motherhood as requiring openness toward another woman with whom I shared a child. Moreover, it was not until after I had experienced postpartum depression following the birth of my second child that I came to query my own status as a "good" mother deserving of approval as a parent. It is, thus, as a straight married woman undertaking biological reproduction (as a "breeder") that my perspectives on motherhood took their first queer turn, as I began to resist the ideology of monomaternalism and its closely affiliated practice of maternal profiling. Here I frame this queer turn in terms of phenomenologist Sara Ahmed's (2006) notion of queer orientations, suggesting that what she terms "oblique" or "slantwise" perceptions may sometimes emerge from rather straight positionings.

Prior to examining my own beginnings as a mother, however, I return briefly to the more distant past of my own childhood. It is here, after all, that my desire to become a mother begins to take shape. And it is here that my later sense of entitlement as a consumer of adoption services becomes intelligible.

The Inheritance of Privilege

In her *Queer Phenomenology: Orientations, Objects, Others*, Ahmed (2006) explores provocatively the ways in which our orientations to objects and other subjects both shapes and is shaped by that which is within our bodily horizon. Arguing that orientation is "a matter of how we reside in space," she suggests that what we are oriented toward, as well as what we are oriented around, is a function of what is "behind us" (1, 62). This is to say that our inheritance shapes what is "before us" or "within our reach" by giving us a certain direction (126). For example, if our childhood home features wedding photographs, baby pictures, and family portraits (as mine did), we inherit a heterosexual orientation, thus increasing the likelihood that in our own future we will become wives and mothers. If our family of origin is white and middle class, then one's childhood home may feature (as mine did) objects such as classical (European) music, books, and magazines (featuring white faces and heroines), photo albums of vacations to places like Disneyland, and so forth. In inheriting a white middle-class orientation, I also inherited a presumption of "belonging" in the world.

In the small town in which I grew up I encountered few non-white faces. Some years ago, my mother recollected, with embarrassment, the time I first encountered a black man; apparently I pointed and asked my mother to "look at that man with no face!" She told a similar story—also embarrassing to her—of the first time my sister encountered a Hutterite woman dressed in traditional garb, including a polka-dotted head scarf, and asked "why is that woman dressed like a clown?" My mother's embarrassment did not stem, I think, from our lack of knowledge about difference (as I don't recall her ever educating us on the differences between us and these rare "others" we encountered), but instead from the fact that we were—as small children are apt to do—showing a lack of middle-class decorum by pointing, staring, and speaking audibly about differences that we were supposed to pretend not to notice. We later learned to talk in hushed tones about difference or to ignore it altogether. Although my sisters and I never did fully inherit our mother's concern for what "the neighbors might think," we did inherit the white, middle-class ethos of colorblindness—which we, raised as good liberals, identified with a lack of racism.

It is possible, of course, to fail to return our familial inheritance, to abandon the sexual, ethnic, class, or other orientation we have been given, to take a different direction. But typically this is not the case as the familial objects around which we are raised frequently obscure other possibilities. As Ahmed puts it, queer objects—say same-sex objects of desire, Muslim prayer mats, or something else that would shift our direction—"may not even get near enough to 'come into view' as possible objects to be directed toward" (91). Of course, what "comes into view" is not simply a matter of what enters our horizons, but of what and how we learn to see. If we learn to ignore that which is non-normative, we will not see it even when it is in our midst. Only in retrospect, having learned to see queerness, do I now recognize that many of the male friends of my (now deceased) mother—fellow musical theatre performers—were queer. But this, like issues of race, was never revealed or spoken about in my childhood home. Nor was it spoken about in the larger community in which I lived—a small town in which "don't ask, don't tell" seemed the key to harmonious living.

Taking seriously the spatial (and temporal) connotations of the term "straight," Ahmed investigates the ways in which certain bodies are viewed as being "on-line" or "in line" as a function of their alignment with the directions and directives of heteronormativity and whiteness. Bodies that are well aligned with normative spaces are able to "extend their reach" as a function of their inheritance. The heterosexual body, for example, takes up its place within the family by directing its desire toward marriage and reproduction of the family line, thus extending its normative reach into the future. The white body inhabits the world readied for it by colonialism with ease, finding most objects within reach and, in extending that reach, reproduces whiteness. The middle-class body inherits resources that enable the accumulation of material and cultural capital, thus propelling it both forward and up and, in following this direction, extends the reach of bourgeois values. Exploring the relation between what is "behind social action" (our inheritance) and "the process of social mobility," Ahmed uses Merleau-Ponty's example of the blind man's stick (131). The blind man extends his reach by means of the walking stick and thereby increases his motility and mobility. In using the walking stick habitually, moreover, the stick ceases to be an object for him, becoming incorporated into his body. Similarly, Ahmed suggests, heterosexual, white, middle-class bodies expand to incorporate "objects, tools, instruments and even 'others'" (132). In this way, what is within reach as a function of our inheritance (i.e., the privileges to which we have become habituated) further extends the reach of normative bodies. Like the blind man who stays on the well-worn path, navigating with his walking stick, heterosexual, white, middle-class bodies that remain "in line," typically have their "bearings"; they know "what to do to get to this place or to that place" (1).

Although my orientations will subsequently change, it is as a well-aligned heterosexual body that I pursue the project of motherhood as I enter my thirties and it is as an acquisitive white, middle-class body that I pursue a particular route to motherhood—a route that includes incorporating a child of color into our family.

Becoming a Mother: Adoption

April 30, 1992: Spring classes are over and I am tallying my final grades—already feeling that sense of deep freedom that comes from summer vacation stretching itself out in front of me—when I receive the phone call. "Congratulations! We have a baby for you. She was born yesterday—a healthy, biracial baby girl. Can you pick her up at Princeton Hospital tomorrow?

As a heterosexual, white, middle-class couple, my husband and I were not thrown off-line by discovering we were infertile. Having a family remained a future goal and infertility did not put having children outside of our reach. We knew exactly what to do in order to make a family; we would simply adopt children. Thus, upon receiving the phone call from the adoption agency, congratulating me on the child we have been awarded, I continue to have my bearings. Matter of factly, I turn in my grades, explore class rolls for a baby name (deciding on "Tomeka"— a variation of "Tamika" that will allow for the gender-neutral nickname, "Tomi" rather than "Tami"), call my husband to give him a shopping list (we will need a bassinet, a car seat, diapers, some basic infant clothes, bottles and formula for tomorrow), and leave the office to attend an end-of-the-term women's studies dinner to which I have been looking forward. When I announce my impending motherhood to my feminist colleagues, they raise their glasses in "congratulations," remarking on my apparent calmness.

Both my colleagues' congratulations and my own calmness illuminate further Ahmed's notion of straightness as being "on-line." The fact that I am congratulated on my forthcoming motherhood—first by the adoption agency, then by my colleagues, and later by family members, friends, and others—connotes motherhood as a measure of success. When we congratulate someone, we communicate our pleasure, approval, or praise for her actions. It is commonplace to congratulate people on the occasions that mark certain points deemed significant markers of a successful life journey, for example, on the occasion of their Bat or Bar Mitzvah, their confirmation, their graduation from high school or college, their promotion at work, their engagement, their marriage, buying their first home, their birthdays and anniversaries, and the arrival of children or grandchildren. Whether or not these are occasions of accomplishment, (good or bad) luck, or simple inertia, these occasions are celebrated as milestones in a normative life. A life that follows this straight line is praised and commended as a life well lived.

My calmness, in turn, on which my colleagues comment, reveals that this straight line marking a normative life journey is presumed by me to be my inheritance. There is, after all, nothing shocking about the phone call I receive. I have assumed all along that my husband and I would be given a child, as we fit the profile of good parents. We are a well-educated, middle-class, married couple who come from intact middle-class, educated families. Indeed, today's phone call was not the first offer of a child that we have received. Within the past three months, we have received two others: one offering us an infant with a cleft palette and another offering an infant with a potential heart problem. My husband and I declined both previous offers of parenthood—primarily out of fear that unknown medical costs would be beyond our means (or at least this is what we tell ourselves). We have thus made clear to the adoption agency that although we are prospective parents for a "special needs" child, we do not desire to adopt a child with potentially major medical difficulties. Of course, this is ridiculous—there is no guarantee that any child might not require special medical care during her or his life and if one were to have a child the "natural" way, one would simply cope with whatever difficulties arose. Yet, as adoptive parents, we have been presented with a menu of options and this is what we

have chosen: physical disabilities acceptable, but no major physical ill-
nesses, no major cognitive impairments, no children over the age of
three, sibling groups acceptable, any race or ethnicity welcome.

Adoption here reveals itself as a consumer choice. As David Eng
(2010) suggests in his analysis of lesbian adoption, "family is not only
whom you choose, but on whom you choose to spend your capital" (99).
Arguing that adoption is a form of "consumptive labor" that "serves to
produce and to organize social community as a supplement to capital,"
Eng highlights the ways in which the boundaries of the white, heteronormative, middle-class, nuclear family are expanded by the reproductive labor of less privileged women and consolidated by the affective
labor of adopted children (108–09). This is a point to which I later
return. For now, however, suffice it to say that for those accustomed
to having what we want within our reach, the asymmetrical processes
of economic exchange through which we benefit from the exploitation
of others' labor is rarely noticed. Indeed, in going to pick up Tomeka
at the hospital, my husband and I do not see ourselves as purchasing
a commodity at all; instead we view ourselves as providing a stable and
loving home for a child in need. Thus, when "our" baby is brought to
us in the hospital waiting room on May 1, 1992, we take her home joyfully—without ever considering the possibility that we have expanded
our family through the appropriation of a child who is the product of
another woman's labor.

As a new mother, my direction does shift as I must reorient myself
from a planned summer of research to new and competing responsibilities. Paying attention to the needs of the small, fragile, dependent body
we have brought into our home consumes most of my attention and my
time. Tomeka is a delight during the day—looking into my eyes while
she has her morning bottle, falling contentedly back to sleep, enjoying
the world around her during her waking afternoon periods, alert to
sounds and sights and tactile sensations. I cannot ascertain, however,
why our lovely infant transforms into a screaming banshee around
five o'clock each evening. It does not occur to me, in trying to inhabit
my daughter's perspective, that she has been separated from what was
familiar and familial territory before birth. Marking her beginnings in
this world as more-or-less simultaneous with my own beginnings as
her mother, I do not consider the possibility that this infant may be
experiencing loss as well as the shock of the new. Thus, my husband
and I simply learn to adapt to her daily transformations (as we will
later do again, less successfully, when Tomeka metamorphoses into a

teenager). One of us cooks supper while the other attempts to soothe her. Then we switch and take turns eating, each orienting ourselves toward our child rather than toward each other. After dishes are done and bottles sanitized, we take shifts walking and rocking our daughter until she finally collapses from exhaustion around midnight. This daily routine makes a concentrated focus on my research feel impossible; thus I make a conscious decision to turn my back on my desk in order to be present in the nursery.

Making such a choice is, of course, a privilege. As a university professor, I have an extended summer vacation and I make enough money to be able to support a stay-at-home husband working on his PhD. Hence, we can give our new baby the attention she needs, enjoying her, caring for her, napping with her, and staying gentle with her when she is inconsolable. I don't know how people with other responsibilities—daily work routines, other children, or other caregiving responsibilities, and no around-the-clock helpmate do this. It occurs to me that this is the situation faced by many birth mothers who relinquish their children for adoption—mothers who are young or poor or single and who face the impossibility of balancing the demands of full-time motherhood with the demands of full-time wage work (if they are fortunate enough to have such work). This is but a fleeting thought, however, and I quickly turn my attention back to my daughter, relegating her birth mother, along with half-written philosophy papers, to a filing cabinet that is rarely opened.

By August, as we near the completion of our probationary period as potential adoptive parents, however, Tomeka's birth mother once again enters our line of vision. We are anxious and uneasy as the obligatory notice goes in the paper alerting any interested parties to our intention to adopt Tomeka—hoping that her birth mother or birth father or other family member won't come out of the woodwork to claim her. No one does. Thus, on October 13, 1992, my husband and I joyfully adopt the four and a half-month-old baby girl who has lived with us since her third day of life. After the court proceedings, we take numerous photos of ourselves, baby in arms, and celebrate. Tomeka Guyana Park-Ozee, a beautiful brown-eyed, ebony-haired, olive-complexioned infant, is now finally *ours*.

Tomeka's birth mother was not present at the proceedings that day, nor had we previously met her. Indeed, at that time, we knew little about our new daughter's birth mother save that she was dark-skinned and beautiful (we'd been shown a photo), was twenty-one years old, had no known medical difficulties, and was of Guyanese heritage (we'd been provided with her medical history, which contained this minimal personal information). We were equally uninformed concerning the specific circumstances that led her to relinquish her infant into our care, knowing only that she was single, had no continuing relationship with the birth father and hoped to go to college. However, none of this bothered us at the time—we were entirely focused on *our* baby.

In thinking about neoliberal narratives of kinship, Eng argues that the logic of neoliberalism renders queer diasporic figures "ghostly" through a process of racial forgetting and colorblindness. The enjoyment of liberal rights and freedoms—including the rights to parenthood sought by both heterosexual and same-sex couples through adoption—is haunted ("ghosted"), however, by these forgotten queer and diasporic subjects. Tomeka's birth mother is just such a ghost during much of the first year of my motherhood. This ghost haunts the hospital where we pick up "our" three-day old child. (Perhaps she is still there? Certainly, she has been there recently. What happens if we encounter her?) She lingers, as a generous angel, behind the placement decision itself as someone who has approved us as her daughter's prospective parents. She floats ominously around the adoption proceedings as someone who might "come out" of the woodwork (as what? as a mother?) and disrupt our direction as parents. It is not that I never consider her existence; both before and after the adoption is final, I send photographs and notes about Tomeka's development to the adoption agency on a monthly basis to forward to her. But I do not know where or how she lives nor what she feels when she receives this correspondence. I rarely ask about her life; nor, when I do, does she answer. For some time, I do not even know her name. She remains thus, an abstraction, a ghostly exotic Other: the young, beautiful, dark-skinned woman of Guyanese-American descent who gifted us with a child. It is not until after I become pregnant myself that I begin to see her—and meet her—as a real person.

Becoming a Mother: Pregnancy and Birth

February 1993: After returning home from a winter visit to Canada to visit our family (and show off our new child), I am feeling sick and have put on weight. My husband suggests I might be pregnant; I insist this is impossible. When he returns from grocery shopping with a home pregnancy test, I hope that this will finally put our dispute to

rest. It does. I am pregnant. A hastily arranged doctor's visit confirms
the result of the home pregnancy test shortly thereafter. "Congratula-
tions!" my obstetrician says, "you are going to have a baby!"

When my obstetrician congratulates me on my second entry into
motherhood, I am less than receptive. Although she means well, my
physician seems not to recognize that I am conflicted about my unexpected pregnancy. This pregnancy is ill timed from a professional standpoint. I am halfway through my probationary period as a tenure-track
faculty member and my research already is behind schedule, given it
received little of my attention the previous summer. This pregnancy
also is ill timed from a family-planning perspective. We had hoped to
space our children further and to adopt a second biracial child (a boy)
in order to complete our multicultural family. This pregnancy thus
seems to foil the direction I was headed, reducing rather than expanding my menu of choices. Therefore, I do not announce my pregnancy
to anyone other than my husband for several weeks.

Even heterosexual, white, middle-class bodies may lose their direction. In these moments of becoming lost, one becomes ungrounded,
uncomfortable, disoriented. Ahmed likens the feeling of disorientation
to walking blindfolded into a room (6–7). If the room is familiar—one
into which we have previously extended ourselves, we can reach out
toward objects and the familiarity of those objects allows us to discern
which way we are facing, thus reorienting ourselves. If, however, the
room is unfamiliar, things are not as easy. The objects for which we
reach may not allow us to get our bearings; a lack of knowledge about
them leaves us uncertain about which way to turn.

I am ambivalent about this pregnancy. On the one hand, it disrupts the direction I had laid out for myself. On the other hand, it
brings new possibilities into my reach, an opportunity to experience
pregnancy and birth giving that I had not thought possible. Thus, I am
torn and do not know which way to turn. An abortion would put me
back on track both professionally and personally. Yet, to my surprise, I
find myself imaginatively attached to the idea of being pregnant. And I
know that the opportunity to experience pregnancy—now unexpectedly
within my reach—is unlikely to make a repeat appearance within my
thirty-two-year-old bodily horizon. Thus, in March, after much delibera-
tion and an amniotic fluid test that reveals no chromosomal or genetic
difficulties with the fetus, I breathe a sigh of relief, cease my Internet
search for places that will perform a second trimester abortion, throw

out my research plans and our family planning manual, and prepare, together with my husband, for another baby.

"Moments of disorientation," Ahmed (2006) argues, "are vital," as it is in these moments of being "off-line" that that the "becoming vertical" of ordinary (straight) perception is challenged (107, 156). Moments of disorientation reveal the ground on which we previously walked as unstable; moreover, seeing the world "slantwise" allows other objects not previously within our bodily horizon to "come into view" and "offer[s] us the hope of new directions" (107, 158). It is the ill-timed and unintended (off-line) nature of my pregnancy that disorients me in the first instance, challenging my white, middle-class perceptions of family planning and career development. It is, however, the pregnancy itself (the paradigmatic straight activity of breeding) that disrupts my previous feminist perceptions of reproduction and, for the first time, brings Tomeka's birth mother into view as a real person, rather than a mere ghostly presence.

In being pregnant, I am forced to pay sustained attention to my body for the first time in my adult life. In thinking about whiteness as a "bad habit," Ahmed suggests that "white bodies are habituated insofar as they 'trail behind' actions: they do not get 'stressed' in their encounters with objects or others, as their whiteness goes unnoticed" (129, 132). As a white body, I have not had to face my whiteness; insofar as the world is oriented *around* whiteness, I rarely have to turn my attention back onto myself, as do the black and brown bodies that are "stopped" or "held up" for being out of place (140–41). Similar considerations pertain to the ease of my movement and action in the world thus far as a heterosexual body, a middle-class body and white-collar worker, and a healthy—as well as relatively young and thin—body. It is only by virtue of inhabiting a female body that I have ever felt the need to pay attention to my body. But, given my various other privileges, my orientation toward my body even as a woman has, frankly, been minimal. As a pregnant woman, however, my body now demands attention. I must suddenly pay attention to what I do (or do not) eat or drink, to getting adequate rest, and I must make regular visits to the physician's office. I thus begin to recognize the labor that is involved in reproductive labor, as well as the queerness of pregnancy itself.

As my pregnancy continues, it is the shape and mobility of my body—in addition to its health—that I can no longer take for granted. When I fail to pay close attention to my body, I bump into things a lot. The "boundaries of my body" are, as Iris Young (1984) describes in her phenomenological account of pregnancy, "in flux."

I literally do not have a firm sense of where my body ends and the world begins. . . . I move as if I could squeeze around chairs and through crowds as I could seven months before, only to find my way blocked by my own body sticking out in front of me—but yet, not me, since I did not expect it to block my own passage. As I lean over my chair to tie my shoe, I am surprised by the graze of this hard belly on my thigh. . . . The belly is other, since I did not expect it there, but since I feel the touch upon it, it is me. (410)

My body no longer trails, unnoticed, "behind me." Instead, it protrudes quite obviously in front of me, demanding my attention be continually turned back onto myself. By month eight, I can no longer tie my shoes, nor even see my feet. Getting up requires assistance, as does anything that requires bending over. Reaching out for ordinary objects (the platter on a low shelf, the computer on my desk) once easily within my grasp, becomes difficult. In being compelled to look upon my body as an object that impedes my mobility, I get a partial glimpse of what it is like to be "other." Insight into how abnormal bodies are othered also accompanies my encounters with others, including strangers, who suddenly feel compelled and entitled to reach out and touch my belly. This invasion of my personal space is, I imagine (rightly or wrongly), akin to that experienced by black bodies when white others want to feel their hair or feel entitled to paternalistically pat them on the head. My very large and awkward body that moves uneasily in the world and attracts the attention of others is, however, unlike the black body, the fat body, or the disabled body, only a temporary condition. Unlike these other bodies, I know that this body will not impede me for much longer. Moreover, the pregnant body that I currently inhabit, although frequently exoticized, is rarely reviled.

Thus, while I am, occasionally, annoyed by the fact that my body won't behave as I expect, for the most part, I experience my body in what Young (following Sally Gadow 1980) terms an "aesthetic mode" (Young 1984, 411). My body comes to the forefront of my attention not merely because of its inability to complete everyday projects with its former ease, but also because its changing mass and shape and movements genuinely fascinate me. I engage in what Young describes as "an innocent narcissism," frequently gazing at myself in the mirror and/or caressing my own stomach, "taking pleasure in discovering new things in my body" without judging my shape or appearance or worrying about what it might look like to someone else (Young 1984, 412).

I am, moreover, mysteriously satisfied to know that a new life is growing inside me. It is the emotional attachment I develop toward this life that causes me to reconsider the politics of both abortion and adoption. As I see my new daughter's images on sonograms, feel her begin to move around inside me, and subsequently poke her knees, feet, elbows and fists against my stomach lining, I feel a privileged connection to this life growing inside of me. I cannot imagine (although I do try to imagine) what it would be like to relinquish this life into someone else's care. I joke about feeling like Lieutenant Ripley (Sigourney Weaver) in the film *Aliens* as my daughter's kicks and punches become readily visible from the outside of my body and her movements resemble, in Adrienne Rich's words, "a being imprisoned within me" that is trying to get out (Rich 1986, 63). And yet, she is not alien to me. The "boundary between what is within, myself, and what is outside, separate" has become "fluid" and although I do "experience my insides as the space of another," I also experience it as my own body, myself (Young 1984, 409). She and I are—for now—one complex being. Despite longstanding feminist sensibilities, I can no longer view what is inside me as a mere fetus. I am with child. This is a baby; this baby is part of my body. She is, as Rich contends, neither me, nor "not-me" (1986, 64). Our relationship is more complicated than either pro-choice or pro-life bumper stickers acknowledge.

It is these phenomenological realizations that turn me toward Tomeka's birth mother, to her presence in the world as a real and complex person with needs, desires, fears, love and, I now imagine, grief over the felt necessity of relinquishing a child she had chosen to nourish in her body for nine months. How could I, a self-proclaimed feminist, have been so entirely insensitive to the existential dilemmas faced by a woman whose sacrifice had made my own joy possible? Why did orientating myself toward my adopted child include turning my back on her birth mother?

In retrospect, I see my former insensitivity as, in part, a form of willful ignorance that is akin to other widespread practices of ignorance practiced by those of privilege: celebrating military victories with little thought to those invisible others who have been killed and maimed by our bombing campaigns; delighting in our ability to find cheap consumer goods, while ignoring the exploitation of third-world women, men, and children necessary to their production; congratulating ourselves on our academic successes and career promotions without recognizing the labor of those bodies who, as secretaries, housekeepers, child-care workers, farmworkers, short-order cooks, and so forth, make it possible for a few of us to lead a life of the mind. Yet there is, I suspect, more to it than this. Aiding and abetting an adoptive mother's specific form of willful ignorance are feminist attitudes toward pregnancy, birth, and motherhood. In our quest to escape compulsory motherhood, middle-class white feminists have focused on abortion as the path to reproductive freedom and—for strategic reasons that are understandable, but nonetheless dishonest—reduced the relationship of a pregnant woman to the life growing inside her to the relationship between a host and a parasite.[1] A portrayal of pregnancy and birth giving as either detrimental or inconsequential to women's lives effectively resists pernicious narratives of maternal instinct and the romanticization of motherhood, but it does so at a price. The price exacted is turning our backs on and attention away from those for whom the experience of pregnancy and motherhood is anything other than hostility or indifference. In belittling the experience of pregnancy, many feminists have rendered invisible, inaudible, and inexplicable the emotional, existential, and phenomenological landscape of women who use reproductive technologies to enable biological motherhood, as well as those who refuse medical interventions to end a pregnancy. We also have devalued the considerable grief that many—albeit not all—women experience when separated from their embryos, fetuses, and children through infertility, abortion, miscarriage, stillbirths, and voluntary or involuntary relinquishment of children they have borne. It is this devaluation that makes it possible for an adoptive mother, like myself, to ignore the fact that her gain may well be another woman's—and child's—loss.

It is during my sixth month of pregnancy that Tomeka (now almost a year old) and I meet her birth mother, Trish, for the first time. We have been instructed by the adoption agency not to exchange addresses or phone numbers, but have recently broken this protocol, exchanged phone numbers, and arranged a lunch meeting. My husband is uncomfortable with our meeting, afraid that if Trish sees Tomeka, she will want her back. But I am unequivocally committed to this meeting, convinced by my own experience of pregnancy that a birth mother should not be irrevocably separated (at somebody else's will) from the child to whom she was attached for nine months. I am nervous—not because I think Trish is going to steal our (or is it her?) child, but because I want her to be a part of our lives. Thus, I want her to like us. I fret about how to make conversation with this woman who is both intimately connected to our lives and yet also a virtual stranger. I don't wish to make the wrong impression by erring in the direction of being inappropriately intimate, nor do I wish to come across as cold and distant. We meet at a restaurant and my fears are almost immediately alleviated as she greets us with a wide smile and a hug. We talk about her job and mine, about her pregnancy and mine, and about Tomeka who, after we finish eating, becomes the centerpiece on our table. The photograph that my husband took of us this day depicts our triangulation perfectly. Trish has her hands protectively placed on Tomeka's midriff to ensure she won't topple from or crawl off the table, directing a loving gaze at her (our) daughter. Tomeka doesn't resist Trish's attentions, but reaches out to me, looking in my direction for reassurance that everything is fine. While Trish gazes at Tomeka and Tomeka gazes at me, my own loving gaze and smile is affixed on Trish. I really like her. I leave the restaurant, after what feels a bit like a successful first date, optimistic that this is the start of a real connection between all of us.

Postpartum Reflections

On August 15, 1993, I give birth to my second daughter, Dakota Elizabeth Park-Ozee. Her middle name, like her sister's, celebrates her maternal lineage. (Elizabeth is my mother's name.) It is in the aftermath of this birth that I once again suffer disorientation. As second-time parents, we have all of the necessary material items for infant care in our possession. Emotional resources are scarcer, however. I am grieving my mother's recent diagnosis of stage IV breast cancer and my inability to be by her side. My sister who has come down from Canada to help me in my mother's absence has to leave in ten days; my husband, who has just started a new vocation as an apprentice carpenter, has no vacation time accrued; and the fall semester is about to begin. Unable to afford leave without pay, I have reluctantly accepted a senior colleague's gracious offer to cover my classes for the first six weeks, but I will need to return to the classroom by October. In September, I begin searching for child care, with both children in tow. However, my newest daughter wants to nurse around the clock and, if detached from me, screams with a persistence that matches—and a shrillness that far surpasses—her sister's earlier squalling. This does not endear her to potential caretakers, nor always to me.

I am physically and emotionally exhausted. Hormonal upheavals combined with sleep deprivation, grief, social isolation, and stress spiral quickly into what I later recognize as a postpartum depression that leaves me feeling quite literally insane. Like the narrator in Sartre's *Nausea*, I feel that I am losing my grip on the world. More aptly, perhaps, I find myself identifying with the narrator in Charlotte Perkin Gilman's (1892) short story, *"The Yellow Wallpaper,"* a woman confronted by the horrors that transpire within the walls of her home. Like Gilman's narrator, "[i]t is getting to be a great effort for me to think straight" (7).

In Gilman's story, the straight lines of heteronormativity and its reproductive narrative are personified by John, a husband and physician advocating a rest cure for postpartum woes and John's sister who helps to enforce this "cure," despite the desire of the protagonist to work and to socialize. Finding herself increasingly straightjacketed by these characters who strive to keep her "in line," the narrator becomes fearful of her family and of her home itself. Both her husband and the walls of her room, she notes, have become "very queer" (10). At first she sees "a strange, provoking, formless sort of figure, that seems to skulk about" behind the design of her wallpaper (6). Subsequently, she describes the wallpaper's pattern as "slanting waves of optic horror" behind which there are "interminable grotesques" that "seem to form around a common centre and rush off in headlong plunges" (7). Finally, as the narrator examines the character of the wallpaper more closely and carefully, she becomes "quite sure" that the previously seen ghostly figures are "a woman"—or perhaps "a great many women"— who are attempting to "climb through" the bars that pattern the paper (12). As they attempt (unsuccessfully) to climb through these bars, she notes, their eyes become "bulbous" as they are "strangled" and turned "upside down" (14). In coming to this slanted perception of her home, Gilman's narrator, herself, becomes irretrievably queer. No longer simply content to observe these other caged women, she attempts to help them (herself?) escape by destroying the wallpaper and skulking alongside them. As the distinction between the narrator and the monstrous Other is blurred, the story concludes with the narrator herself "creep[ing] smoothly on the floor, [where her] shoulder just fits in that long smooch around the wall, so [she] cannot lose [her] way" (15).

Like the narrator in *The Yellow Wallpaper*, I am socially isolated after giving birth and unable to write—or even speak—intelligibly. "I cry at nothing, and cry most of the time" (6). Still clinging to my self-perception as a good woman, however, I do not tell anybody else that I am falling apart, doing my best—although quite unsuccessfully—to perform as strong, resilient and capable. Unlike the somewhat giddy disorientation of being a pregnant body-in-flux, this disorientation feels "too shattering to endure" (Ahmed 2006, 176). I cannot, however, reorient myself by clinging to the familiar, as it is the familiar itself that has become strange.

Noting the unsustainability of the differentiation between "strange and familiar," Ahmed explains that "[e]ven in a strange or unfamiliar environment we might find our way, given our familiarity with social form, with how the social is arranged" (7). Returning to the example of being blindfolded in a strange room, Ahmed reminds us that our knowledge about rooms, even unfamiliar ones, allows us to navigate them in the dark. We know what a wall feels like and that it marks the boundaries of a room, thus making it possible to find our way to a doorway by reaching for the wall and slowly following it until we find our way out. What happens, however, when the walls of the house take on a life of their own and no longer lead us to a perceptible exit? What happens when we are lost not because we inhabit an unfamiliar space, but because we can no longer find our bearings within that which is familiar? Will we find ourselves, like Gilman's narrator, forever "creep[ing] smoothly on the floor," in circles?

As the neediness of my own children becomes unbearable, I suddenly understand—even empathize with—mothers profiled in sensationalist news stories who have abused, neglected, or abandoned their babies. Like the narrator in Gilman's short story, I suddenly see the ghostly figures of other women—"a great many women." And from my newly slanted perspective, I understand that these women—typically imagined as monsters—simply might be struggling to escape the barriers that constrain them. Although I never harm my children, the distinction between good and bad mothers, between the monstrous Other and me, has been irretrievably blurred.

The Good, the Bad, and the Mad: Profiles of Motherhood

The turn of the century witnessed a spate of attention to maternal abuse and neglect of children in the United States, including some highly publicized cases of maternal infanticide and filicide. In 1987, Sheryl Lynn Massip bludgeoned her infant son and then drove over him with her Volvo. In 1994, Susan Smith was accused of murdering her two young sons by strapping them in car seats and rolling the car in which they were seated into a lake. In 1996, Darlie Router was arrested for stabbing her two young sons to death; Susan Eubanks was convicted in that same year of killing her four sons with a revolver as they watched television and played Nintendo. In 1997, Melissa Drexler gave birth to a baby in a bathroom during her high school prom, subsequently wrapping it in plastic bags and depositing it in the trash. In 1998, Sandi Nieves killed her four daughters by setting fire to the house in which they were sleeping. In 2001, Andrea Yates confessed to drowning her five children in a bathtub after hearing God instruct her to do so. In 2003, Deanna Laney confessed to smashing her three sons' skulls with rocks and, in 2004, Dena Schlosser killed her infant daughter by amputating both her arms. Both Laney and Schlosser, like Yates, cited God-given signs for their actions. In 2008, Casey Anthony reported her daughter Caylee missing a month after Caylee's disappearance and was subsequently arrested for child neglect, obstruction of justice, and finally first-degree murder.

The shock elicited by these cases suggests that infanticide and filicide are obscure crimes—crimes so queer as to be unimaginable. In fact, however, almost 10,000 children under the age of five suffered homicide at the hands of a parent between 1976 and 2005 in the United States with several thousand more killed by other family members or intimate friends of the family (U.S. Bureau of Justice Statistics 2010). Statistics on infanticide and filicide in the United States suggest that the problems are systemic and require complex, multipronged solutions (Friedman et al., 2005). Several motives for parental murder of children have been identified—for example, systemic problems of family violence (Fujiwara et al. 2009), economic stress (Gauthier, Chaudoir and Forsyth 2003), mothers' feelings of inadequacy and frustration (Smithey 2001), and the "social construction of and constraints upon mothering" (Meyer et al. 2001, 2). However, sensationalist media stories concerning child homicide rarely discuss the familial, social, or economic factors that might contextualize the problem of infanticide and filicide, choosing instead to pathologize individual perpetrators. Moreover, the cases on which the media chooses to focus almost always feature "murderous moms," whereas it is men (fathers and boyfriends) who are responsible for the majority of cases of murdered and abused children older than one week (Overpeck et al. 1998; U.S. Bureau of Justice Statistics 2010).

Noting that we have implemented few child protection policies (addressing, e.g., poverty or male violence, as well as postpartum depression or other sources of maternal mental illness), feminist legal scholar Elizabeth Rapaport (2006) suggests that high-profile infanticide cases are "less about the protection of children than the regulation of women" (530). In widely publicized infanticide and filicide cases, we witness something we might call maternal profiling. I use the term *maternal profiling* to deliberately evoke the connotations associated with the term *racial profiling*. Practices of racial profiling by police officers, private security agents, and national security personnel disproportionately target people of color for surveillance, investigation, and law enforcement, making black and brown people the scapegoat for community concerns about safety and security. Racial profiling takes place not only in matters of criminal investigation, but also in the cultural depiction of crime (wherein people of color are more likely to be portrayed in the evening news, in television series, and in films as violent criminals than they are to be depicted as victims of interpersonal and systematic violence). In a parallel fashion, practices of maternal profiling by social workers, police officers, and others disproportionately target mothers for regulation and punishment, making women the scapegoat for community concerns about child welfare. Not only are mothers most likely to be profiled in the media as the perpetrators of infanticide and filicide, they also are more likely than fathers or others to be blamed for children's ill health (both physical and emotional), children's educational deficiencies (learning disabilities and high-school drop-out rates), children's antisocial behavior (everything from poor manners to teenage delinquency to serial murder), and any failure to protect a child from harm (mothers, for example, are frequently blamed for allowing their children to be sexually victimized by male family members). In popular culture, as in the implementation of child welfare guidelines, mothers are much more likely to be portrayed as perpetrators of abuse and neglect than as victims of interpersonal and institutional violence and neglect.

Maternal profiling does not merely parallel racial profiling, however; it also intersects with it. It is not, after all, every mother who is selected for investigation of child neglect and abuse. Nor are all mothers equally likely to be portrayed as bad mothers in the news media or other facets of popular culture. In selecting some mothers as particularly apt to endanger their children (and the broader communities those children inhabit), social workers, police officers, journalists, filmmakers, and others engage in practices of maternal profiling that are frequently racialized. Just as we presume that those who would terrorize our nation are apt to be of a particular complexion and ethnicity (including a presumed religious affiliation), so too do we presume that those mothers most apt to abuse or neglect their children have particular racial and ethnic characteristics (as well as class and age characteristics) that can be used to identify them. Such racialized profiling of bad mothers was particularly evident during the moral panic surrounding an alleged epidemic of "crack babies" during the 1980s and 1990s. Photographs of tiny babies hooked to ventilators, or of crack-addicted mothers, usually African American, living in substandard conditions, forwarded a narrative about the supposed moral depravity of poor women of color. This press coverage, in turn, prompted numerous punitive legislative proposals permitting the arrest, incarceration and sterilization of women accused of drug-use while pregnant (Cox 2011).

Indeed, it is only against the background of a racialized profile of the "bad" mother that public shock concerning cases of infanticide and filicide sensationalized in the news media makes sense. Massip, Smith, Router, Drexler, Nieves, Yates, Laney, Schlosser, and Anthony are all white; many of them are middle class. It is the failure of these women (women who are supposed to epitomize feminine virtue) to orientate themselves appropriately as protective and nurturing mothers that fuels public fascination (Rapaport 2006, 558). The public is less easily shocked when someone such as Melissa Lucio, a janitor and Latina mother of 14 children, is charged with killing her youngest daughter through excessive abuse. Poor women of color—stereotyped as promiscuous, irresponsible breeders, and drug addicts—are those most likely to be suspected of child maltreatment. Indeed, African American, Native American, and Hispanic mothers (almost four times as likely to live in poverty as whites) are "nearly twice as likely to be investigated for abuse or neglect" (U.S. Dept. of Health and Human Services, Children's Bureau 2011. Tables 3–12).

Whereas poor women of color are commonly viewed as "bad" mothers, white, middle-class women who kill their children are pathologized (like Gilman's narrator) as "mad" (Rapaport 2006). Thus, many cases of infanticide capturing public attention feature mental illness as the primary factor explaining why otherwise good women might kill their children (Resnick 1969). This explanation enabled Massip, Yates, Laney, and Schlosser to escape imprisonment, secured Drexler a reduced sentence, and saved Smith from receiving the death penalty as a punishment for her actions. Although a jury convicted Massip, a young housewife, of second-degree murder, the trial judge who declared her not guilty by reason of insanity overturned her conviction and committed her to outpatient psychiatric treatment and ongoing supervision by a Forensic Conditional Release Program. Yates, Laney, and Schlosser—all stay-at-home, married mothers and devout Christians, portrayed as good wives and devoted mothers to their children—were each found not guilty of their crimes by reason of insanity and were committed to mental health institutions.[2] Drexler's middle-class upbringing earned her the benefit of the doubt as a young woman who suffered from "pregnancy denial," enabling her to plead guilty to aggravated manslaughter rather than murder; she was released on parole after serving a little more than three years of her fifteen-year sentence. In the Smith case, a prosecutorial case that attempted to position her as a bad mother (who viewed her children as an impediment to starting a new life with a recent boyfriend) led to her conviction for the dual murders of her sons. However, Smith's defense focused on her tragic childhood, her husband's infidelity, and her boyfriend's rejection of her as causes of mental illness leading to Smith's heinous act (Dozier 1995), providing evidence that Smith was a doting mother to her sons up until the time of her crime. Smith was thus spared the death sentence by a partially sympathetic jury, receiving 30 years to life in prison (Rapaport 2006, 562–64).

Router, Eubanks, and Nieves, like Lucio, were less fortunate. All are on death row for their acts of filicide. These cases illustrate that white skin, on its own, is insufficient for passing as a good mother: "the white body must also be a respectable and clean body . . . a body that is 'in line'" (Ahmed 2006, 136). Router, Eubanks, and Nieves all failed to exhibit the middle-class decorum necessary for gaining the benefit of the doubt as proper women and thus good mothers. Although married, Router was successfully portrayed by the prosecution as white trash: she was deeply in debt, she dressed in revealing ways, had breast implants, body piercings, and tattoos, owned sex toys, and partied with girlfriends at a male strip club. Viewing Router's crass materialism, brashness, immodesty, and raunchy behavior as incompatible with the virtues of middle-class motherhood, the jury believed the prosecutorial case that she had killed her children to relieve herself of the financial drain and physical labor of caring for them (Rapaport 2006, 565–68). Eubanks and Nieves were both positioned as angry and vengeful women, also lacking middle-class restraint. Although the defense argued that Eubanks was in a "diminished mental state" when she shot her sons, due to extended alcohol and prescription drug use combined with a domestic dispute earlier that day, in the end, Eubanks' alcoholism and domestic disagreements with both her current boyfriend and her ex-husband proved her undoing. Public intoxication and public displays of anger (she slashed the tires on her boyfriend's car) could not be reconciled with the notion that Eubanks was a good (virtuous) woman; thus, prosecutors succeeded in convincing the jury that Eubanks had killed her sons as an act of revenge against their fathers, who had all left her. Similarly, Nieves' actions were portrayed as lashing back at the men in her life with whom she had experienced failed relationships, including two ex-husbands (the fathers of the girls) and a boyfriend who was threatening to undo his adoption of the girls. The defense argued that Nieves, who had a history of epilepsy, was in an unconscious, sleepwalking-like state induced by a combination of hormonal imbalance, stress, and an adverse reaction to prescription drugs at the time she set her house ablaze with her children inside it. The defense's argument that Nieves was a good woman and devoted mother whose children "were her world" was undermined, however, by her unseemly sexual history (not only did her children have different fathers; at one point Nieves had been married to her own stepfather) and a fourteen-year-old son who escaped the blaze and testified against her in court.

Prosecutors sought the death penalty for Anthony as well, portraying her as a promiscuous, self-centered, unmarried young woman who sought a carefree life without the responsibilities of motherhood. After a lengthy trial, however, the jury quickly found her "not guilty" of killing her two-year-old daughter, Caylee. Determining the prosecutorial case to be based solely on circumstantial evidence (failing to prove "beyond a reasonable doubt" that Anthony had committed the crimes of which she was accused), the jury also found Anthony "not guilty" on the charges of aggravated child abuse and aggravated manslaughter of a child, convicting her on only one charge: misleading law enforcement. The general public was outraged at their "not guilty" verdict. Even a host of celebrities from Miley Cyrus to Kim Kardashian expressed their disbelief on television, Facebook, and Twitter feeds. Like the other women currently awaiting execution, Anthony had been portrayed consistently and incessantly by the media—for almost three years—as lacking the virtues of middle-class womanhood. Photos of her partying and drinking with friends during the time of Caylee's absence were widely circulated on the evening news and social media. Also covered in excruciating detail were Anthony's conviction for check fraud and the subsequent defamation suit brought against her by a babysitter she had named as a potential suspect in Caylee's disappearance (Boedecker 2009; Karas 2010). Particularly damning to Anthony was the fact that she did not report her daughter missing for a month after her disappearance and, as the news media frequently noted, her seeming lack of grief about her daughter's death. This failure of maternal duty, combined with a failure of appropriate demeanor, literally blackened Anthony's record, ensuring that she could not pass as a good (respectable) mother. Thus, moments after the verdict was read, masses of people outside the courthouse began crying and screaming "Justice for Caylee" and "Fry Casey." When Anthony was released from prison, a SWAT team transferred her in secrecy to an undisclosed "secure" location and then later transferred her from there to elsewhere in fear that an angry mob might execute her themselves. Whether or not Anthony killed her daughter is unknown, but as public outrage demonstrated, Anthony clearly fit the profile of a "bad" mother and thus, many concluded, a mother capable of murder.

Cases of infanticide and filicide are not, of course, the only cases in which we can detect maternal profiling at work. Indeed, the intersection of maternal and racial profiling extends beyond reports of child maltreatment into all stages of the child welfare process: which reports of abuse are selected for investigation, which accusations are found to be substantiated, which families are offered services related to keeping children in the home, which children are removed from their homes and placed in foster care, how long such children remain in foster care, and which children are ultimately placed for adoption, severing their birth families' parental rights.[3] Examining cases in which mothers kill their children is instructive, however, in bringing to our attention just how far "off-line" some mothers—including biological mothers—may wander. Public shock and outrage at such cases, moreover, illuminates our desire to distance ourselves from such monstrously queer mothers. Our fascination with mothers who kill their children both "leads [us] toward and separates [us] from them" (Kristeva 1982, 2). We recoil from these subjects as Other and yet they confront us with the fragility of the boundaries by which we define ourselves as (good or pure) subjects, both individually and collectively.

The queerness of the mother who kills her children (and the ways in which we recoil from this image) bears a certain resemblance to the queerness of the terrorist (from whom we so carefully distance ourselves) as insightfully analyzed by Jasbir Puar (2007). In *Terrorist Assemblages: Homonationalism in Queer Times*, Puar argues persuasively that the figure of the Muslim terrorist (as well as "the turbaned Sikh man so often mistaken for him, and the woman in hijab who must be rescued from them") is "always already sexually pathological" (173). Noting how gay patriots, such as Mark Bingham, are characterized as "one of us" by emphasis on their positive (normative) attributes (he was masculine, athletic, white, heroic, and called his mother), whereas the terrorist, such as Osama Bin Laden, is characterized as Other by emphasis on his racialized sexuality (he was feminine, perverse, dark, pedophilic, and disowned by his family), Puar argues that "what is at stake here is not only that one was good and the other evil; the homosexuality of Bingham is converted into acceptable patriot values, while the evilness of Bin Laden is more fully and efficaciously rendered through associations with sexual excess, failed masculinity (i.e., femininity) and faggotry" (46). Similarly, what is at stake, it seems, in distinguishing between "mad" mothers and "bad" mothers is not merely that one is good (and deserving of mercy) and the other evil (and deserving of the most severe punishment we can dole out). The crimes of women such as Yates, Laney, and Schlosser are converted into excusable acts by the heteronormative characterizations of the women who committed them (married, Christian women, devoted to their husbands and children), whereas the evilness of Router, Eubanks, and Nieves is communicated through associations with sexual excess (Router's revealing attire, breast implants, body piercings, sex toys, and raunchy behavior), failed femininity (Eubanks' and Nieves' failed marriages and relationships and a lack of feminine docility), and perversity (promiscuity, incestuous relationships).

The legal distinction between "mad" and "bad" mothers as analyzed by Rapaport thus reveals itself as akin to the homonationalist distinction between "good" and "bad" queers as analyzed by Puar. In the case of heteronormative women who kill their children, as in the case of homonormative subjects such as Bingham, we may hate the sin, but love the sinner. But in the case of non-normative (perversely racialized and sexualized) women who kill their children, as in the case of terrorists such as Bin Laden, we hate both the sin *and* the sinner. As the term "hate" rightly suggests, our reaction to the perverse bodies of baby killers and terrorists is not so much a cognitive evaluation of their behavior as it is an affective reaction to their body, to their being in the (our) world. We recoil from such subjects, literally distancing ourselves from them because we are repulsed. Through such affective reactions as love and hate we align ourselves with some bodies while aligning ourselves against others (Ahmed 2004). We behave mercifully toward the heteronormative body of the woman who in an episode of madness kills her children not because of her circumstances (which are, after all, quite privileged). Instead she is the object of our mercy because she is perceived as "in line" with "us"; in pitying her, we align ourselves with her. The racialized, sexually perverse body of the baby killer, in contrast, is shown no mercy. She is the object of pubic hatred and in hating her (or the specter of her), we disalign ourselves with her. She becomes the dreaded, unintelligible, queer Other who must be ousted from our midst.

What might happen if, instead of pitying "mad" mothers and hating "bad" mothers, we were unmoved by the distinction between the heteronormative body and its queer Other? What if we did not align ourselves with "good" breeders (and "good" queers), while drawing the line against "bad" breeders (and "bad" queers)? We also might ask how to imagine a world in which mothering isn't a "line" at all, but a queer triangulation wherein the distinction between breeders and queers, itself becomes blurred. Such a picture may threaten loss of our moral compass and our theoretical bearings. Yet, as Ahmed reminds us, "'getting lost' still gets us somewhere" (7).

2

The Adoptive Maternal Body

Queering Reproduction

> Queer, as a marker of both identity and politics has always signified in opposition to heterosexuality as denoting not only different-sex object choice but also [opposition to] an ethos of reproduction and familialism; hence the pejorative term 'breeders' that queers apply to straights, a term that ridicules and denounces the heterosexual commitment to this ethos. But what happens when queers begin to breed?
>
> —Amalia Ziv (2011)

In her paper, "What's Queer About Queer Breeders?" Ziv (2011) examines "the contradictory implications of queer parenting," arguing that gay and lesbian parenting "subverts key elements of the heteronormative ideology of the family, and revolutionizes kinship" at the same time as it succumbs, perhaps, to the pressures of "normalization and assimilation." In this chapter, I contest the border between queers and breeders from another angle, asking not about queers (e.g., lesbians) who breed, but instead about breeding (e.g., mothering) that is queer. What happens when mothering occurs queerly? And what might examining queer forms of motherhood teach us about normative forms of mothering?

Like queer theorists, feminist theorists often have been suspicious of mothering as a practice that succumbs to heteropatriarchal
norms. Until its re-emergence as a somewhat romanticized practice
under third-wave feminism, motherhood was largely perceived and
theorized by feminists as a "burden" or "problem" for women (Fineman 1995a, xi). Many feminist critiques of motherhood, like queer
critiques of breeding, presuppose the biological paradigm of motherhood that accompanies conservative idealizations of motherhood. In so
doing, they erase the possibility of "unnatural" forms of motherhood
that may embody resistance to conservative discourses and practices
of mothering. Here I suggest that taking biological maternal bodies
as the paradigm from which we think about issues of mothering and
family obscures important facets of mothering more readily visible
from the (slanted) perspective of more marginal maternal bodies—
bodies marked as "deviant" in some fashion. My focus here is on the
adoptive maternal body; however, many of the reflections below apply
also to stepmothers and lesbian co-mothers as mothers who adopt
children into their lives and whose bodies deviate from biocentric
norms of motherhood whether or not they are *legally* recognized as
adoptive parents.

A pronatalist perspective on maternal bodies defines motherhood
as a natural, biological phenomenon including both a gestational and
genetic connection to one's child. From this perspective, there is something queer about any adoptive maternal body—a body that poses as,
yet is not a "real" mother; a body that presupposes, yet is defined in
opposition to, procreative activity; a body that is marked as defective,
yet is chosen as capable. This position of the adoptive maternal body on
the borderlands of maternity—a body that has been given an entry visa,
but not full citizenship in motherhood—provides the opportunity for a
critical perspective on the dominant scripts of motherhood. Viewing the
maternal vista "both from the outside in and the inside out," adoptive
mothers, like stepmothers and lesbian co-mothers, may embody a dual
consciousness related to our firsthand experiences of mothering combined with a critical awareness of how biological ("natural" or "real")
mothers—and others—perceive us (hooks 1984).[1] In addition to revealing the ways in which all maternal bodies are discursively mediated and
socially regulated, exploring motherhood through the lens of adoption
reveals important heteronormative and monomaternalistic assumptions
that frame normative views of the biological family.

Is There an Adoptive Maternal Body?

My claim that a focus on the production and experience of adoptive maternal bodies can queer motherhood presupposes that there is a distinction between adoptive maternal bodies and other parental bodies. But can we—without slipping into essentialist rhetoric—talk meaningfully about adoptive maternal bodies, as distinct from both biological maternal bodies and from adoptive (or other) paternal bodies?

Margaret Homans (2002) claims that adoption teaches important lessons in anti-essentialism: "to seek adoptive parenthood—especially across lines of nationality, race, and ethnicity—both requires and helps one to think beyond essentialisms of gender, race, ethnicity, culture, and even the body" (257). These lessons must be applied to thinking about the adoption experience itself. In speaking here of the adoptive maternal body, I do not wish to suggest that there is a singular adoptive experience. White adoptive mothers of black babies, American mothers of Chinese toddlers and able-bodied mothers of children with disabilities, for example, must negotiate culturally significant differences not experienced by those participating in same race, intranational adoptions of healthy newborns. Adoptive experiences vary widely: adoptions may be private or public, domestic or transnational, open or closed, formal or informal; they may involve the adoption of infants, toddlers, or older children; they may be same-race adoptions or transracial adoptions; they may involve grief over infertility or personal and political choices not to procreate biologically. In some cases, as with stepparent adoptions, the experience of mothering may not even originate from a desire for children, but simply be a (fortunate or unfortunate) byproduct of erotic desire and/or affection for another adult.

Similarly, there are a variety of experiences of biological mothering. Biological mothering may include a range of difficulties with conception, birthing, or parenting or none of these. Biological mothering may result from conscious personal choices to become pregnant, from unplanned pregnancies (such as my own), or from violations of rape and incest. Whether consciously chosen or not, biological mothering, like adoptive mothering, may be experienced as satisfying and fulfilling or rife with challenges and regret. Noting the vast range of different maternal experiences highlights the ways in which adoptive and biological maternal bodies may share analogous traits and experiences. Some biological maternal bodies, like some adoptive maternal bodies, may have experienced infertility issues. Some adoptive maternal bodies, like some biological maternal bodies, may have genetic connections to the child they adopt.

So *is* there an *adoptive* maternal body, distinct from a *biological* maternal body? If this is a question about essential differences, the answer is "no." As I suggest here, the distinction between adoptive and biological mothers is a historically contingent one. Nonetheless, we can point to patterns and threads of experience and meaning that run through many, if not all, contemporary narratives of adoptive mothering and that distinguish these experiences from those of (most, not all) biological mothers. As these narrative threads center primarily on issues of material, physiological difference, we can speak intelligibly about adoptive maternal *bodies*.

There are two different ways to become a biological mother: genetic and gestational. Historically, these two threads have been closely interwoven. However, the use of new reproductive technologies have pulled apart these strands, making clear that the genetic and gestational connections to one's child each provide a different, specific meaning to the maternal experience (Mahoney 1995). As Christine Overall (1987) observes, "in rearing one's genetically related offspring, very real experiences are involved in discerning and appreciating the similarities between oneself and one's children . . . there is a sense of continuity and history created by the genetic tie" (cited in Berg 1995, 82). As Michael Warner (1991) suggests—a point to which I return below—biological reproduction provides a sense of personal identity derived from embedding oneself in a narrative of generational succession. Yet, women's preference for giving birth over adopting reveals "not only a value placed on the genetic linkage," but on the uniquely female experiences of pregnancy and childbirth (Berg 1995, 81). As I learned in becoming unexpectedly pregnant after adopting my first child, "[t]he process of watching one's own body undergo transformation during pregnancy, establishing emotional connections with the fetus by feeling movements through the abdomen, and giving birth are unique to biological parents" (83). The meaningful element of biological motherhood is understood here as the establishment of an intimate relationship between a mother and child during gestation.

Some cases of adoption include genetic ties to children (as when one adopts a child neglected, abandoned or predeceased by a family relative), but most adoptive maternal bodies—like the bodies of stepmothers and lesbian co-mothers—are bodies that have neither a genetic, nor a gestational, connection to their adopted children. Adoptive maternal bodies thus understood, lack both of the threads of bodily connection to their children that are typically part of the experience of biological mothering. Adoptive mothers do not experience conception, pregnancy, or giving birth to their children, nor do they (typically) nourish them with milk from their breasts, nor do their children carry forward their DNA or resemble them in socially salient ways. Because an adoptive maternal body lacks the obvious bodily connections to her children that ground a traditional conception of motherhood as based on a natural (and also, it is sometimes alleged, instinctual) bond, adoptive mothers are, *qua* mothers, deviant. The experience of adoptive mothering, thus, differs both phenomenologically and narratively from that of gestational and genetic mothers.

It is tempting—and very common—to define adoptive maternal bodies in terms of the bodily experiences that they lack. Indeed, the number of women who undergo expensive, painful, and potentially harmful fertility treatments (rather than choosing adoptive mother-hood) can be explained largely by the desire to experience genetic and gestational connections to their offspring, as Barbara Berg (1995) observes in her analysis of women seeking medical assistance with fer-tility. From this pronatalist perspective, adoptive bodies are frequently characterized as infertile (and thus damaged) bodies and adoption is considered a "second-best" solution to the problem of discovered infer-tility: adoptive motherhood is better than being childless, but inferior to having a child of "one's own."

To avoid depicting adoptive motherhood as inferior to (less real than) biological motherhood, we must move away from a pronatalist perspective. One way to do this is to shift our focus from nature to nurture—or put another way, from the absent to the present embodi-ments of mother–child relations in adoptive families. There are many nongenetic, nongestational, bodily relationships between mothers and children that serve to connect parent and child in both momentary and in fundamental and long-lasting ways. As Margaret Homans (2002) indicates, all forms of parenthood include intense bodily experiences— "there are the same pleasures of plump baby-flesh, almost the same number of diapers to change and sleepless nights" (266). There are the same joys of and responsibilities for bathing, feeding, singing lullabies, and reciting stories to one's child. Adoptive mothers carry infants in our arms and potty train our toddlers. As the mothers of infants, toddlers, and/or teens, we too are familiar with the tears, screams, laughter and smiles that "enter one's bones" (266).

A difficulty with defining adoptive maternal bodies in terms of their participation in these nurturing roles is that adoptive maternal bodies now appear to have no essential difference from the adoptive paternal body.[2] And, indeed, there is no essential difference. At the same time, it is a mistake to conclude, as does Homans, that when mothering is detached from the unique reproductive capacities of a woman, then a "mother is no more or less physically connected to her baby than is her partner, male or female" (269). As Sara Ruddick (1997) suggests, there are important differences in maternal and paternal practices that cannot be captured by speaking in terms of a generic "parental" body: "parenting is a complex ongoing work of responding to children's needs in particular economic and social circumstances . . . this work is not *prima facie* associated with either sex . . . (but) the younger the children, the more physical their demands . . . the more likely to be assigned to women. (206)

The "neutering" of the term "mother" that occurs when we speak of men mothering or when we shift from talking about mothering to the more generic parenting, Ruddick argues, "denies the history and current practice of female mothering—including women's dispropor-tionate responsibility for childcare" (216). This becomes clear to me as the mother of young children when, in order to provide our children access to better public schools, my husband and I move from the city into the dreaded suburbs. In this new neighborhood, I find myself surrounded by white, Christian, middle-class families embodying tra-ditional gendered divisions of labor. I am invited to Tupperware parties (which, after accepting the first one, I learn to politely decline). My children are invited to church services and vacation bible school (no doubt because they are showing the signs of being raised by a heathen mother). When I go away to a conference, neighborhood women bring my husband casseroles and ask him if he needs assistance with the children. I do not receive similar offers when he is absent.

As other feminists have noted, women's function in the patri-archal family includes not only biological reproduction, but also the physical sustenance of children (e.g., shopping for food, preparing meals, sewing, ironing and laundering clothing, maintaining a clean and healthy home environment, and ensuring their children's physical safety) throughout their non-adult years. As mothers, we also bear primary responsibility for the cultural reproduction of a new generation, as the primary conveyors of cultural and family values. Although men often define those values, it has fallen on our shoulders to teach and enforce them. Adoptive maternal bodies are thus distinct from adoptive paternal bodies insofar as the former but not the latter are mediated by cultural expectations and norms for mothering.

Foucault (1980) speaks of power as reaching right into our bodies, permeating posture, gesture, speech, relationships, and ways of living (98). Following Foucault, we can speak of power as "producing" adoptive maternal bodies. Some of the ways in which power produces (Western) adoptive maternal bodies are similar to the ways in which power produces (Western) biological maternal bodies. Through multiple social pressures—exerted by families, friends, neighbors, churches, schools and the media (e.g., parenting advice books and television talk shows)—female bodies become the maternal bodies who coo softly at and sing lullabies gently to their infants, rocking them to sleep or walking the floors with them when they cry. Female bodies are typically the bodies who carry toddlers on their hips while warming bottles or preparing meals, who let their elementary school children crawl into bed beside them when they have a nightmare, and who lay awake at night worrying about the whereabouts and well-being of their teenagers. Maternal bodies are the bodies who teach their children religious, ethical, and emotional lessons. Western maternal bodies also are produced as bodies that drive carpools and serve on PTA committees, who arrange birthday parties, buy or make clothing for their children, and decorate and bake for holiday festivities. This is largely so whether or not the mother in question also works (as I have) outside the home. The maternal body is the parental body that is expected to juggle calendars and schedules and competing needs. My husband helps with (some of) these tasks, but it is I who must keep everyone's needs in mind and make the task list for him to follow. Moreover, whereas he is applauded for his helpfulness, like most mothers, I receive little in the way of praise or accolades for my parenting work. This has everything to do with gender and is largely unaffected by one's status as an adoptive or a biological parent.

Adoptive maternal bodies also are produced in ways that are distinct from biological maternal bodies, however. Most notably, expectations of social service agencies and legal regulations play a specific and visible role in the creation of adoptive mothers. Noting the techniques of surveillance to which adoptive mothers are subjected illuminates the ways in which biological motherhood is itself regulated through normalizing discourses, albeit differently and less visibly and explicitly.

Maternal Bodies Under Surveillance

Fall 1991: I am kneeling on the floor, attempting to comfort my pretend child who is upset about something. I'm not certain what. Playing the role of my would-be child is another adult participant in the Model Approach to Partnership in Parenting (MAPP) training in which my husband and I have been "invited" to participate. Under the watchful eye of social workers, I keep my voice soft and low, attempting to maintain eye contact with my "child," listen carefully, patiently, and respectfully to his painful and somewhat unintelligible whining, and determine how to modify his bratty behavior. I do not succeed in behavior modification (my co-participant is clearly enjoying his opportunity to act like an out of control child), but I do not make any major gaffs either.

I would give my performance on this task a B+—or at least this is what, I imagine, the caseworkers who are observing me from the sidelines might think. This is good. It means that I am still in contention for a child. And I vow to perform even better on my next opportunity. I am aware throughout the process of seeking to be approved as an adoptive parent that I am being watched and critiqued, that my potential as a "fit" parent is under evaluation. From the beginning, caseworkers have queried my health, age, race, familial history, professional status, income, neighborhood, and home. They have asked me about my religious views and practices, my feelings about child discipline and corporal punishment, my present relationship with my family of origin, my reasons for wanting to adopt and much, much more. They want to know everything about me and how my husband and I live, think, feel, and eat. We, in turn, have written endless pages of narrative to our caseworkers, kept our emotional and physical houses in order so that we might pass inspection (hoping that they will not look too closely at the items we may have swept under the rug), and faithfully attend recommended trainings—clearly intended to weed out those "unfit" to parent, as much as to instruct participants about the best (i.e., normative) practices of childrearing.

As gatekeepers to parenthood, social workers, lawyers, and others have the power to provide or withhold from you your desired status as a parent. But their expectations are not formed in a vacuum. As Foucault (1980) notes, power is "a productive network which runs throughout the whole social body" (119). The norms for good parenting that govern prospective adoptive parents and produce the adoptive maternal body reflect widespread social ideals governing "good mothers," "good fathers," and "good families."

As noted in earlier discussions of maternal profiling, good families and the good mothers who inhabit them are typically middle or upper class. They have spacious, clean homes. Good families include heterosexual, married parents. These parents care about education and know how to discipline children without resorting to corporal punishment. They have strong and healthy relationships with their own families of origin. Ideally, they are Christian or, perhaps, Jewish. If not affiliated with a mainstream Western religious denomination, the prospective parents will at least subscribe to mainstream Western religious values, including a strong work ethic. They will drink in moderation only, if at all. They will not have an arrest record for drugs, nor will they have committed other infractions of the law—or of good taste. They will practice good personal hygiene and wear fresh, unrumpled clothing.

Good families afford their children race and class privilege. They live in suburban neighborhoods featuring good schools and allegedly safe streets. They enroll their children in piano and ballet lessons. They do not let their children watch too much TV or hang out with the "wrong" crowd. They take their children on vacations. They have college funds for their children. They feature stay-at-home mothers or, failing this, hire full-time nannies to care for their children.

Good families enjoy heterosexual privilege. They do not embarrass or "damage" their children by participating in sexual or affectional relationships that depart from the norm. They provide both male and female role models for their sons and daughters. As this suggests, good families also exemplify traditional gendered divisions of labor. Good fathers are good breadwinners. Good mothers are good homemakers. Good fathers are stable and dependable and know how to enforce discipline. They coach little league and mow lawns. Good mothers are emotionally available and know how to develop self-esteem in their child. They make cookies for bake sales and arrange play dates for their children.

Few families fit this profile in all of its dimensions. However, families (such as my own) who are successful at adopting a child typically fit several aspects of this profile—or, at any rate, are knowledgeable enough about this profile to provide answers to questions and dress and act in ways that make us appear desirable as parents. Adoptive maternal bodies are not, thus, natural bodies. We are bodies simultaneously marked as "damaged" (i.e., infertile, whether or not this is true) and yet bodies chosen for motherhood on the basis of being marked as "desirable" by gatekeepers. We are bodies who know how to announce ourselves as normal, even as we are marked as "abnormal." We know the dominant social script for mothering and thus know how to pass as a real mother. In this respect, adoptive mothers share certain affinities with light-skinned persons of color who know how to perform the script for whiteness and with closeted lesbians or gays who know how to perform the script for heterosexuality.[3]

Biological maternal bodies may escape the closet, but do not escape surveillance, as often is thought. Berg (1995), for example, explaining why women use reproductive technologies, claims that biological parenting is meaningful because it allows women to participate in a "remarkably natural process." She contrasts this "natural" process of gestation and birth giving to the process of adoption wherein "parents receive their child from a stranger in a process regulated by lawyers, adoption agencies and the courts" (83). Yet, the notion that biological parenting is natural requires critique in the social context of contemporary Western medicine. Here doctors play the role of gatekeepers, determining how the good mother will act (e.g., she will eat only healthy foods, get adequate rest, take prenatal vitamins, refrain from smoking and drinking, avoid strenuous exercise, and abstain from certain sexual practices). The physician also determines who will have access to medical services. This is the case especially when reproductive technologies are used, but it is also the case in so-called "normal" cases of conception, gestation, and childbirth.

I discover this in my third trimester of pregnancy: Having discovered on a sonogram that my placenta is displaced, my obstetrician orders me to bed rest. When I resist her suggestion, indicating that I am our family's primary breadwinner and we require my summer teaching salary (something that I hope another professional woman might understand), she looks at me disapprovingly, noting that my refusal to follow her instructions will put my pregnancy and baby at risk. She also cautions me that I have gained too much weight and need to more carefully monitor my caloric intake. Later, as I successfully reach my due date (despite a lack of full-time bed rest), she indicates that my labor will need to be artificially induced if I have not given birth within the next ten days. I am not altogether certain I wish to follow these instructions, but do not argue with her at this moment, as I have another issue I wish to discuss with her. "Will you tie my tubes after I have given birth?" I ask, noting that it is my understanding that this is a relatively simple procedure if done at the time of birthing. She responds that this is unadvisable, as I might want another child. When I remind her that I am thirty-three years old, already have another child, and explain that my husband and I will be happy to adopt another child should we consider more children a necessary addition to our life, she conjectures that I "might feel differently" after I have a child of "my own." Too tired to address the presumptions included in this nonmedical advice, I depart and prepare to tell my husband that he will need to have a vasectomy.

As Laura Woliver (1995) indicates, "the medical profession's gate-keeping role," including "its monopoly over birth control information and services" displays a tendency to "control and medicalization" that precedes its involvement in designing and implementing new reproductive technologies (347). The bodies of birth mothers, like those of adoptive mothers, are created by disciplinary discourses (e.g., the languages of medicine, sociology, and psychiatry) operating in conjunction with social institutions (e.g., hospitals and social service agencies). The medical language of "fertility" and "infertility," for example, produces subjects who are viewed as—and who, thus, come to view themselves as—beings defined in terms of their procreative capacity. Taken in conjunction with theories of social psychology (and, notably, Freudian psychoanalytic theory) that deem a woman's fulfillment to reside in procreation, these discourses serve to define an "abnormality" in particular women that is to be resolved by the practices and technologies of modern medicine.

As Foucault (1978) indicates, persons who engaged in particular sex acts came to be seen as a type of person (homosexuals) during the eighteenth century. The marking of homosexuality as a deviant identity (comprising much more than a sex act) simultaneously produced compulsory heterosexuality as the norm (125). Similarly, we see in the late twentieth century the emergence of a *type* of person who is "fertile" or "infertile." The marking of infertility as an abnormal identity produces procreative sexuality as the norm, reinforcing compulsory motherhood and heteronormativity. Compulsory (heterosexual) motherhood preceded medical discourses concerning fertility, but now take a particular form that marks biological motherhood as the essential form of mothering. Practices of adoption—like homosexual behavior—have long existed, but adoptive motherhood as an *identity*—like homosexual identity—only emerges at a particular historical juncture. Moreover, the deviance of the adoptive maternal body serves to mark out biological motherhood as natural. Neither adoptive mothers, nor biological mothers have an *a priori* essential nature, however. Indeed, throughout much of history—and still within many indigenous cultures—the distinction between adoptive mothers and natural (or real) mothers would not be a salient distinction (Carp 1998; Novy 2001).

Foucault (1978, 1979, 1980) observes that surveillance is a disciplinary mechanism that constitutes and regulates subjects into oppositional relations. At the same time, power also essentializes the oppositional categories it has constructed, making them henceforth appear both natural and immutable. In order to interrogate the categories that pose as "natural" in the oppositions thus created (e.g., heterosexual/homosexual, fertile/infertile, biological/adoptive, normal/queer), it is useful to view them through the lens of their allegedly opposing construction. If, for example, we look at mothering through the lens of adoption, the social regulation of "having" children is made explicit and the social rules and discourses governing motherhood obscured in cases of biological motherhood are rendered visible. Gatekeepers may sometimes differ (with social workers, courts and, in the case of transnational adoption, consulates and immigration authorities, mediating maternity for adoptive mothers and nurses, physicians, pharmacists, and drug companies mediating maternity for biological mothers), but the gates are still kept. Moreover, the gatekeepers do not always differ, as women deemed "unfit" for parenting know all too well. Physicians act in concert with the courts that mandate birth control for mothers convicted of drug offenses. Social service agencies regulate the activities of poor mothers receiving welfare. Social workers enlist the help of the legal system to remove children from mothers identified as unfit. Children thus removed are returned, if at all, only if their mother follows court-ordered rules governing her conduct. Lesbian mothers risk having their fitness queried by ex-husbands and the custody of their children revoked by the courts. Teen mothers and mothers with cognitive disabilities are routinely assumed unfit and encouraged by their own family members as well as social service agencies to relinquish their children.[4]

In light of these issues, it makes little sense to consider biological maternal bodies as natural objects outside of social contexts. Biological maternal bodies, like adoptive maternal bodies, are always embodied in social, cultural, economic, and political contexts—contexts marked by racism, classism, sexism, heterosexism, ageism, and ablism. In both cases, therefore, it makes sense to speak of motherhood as a status that may be conferred or withheld in processes involving the potential intervention of strangers—as well as the potential intervention of friends, neighbors, and family members. Those for whom motherhood is experienced as natural are precisely those who have—like the adoptive mother—successfully embodied what Nancy Miller (1995) terms "the dominant social script" about mothering. The difference between biological mothers and adoptive mothers is an epistemological one: adoptive mothers know that their status as mothers depends on mastery of the social script for good mothering; the contingency of their status as mothers is largely invisible to biological mothers who embody the norms regulating their status as mothers—unless and/or until such time as they inadvertently deviate from that script.

The different epistemological standpoints inhabited by adoptive and biological mothers with regard to social scripts of motherhood parallels the epistemological standpoints on "role playing" inhabited by straights and queers as described by Marilyn Frye (1983):

> [H]omosexuals and lesbians are mocked and judged for "playing butch-femme roles" and for dressing in "butch-femme drag," [but] nobody goes about in full public view as thoroughly decked out in butch and femme drag as respectable heterosexuals when they are dressed up to go out in the evening, or to go to church, or to go to the office. Heterosexual[s] . . . ought to look at themselves in the mirror on their way out for a night on the town to see who's in drag. The answer is, everybody is. Perhaps the main difference between heterosexuals and queers is that when queers go forth in drag, they know they are engaged in theater—they are playing and they know they are playing. Heterosexuals usually are taking it all perfectly seriously, thinking they are in the real world, thinking they are the real world. (29)

Not unlike heterosexuals in drag, biological mothers frequently think of themselves as "real," intimating that adoptive mothers are just role-playing. This notion, however, presumes that the social script for good mothering simply *describes* what real (i.e., biological or "natural") mothers do. Adoptive mothers know that such role playing is *prescribed* by the dominant view of motherhood and that *all* mothers are playing a role as mandated by this script or, if refusing to conform to such a role, are still subject to its imposition by those who are gatekeepers to motherhood. As Homans (2002) suggests:

> The experience of adoption reveals that all parenthood is fundamentally adoptive, for adoption is not just a poor copy of a sterling original but rather . . . the copy that reveals there is no original, no tenable distinction between copy and original. Even biological parents must make an active choice to keep and bear the children they bear. There is no purely natural or physical parenthood or even maternity. (265–66)

Yet, choices to keep and/or bear children are not made in a vacuum; they are choices heavily influenced by prevailing social norms, discourses, and practices—all of which privilege biological motherhood as real. As Frye contends, heterosexuals are not merely pretending to be "the real world"; their behavior "has a function in the construction of the real world" (29). So too the linguistic and other practices surrounding mothering construct a reality that privileges biological mothering: "whether feminist or not, the discourse of parenting is heavily weighted towards bodily experience, just as leading myths of what constitute the 'real' for adopted children privilege biological 'roots' over adoptive families" (Homan 2002, 266). Thus, although we can imagine, as Beizer (2002) does, a world in which adoptive mothers weren't contrasted to "real" mothers and adopted children were not contrasted to children of "one's own," a world in which "biological relationships were made in the image of adoptive relationships" (249) and featured choice and responsibility more prominently than nature and instinct, imagining won't make it so. Other forms of resistance are also necessary.

Adoptive Maternal Bodies as Sites of Choice and Resistance

Despite the effects of discourse, surveillance, and regulation on the social construction of motherhood, it would be a mistake to view maternal bodies as simply docile and passive. Maternal bodies also are capable of resistance both to compulsory motherhood and to prevailing definitions of motherhood. This potential for resistance, like the realities of surveillance, may be more readily visible from the slantwise perspective of marginalized maternal bodies. Adoptive maternal bodies provide a unique vantage point for subversion of the dominant script governing motherhood because of their ambiguous status as maternal bodies.

In *The Epistemology of the Closet*, Eve Sedgwick (1990) lists her experience as a "nonprocreative adult" alongside her experiences as a "fat woman," a "sexual pervert," and a Jew, as those most salient to her epistemological outlook (63, see also, De Lauretis 1990b). Miller (1995) agrees with Sedgwick that "self-identification as a woman who has not had a child" is an important "marker of social difference" central to "a cultural critique of marginalities and dominations" (9). Both Sedgwick and Miller assume here a privileged—or at least unique—epistemological vantage point that comes from living outside the norms of compulsory motherhood. Yet, the notion of "nonprocreative adult" or "woman who has not had a child" is a complicated one. What does it mean to "have" a child? Do adoptive maternal bodies "have" children? Do we procreate? On the one hand, we choose motherhood (and in so choosing, could be viewed as participating in compulsory motherhood). On the other hand, in adopting, we do not (biologically) procreate; we do not reproduce ourselves as bodies. Thus we do not "have" children, in the sense of conceiving, gestating, or genetically "owning" children. This is why family, friends, and strangers are apt to pity us for not having children "of our own" (Beizer 2002).

Indeed, the notion of "nonprocreative adult" is complicated even if "procreation" is read in a purely biological sense. As Miller suggests, there is a difference between those who refuse to reproduce—in conscious defiance of social norms—and those who "fail" to have children. Recounting her own experience, she says:

> I cannot . . . claim that I have *refused* to reproduce, since at various times in my life I flirted with the possibility and tried to conceive a child—strenuously for three miserable years— at the borderlines of my fertility and failed a decade ago; rather by virtue of a tenacious ambivalence and treacherous propensity for deferral I have not had a child, and probably never really wanted to in the first place. (N. Miller 1995, 9)

As the phrase "probably never really wanted to in the first place" suggests, however, this distinction between refusing motherhood and deferring motherhood is not clear-cut. Miller continues:

> For me, as for many women of my generation in the Unit-
> ed States who modeled our identities on Beauvoir's famous
> split—intellectual accomplishment *or* babies—it might be
> more accurate to say that . . . we refused to reproduce *as*
> *women*, as though anatomy were our destiny instead of his-
> tory, on schedule as though we had no say; only some of
> us then changed our minds (or thought we did in a fren-
> zy of belatedness), and it turned out that for some of us
> "nature" (or maybe it really was history) would have the
> last word after all. . . . Choosing motherhood or refusing
> it has proven to be more complex than seventies feminists
> had imagined. (9)

Miller suggests that the complications unforeseen by seventies
feminists stem from a historical juxtaposition of "massive infertility"
coupled with "dizzying adventures in reproductive techniques" (9).
However, the complications involved in choosing and/or refusing motherhood preceded both this historical moment and the advent of second
wave feminism. The complexity of choosing or resisting motherhood
has long been evident from the perspective of adoptive maternal bodies.

Adoptive mothers—like many other mothers—choose motherhood. However, we do so in a way that simultaneously rejects the idea
that woman's anatomy is her destiny. Adoptive mothers make conscious choices whether to become a mother and how to become a
mother. Motherhood does not just happen to us; in becoming an adoptive mother, no "accident" befell my body as it did when I became a
biological mother. Nor did anatomical destiny drive my decision to
become a mother. My first story of motherhood is, like the stories of
all adoptive mothers, a story of social agency. Adoptive maternal bodies are active, not passive bodies. Moreover, at the same time that we
choose motherhood, adoptive maternal bodies—unlike other maternal bodies—can (and, in different ways, do) refuse to bear children.
Some women choose adoption as a route to motherhood because of
infertility. Others select adoption, rather than procreation, as a way
of creating a family for personal and/or political reasons. In my own
case, all of these factors pertained. I had been diagnosed as infertile
and—after a mere three months of hormone treatments that made
me crazy, temperature-taking routines that I wasn't quite organized
enough to manage, and sex-on-biological-demand that was in tension
with spontaneous erotic pleasure—I decided to embrace my infertility

as much preferable to medical interventions. Adoption would give us an opportunity to create a family in an alternative fashion, as a family of personal and political choice.[5]

Infertile maternal bodies, although frequently portrayed as "damaged," "inferior" or even "desperate" bodies (see, e.g., Berg 1995), can also be interpreted as healthy and resistant bodies. Adoptive mothers do not have to adjust to the rapid changes in embodiment that accompany pregnancy and post-partum; we are less physically exhausted and/or traumatized from childbirth than biological mothers of infants and thus have more energy; we do not suffer the tenderness of breasts laden with milk; we are thus better able to retain some degree of independence from our children, and so forth. Adoptive mothers do not, moreover, risk the short and long term health consequences of the prolonged hormone regimens that are a part of fertility treatments and we avoid the cost and invasiveness of expensive, complicated medical procedures. Many infertile maternal bodies are bodies who, like Miller and myself, delayed childbearing until after the completion of their education and the establishment of their careers. As such, we are female bodies who have established an identity and meaningful relationships for ourselves outside of the norms of compulsory motherhood. We are also bodies who have resisted procreation during our most fertile years. We are bodies who, for years or decades, have uncoupled sexuality and procreation. And in discovering our infertility and choosing to pursue adoption over fertility treatments, we are bodies who continue to resist making sex into a procreative ritual.

The personal and political reasons for which women may choose adoption over procreation as a means of creating a family are varied. For some fertile women—like infertile women who refuse fertility treatments—adoption represents a conscious personal choice to maintain a nonprocreative sexual body. For others, such as those who adopt "special needs" children, adoption may represent a way of sharing resources with children in need and/or of creating families that embody diversity. For at least some of those who pursue transnational adoption, this route to motherhood may represent the ability to avoid U.S. norms mandating two-parent, heterosexual, nuclear families. For yet other women, adoption represents an environmental choice related to concerns about global overpopulation.

None of these motives are uncomplicated. Some women who choose not to become pregnant may do so for reasons linked to questionable beauty ideals. Some white women who adopt children of color or disabled children may do so, consciously or unconsciously, for reasons linked to self-aggrandizement, religious principles or even humanitarian motives (such as I address in the next chapter) that are questionable from a queer, feminist, anti-racist and/or anti-ablist, point of view. Single women and lesbian women who adopt transnationally may turn a blind eye to issues related to the western appropriation of global resources. Similarly, some Western women who choose adoption to resist contributing to global overpopulation may remain oblivious to the ways in which Western consumption of global resources damages environmental stability. Nonetheless, these maternal bodies also can be read as resisting romanticized versions of the gestational maternal body, as refusing to define family in terms of genetic inheritance and ownership, and as rejecting notions of motherhood and of two-parent, heterosexual families as "natural." In this sense, adoptive maternal bodies are a close relation to the "nonprocreative adult" bodies of Sedgwick and Miller. Our bodies mark social difference in a way that enables a cultural critique of the dominant social script governing motherhood.

This is so whether or not we consciously resist social norms governing motherhood. In fact, however, adoptive mothers will typically be conscious of their resistances. The myriad questions that we answer in applying to become an adoptive parent are not merely invasions of privacy; they are also cause for self-reflection about one's maternal desires and capabilities. In completing the application for adoption, one is forced to think about whether and why one wants to become a mother and about one's own capacities for mothering. One must also think about why one views adoption as preferable to other alternatives. One thus formulates a story that is both about desire (what one wants) and about repulsion (what one doesn't want). In circulating these stories, we authorize ourselves "to have the decisive role in deciphering [the] meaning [of our bodies] and adjudicating their circulation in the world" (N. Miller 1995, 9).[6] This is especially prevalent in cases of transracial adoption and open adoption. Here no sustained secrecy or pretense of being a mother within a "normal" biological family is possible.

Bringing Adoption Out of the Closet

Spring 1999: I am enrolling my children in a new school. The secretary behind the desk welcomes us, but assumes that I am only enrolling the one daughter (the tall, blonde, skinny one who looks like me) and

I have to politely correct her assumption, clarifying that my daugh-
ters (plural)—not daughter and friend—both need to be enrolled. Later,
meeting other school families at an ice cream social, a PTA mother
comments that my elder daughter (I have introduced her as such) must
have got her beautiful black hair from her dad's side of the family. These
conversational interludes have become commonplace. For years, I have
encountered such casual conversational remarks about the presumed
heteronormative source of Tomeka's difference from me (and/or from her
sister) in grocery stores, playgrounds, and elsewhere. If I am behaving, I
patiently explain that I am Tomeka's adoptive mother. But, frankly, this
gets tiresome and so I have developed other stock responses intended to
confuse the heteronormative assumptions embedded in casual diagnoses
of the difference between my daughter and me. On this occasion, I con-
sider indicating, simply for the shock value inherent in telling partial
truths, that it's hard to say if Tomeka gets her coloring from her dad,
since I have no idea who Tomeka's (birth) father is. But I opt against
the "skanky whore" strategy this time, settling instead on the "oh, she's
a lesbian" strategy, indicating that Tomeka inherited her hair color from
her other mother. It is quite remarkable, really, how my ambiguous
relationship to Tomeka is so quickly interpreted as a reflection of my
presumed non-normative (i.e. promiscuous or homoerotic) sexuality.
Only rarely does my interlocutor consider that our relationship may
be the product of non-normative (i.e., asexual) reproduction.

Adoptive mothers have a unique perspective on mothering that
could be described as being "closeted." Lesbian feminists such as Frye
(1983) and queer theorists such as Sedgwick (1990) argue that non-normative sexual and affectional practices render queer identities invisible.
Frye, for example, argues that lesbians are rendered invisible within
a phallocratic, heterosexist conceptual framework, insofar as the term
"lesbian" (a woman who has sex, i.e., intercourse, with another woman)
names something both empirically and logically impossible (152–83).
The invisibility of non-normative sexual identities is linked to the experience of being closeted, which Sedgwick describes as the shaping presence in the lives of lesbians and gay men. Like the term "lesbian," the
term "adoptive mother" is oxymoronic; insofar as "mother" is defined
as a procreative being, adoptive mothers (as nonprocreative beings) are
impossible. This frequently renders the adoptive mother invisible giving
rise to the phenomenon of being closeted. Like the "deadly elasticity
of heterosexual presumption" that perpetually re-closets even the most

openly queer person (Sedgwick 1990, 46), the presumption that reproduction is a biological phenomenon rooted in (hetero)sexuality forces
adoptive mothers (including those participating in open adoptions) to
either dissemble or to continually reveal anew the secret of their deviant motherhood.

Although informal adoption has been practiced openly throughout history and continues to be practiced in many parts of the world,
when adoption was formalized as a legal procedure in the United States
in the latter half of the nineteenth century, adoption became largely
a secretive practice (Grossberg 1995). In such secretive, closed adoptions, members of the adoption triangle live under what Margot Backus
(2001) describes as a "discursive interdiction," akin to the "burden not
to tell" experienced by lesbians and sexual abuse survivors—a burden
that can, as noted by Ann Cvetkovitch (1995), "create . . . its own network of psychic wounds [exceeding] the event itself" (Backus 2001, 139;
Cvetkovitch 1995, 380). Under such circumstances of secrecy, adoptive mothers had little role, much less a decisive one, in interpret-
ing the meaning of their bodies or practices. Thus, far from marking
social difference, adoptive maternal bodies (as well as the gestational
maternal bodies whose children were surrendered for adoption, and
the adopted children themselves) were largely rendered invisible and
silent—except insofar as they "mimic[ked] certain idealized images of
the mainstream family and . . . prop[ped] up the idealization" (Kirk
and McDaniel 1984, 77). Invisibility and silence—and related to this,
the association of adoption with stigma and loss—made it difficult for
adoptive mothers, birth mothers, or adopted children to form communities. Thus they dealt with these aspects of their identities largely
in isolation from one another.

In recent decades, however, practices of open adoption, as well as
the practices of transracial and transnational adoption, have brought
adoption out of the closet. In coming out, adoptive mothers have joined
with birth mothers and adopted children to confront the stigmatization
of adoption and develop alternative family formations openly embodying a critique of conventional family structures and values. In particular, new adoptive practices explicitly resist what Michael Warner (1991)
terms "reprosexuality" and "repro-narrativity."

"Reprosexuality," as defined by Warner, is an "interweaving of
heterosexuality, biological reproduction, cultural reproduction, and
personal identity" (9). The straight personal identity interwoven with
biological and cultural reproduction is a "breeder identity"—a self-

understanding (along with fantasies of self-transcendence) that is tied to one's status as procreative. As Warner claims, "reprosexuality involves more than reproducing, more even than compulsory heterosexuality: it involves a relation to self that finds its proper temporality and fulfillment in generational transmission" (9). As such, reprosexuality is closely aligned with "repro-narrativity" or the notion that "our lives are somehow made more meaningful by being embedded in a narrative of generational succession" (7).

Adoptive relationships, when brought out of the closet, have the potential to queer the family by openly resisting both reprosexuality and repro-narrativity. In particular, as nonprocreative adult bodies, adoptive maternal bodies openly resist the notion that "reproduction must be the logic of sexuality and the means of self-transcendence" (M. Warner 1991, 9). As Warner indicates, the notion that reproduction is the goal of sexuality (and hence that if everyone were queer, humanity would become extinct) presupposes "that there are no lesbian or gay parents, that people who have gay sex do not have other kinds, that heterosexuals only have sex when they want to reproduce, that sex always means coupling, that parental narcissism is higher consciousness" (9). Adoptive maternal (and paternal) bodies embody a critique of the notion that reproduction and (hetero)sexuality are inextricably intertwined. Adoptive parents may be single as well as coupled, lesbian or gay as well as straight, and even if straight and coupled, their status as parents bears no essential connection to their sexuality. The fact that most adoptive parents are straight and married highlights the enforcement of predominant cultural values; it is not a function of any "natural" edict.

Adoptive maternal bodies resist reprosexuality also in an even more basic way. As Warner indicates, "the problems with repro dogma" are so obvious—given the absurdity of the notion that humans are in short supply—that it is difficult to know why anyone would believe it. Why then do so many wish to assume "a paradigmatic status for heterosexual coupling?" The real reason, Warner suggests, "is to render the tacit value on reproduction itself unquestionable." Heterosexuality would not find itself necessary, i.e., "meaningfully opposed to something else—were we not invested in a growth economy of population" (10). Similarly, the notion of "real" motherhood might not find itself necessary, that is, meaningfully opposed to something else, namely, adoptive (foster, step- and co-) motherhood, were there no investment in a growth economy of population. Uncloseted adoptive maternal bodies stand openly (even if unintentionally) against a growth economy of

population. Thus we also undermine a primary—albeit absurd—ratio-
nale for both compulsory motherhood and compulsory heterosexuality.

In open adoptive relationships, adoptive mothers also challenge
the paradigms of real motherhood and of the heterosexual nuclear family in another way—by the deliberate inclusion in a child's life of more
than one mother. There is a "physical maternal body presupposed by
adoption—a childbearing body that should not be erased or rendered
invisible" (Homans 2002, 270). The practice of open adoption insists
that this gestational body be considered a maternal body alongside the
maternal body legally authorized to raise her birth child. Thus the
practice of open adoption rejects the monomaternalistic notion that
children must have only one real mother, refusing the logic of "either/
or" embedded in the nature/nurture dichotomy in favor of "both/and"
reasoning. When adoptive mothers and gestational mothers embrace
each other as co-participants in childrearing, we openly challenge both
(biological and legal) "ownership" paradigms of parental rights and the
heteronormative paradigm of families.

As Kate Harrison (1995) says, commenting on lesbian custody
cases, "the law has traditionally recognized only one type of mother—
the person who either gave birth to or adopted the child" (181). Thus
if, for example, two women co-parent a child with an involved sperm
donor acting as a limited father, the existence of three people acting
in a variety of parenting relationships to the child presents the courts
with an unrecognized family structure (Harrison 1995, 177–81). Prior
to the twenty-first century, the courts were reluctant to grant custody
to those in *loco parentis* standing for fear of jeopardizing the nuclear,
heterosexual family as the accepted child-raising unit (182, 190–91).[7]
This was made clear in the judicial reasoning of the court in *Nancy S
v Michele D* (1991), a case attempting to resolve a child custody dispute
between a separating lesbian couple. The couple had raised the children
together since birth (and had also planned the pregnancies via artificial
insemination together) and the court agreed that it would be "tragic"
for the children involved to be separated from one of their mothers.
Nonetheless, the appellate court upheld the lower court's decision to
award the biological mother full custody rights and control over visitation on the basis that the notion of "functional parenthood" was a
"novel theory," the application of which would leave the courts facing
"years of unraveling the complex practical, social and constitutional
ramifications of this expansion of the definition of parent." Indeed. Yet,
this is precisely the unraveling that must occur if the law is to be flex-

ible enough to embrace alternative family structures—including those created by lesbians (and gay men), those created by open adoption and those created by extended, blended families.

In all cases, the barriers to legal recognition of non-normative families of choice are similar. First, the law has traditionally refused to recognize more than one person of the same sex as having parental status with the result that a legally recognized parent (the birth mother) can only create another parental relationship for her child (an adoptive mother) by foregoing her own parental status. Secondly, as Martha Fineman (1995b) notes, family law has focused on preserving the "sexual" family. Prior to the 1990s, this sexual family was interpreted specifically as a heterosexual family, making second parent adoption by lesbian or gay parents a near impossibility and placing the parental status of lesbian mothers at considerable risk, even where such mothers had biological connections to their children. During the 1990s, most (although far from all) states ceased revoking the parental rights of lesbian mothers biologically related to their children and some states began allowing for second parent adoptions through the "stepparent" exception to the rule against recognizing two parents of the same sex (Richman 2009, 35–37).[8] Yet, in many states, second-parent adoptions were (and remain) permitted only in circumstances where the second parent is related to the child through a biological connection (e.g., an aunt or uncle) or through being legally married to the child's biological parent. This has left nonbiological lesbian mothers with no legal maternal status when lesbian unions dissolve (35). As Kimberly Richman's (2009) exhaustive analysis of such cases demonstrates, in thirty-three of the fifty-six cases heard prior to 2005 involving the dissolution of a lesbian couple, the courts decided that the nonbiological mother was a nonparent or "legal stranger" to the child by virtue of the fact that she had no natural or legal link to the child (58–59). The fact that lesbian mothers facing a heterosexual ex-spouse in court were much less likely to be deprived of custody in 2000 than in 1990 cannot, in this context, be understood as indicative of a general trend toward lesbian and gay parents' rights. Rather, the legal status of lesbian mothers at the turn of the twenty-first century was improved "only to the extent that these rights overlapped with their biological status as parents and therefore fit with heteronormative understandings of family structure" (90).

Adoptive maternal bodies—whether straight or lesbian—occupy a position with the potential to resist both the monomaternalist and pronatalist ideologies embedded in the law. By embracing two (or more) mother families and advocating for the legally recognized status of *both* biological mothers and "de facto" (or "psychological" or "functional") mothers, those committed to practices of open adoption challenge heteronormative understandings of kinship. Indeed, in the case of straight adoptive mothers and lesbian mothers whose unions have dissolved, adoptive maternal bodies also challenge the assumption that families involving childrearing are premised on sexuality. As feminists and queer theorists have long argued, sexuality and reproduction must be delinked. The focus of such arguments has largely been oriented toward the embrace of non-reproductive sexuality. Here I am arguing that it may be equally important to embrace nonsexual reproduction.

The challenge of adoptive maternal bodies to heteronormativity goes further than this, however. By denying any necessary connection between childrearing, on the one hand, and pregnancy and childbirth, on the other, adoptive motherhood refuses "repro-narrativity," by complicating the narrative of generational succession. This means that the notion of reproduction must itself be reconceptualized. In choosing adoption, as Berg notes, parents forgo the "sense of continuity and history created by the genetic tie" sought by Warner's breeders. Adoptive mothers "must be able to love a child who does not represent an extension of their own bodies and genetic linkages; one who has the potential to be quite different from either parent" (82).

As I discuss in greater detail later, actively engaging difference and loving those who are different is not always an easy feat. At our best, however, adoptive mothers invite into our homes (and arms and hearts) a body (or bodies) that may be quite unlike our own and give meaning to our lives *through the challenge of difference, rather than the familiarity of replication*. As Beizer (2002) notes, "the decision to adopt often represents a *choice* of otherness and difference and the unknown." Thus, open adoptive maternal bodies "make visible the irrelevance of consanguinity to family bonds and the reality of alternatives to conventional family structures" (248). Describing her relationship to her adopted daughter as an "as is" relationship, rather than an "as if" relationship, Beizer indicates her surprise and wonder at her daughter's "unanticipated talents and skills" which often unfold in "(welcome) contradiction of established family traits":

> I cannot walk on ice or rocky terrain without stumbling; she
> can dangle from trees by her toes. I cannot carry a tune;
> she can imitate any succession of notes on the first hear-

ing. I agonize over every alternative; she leaps spontaneously towards each decision. I turn in circles without a map; she backseat drives with glee and flawless spatial precision. On the other hand, like me, my daughter likes cooking, cuddling, puzzles, red, and irony. Coincidence? Parallel genetic construction? Environment? Nurture? Chance? Magic? Does it matter? (248–49)

Arguably, this openness to surprise and wonder as a child's traits unfold and the willingness to accept a child "as is," should be a feature of all (adoptive and biological) parenting relationships. The potential for children to display significant differences from their parents exists in biological relationships as well, as happens most notably in circumstances where a biological child borne to a healthy mother suffers a traumatic birth or genetic disorder or later accident that results in a disability. As Eva Feder Kittay (1999) illustrates poignantly in discussing mothering her disabled daughter, successful parenting here too must acknowledge and respect such differences, be able to learn from them, and embody a love that does not demand acquiescence to normative similarity. The doctrine of "repro-narrativity," however, with its emphasis on the importance of genetic continuity and the cultural transmission of family values, may often erase or devalue important differences between parents and children and make love appear to be (or actually be) conditional upon the child's conformity to family norms and willingness to transmit these inherited values to a subsequent generation. Nowhere is this clearer, perhaps, than in the case of heterosexual families who disown their gay sons and lesbian daughters.

I am not claiming that adoptive mothers (and/or fathers) never withdraw their love from children who differ from them in ways those mothers (and/or fathers) may find intolerable. Indeed, adoptive parents, like biological parents, may (and many do) erase, devalue, reject or abject their children's sexual (or other) identities where these differ significantly from their own. I do think, however, that the ability to embrace difference—including, importantly, sexual difference—may be enhanced in adoptive families for several reasons. First, adoptive families cannot accept the repro-narrative assumption that generational succession will engender similar bodily appearances, skills, desires, or practices. Of course, we may and often do strive to replicate our manners, tastes, habits, and values. Yet, we cannot assume we will be able to do so in the ways that biological parents might. Nor, in the case of open adoption, can we assume that our manners, tastes, habits, and values will be uncontested by other parents who may embody aesthetic and moral values different from our own. In the case of transracial adoption, our values and practices may, indeed, be contested not only by other parents, but also by larger ethnic communities. "Good mothering" within such interpersonal and political contexts cannot be reduced to self-propagation, but must include a focus on mothers and children (which may include biological children, as well as adopted children) learning to understand, accept, respect, and negotiate difference.

Second, insofar as adoptive parents are themselves nonprocreative adults, they should have less difficulty embracing children whose sexuality is nonprocreative. Adoptive mothers, in particular, are apt to be familiar with having their bodies stigmatized as abnormal—since whether or not infertility is an issue and whether or not it is their own body or their partner's body who lacks fertility, it is the common assumption that all adoptive mothers have bodies unable to uphold the norms of repro-sexuality (Berg 1995). Adoptive families are, furthermore, aware of alternative ways of creating families and alternative configurations of families. Finally, families who engage in open adoptive relationships featuring multiple parents (including, typically, two mothers) are, as I've suggested here, in a sense, themselves "queer."

These and other situational factors (e.g., the transracial and transnational composition of some adoptive families) provide an epistemic advantage to adoptive parents and especially adoptive mothers in understanding and negotiating bodily and ideological difference. A critical vantage point on mothering (or any other topic) does not guarantee, however, a critical vision; even those ideally located to see both the difficulties and the radical possibilities of mothering are capable of being inattentive, of closing their eyes to, or averting their gaze from that which could be seen from their position. And certainly, some adoptive mothers do just this, simply mimicking, as best they are able, the norms and values of traditional motherhood—despite their alternative embodiments as mothers. Like persons of color who advocate colorblindness as an antidote to racism, some adoptive mothers will fail to see and acknowledge the differences between their children and themselves, aiming to raise their children "as if" they were "their own." Or like closeted lesbians or gay men, adoptive mothers may see their differences from their children, but fail to respect and embrace these differences, viewing these differences as a source of shame and hoping they can be transcended, erased, or hidden. This is best counteracted by open adoptive relationships that bring adoption out of the closet, thus shifting family configurations in ways that blur the distinction between the queer and the normal, allowing for—indeed, demanding—the honest negotiation of differences within and across generations.

3

Queer Orphans and Their Neoliberal Saviors

Racialized Intimacy in Adoption

> The adoption of a child, domestically or from abroad, is obviously a material and affective enterprise of great magnitude. In unpacking its political implications and psychic effects, . . . the relentless moralizing that characterizes too much of our contemporary debates on the erosion of "family values" . . . must give way to a sustained discussion of both the ethics of multiculturalism in a colorblind age and the emergence of . . . the new global family.
>
> —David Eng (2010)

As argued in the previous chapter, adoption may be viewed as a potentially queer, feminist practice of mothering. This queer perspective on adoption may make sense, however, only from the perspective of potential or actual adoptive mothers (and fathers)—including gay and lesbian adoptive parents—many of whom, like myself, are white, middle-class subjects. In this chapter, I further unpack the race and class politics of adoption alluded to in Chapter 1, with attention to the ways in which transracial, including international, adoption is both materially and discursively constructed and the effects (and affects) of these constructions on the adopted child. A queer of color perspective attentive to the postcolonial politics of migration is helpful here. To this end, I draw heavily in this chapter on David Eng's (2010) analysis of adoption in *The Feeling of Kinship*. Notably, Eng is one of few queer theorists to address the politics of adoption, demonstrating, perhaps, that queer theoretical perspectives, like homonormative gay politics rooted in identity politics, continue to represent a perspective emanating from the subject position of the "twentieth century western white gay male" (Duggan 2006,155). Universalizing such a perspective—like adopting a middle-class, Western, white feminist perspective—too easily lends itself to a politics of colorblindness that threatens to co-opt potentially queer practices of family making into the service of neoliberal globalization.

My own entry into adoption, two decades ago, was shaped by the colorblind politics of neoliberalism I examine here. As the potential parents of a child of color, my husband and I (like many transracially adoptive parents) entered the adoption process believing that our family-making practices would be a win–win situation. We wanted to be parents, there were many "special needs" children who needed homes, and by adopting a child (or children) of color we would be able to transform our family into a site of racial integration, thus living the values of multiculturalism that we (at the time, uncritically) professed. Our narrative of liberal humanitarianism and political righteousness parallels other narratives of political liberation in which the politics of adoption have been enmeshed. Feminists have sometimes portrayed adoption as a path to the emancipation of women from compulsory reproduction and the attendant exploitation of women's bodies (see, e.g., Allen 1984). More recently, gay and lesbian couples have pursued adoption and adoption rights as a critical step in their quest for equality and liberation, emphasizing the harm done to children who are deprived of loving homes by continued homophobic bigotry.

Unfortunately, these perspectives on adoption largely occlude the perspectives of women who have relinquished the children they have borne, as well as the perspectives of children who are separated from one family and "placed" in another. From these latter perspectives, adoption may seem far from emancipatory. In the words of one birth mother critical of adoption practices, "adoption" is simply a form of "legalized kidnapping," a euphemism for "violently separating an infant from its natural mother and pretending like she doesn't exist, like it's no big deal" (Phillips 1995, 5). "Kidnapping" may seem an exaggerated description to those—namely most of us—who have been trained to view adoption as the result of either a calculated personal decision to give a child for adoption or, alternatively, involuntary relinquishment of a child by a mother so abusive or neglectful as to require intervention for the child's sake. The sanitized language of "gift-giving" and "relinquishment," however, erases the pain of surrendering a child one has borne and disguises the relative powerlessness of many young, unwed mothers, as well as those who must struggle against poverty, racism, or heterosexism in attempting to retain custody of their children. Indeed, the word "surrender" comes closer to the mark with its connotations of giving up an adversarial struggle (a fight, a war) against a more powerful opponent against whom one feels unable to win. As Ann Fessler (2006) reveals in her study of women who surrendered children for adoption in the 1950s and 1960s, many of these women were ill-informed about their rights and often coerced into giving up their children by parents, physicians, social workers, and social pressures that converged to make resistance virtually impossible for a young woman. Resistance has been similarly difficult for incarcerated women and for those whose cultural practices or impoverished circumstances are too frequently interpreted as signs of neglect by caseworkers who remove children from their parents' care.[1] Yet, "surrender" itself is too weak a word to describe other historical and contemporary events that give support to the analysis of adoption as kidnapping—for example, the "orphan trains" that relocated children from coastal U.S. cities into the rural Midwest (Holt 1992); the placement of indigenous children in Mission schools far away from their families, language, and culture (Smith 2009); the brutal separation of African children and other children of color from their parents at slave markets (Campbell, Miers, & Miller 2009); and the international trafficking in children from the East (e.g., Korea, Vietnam, China, and Russia) and the South (e.g., Mexico, Ecuador, Guatemala, El Salvador, Malawi, and Ethiopia) to the United States and other developed Western nations under the forces of globalization.[2] In all these cases, birth mothers were and are largely rendered invisible by colonial, neoliberal policies, as though their connections to their children were "no big deal."

As "quare" theorists and other queers of color have suggested, queer theory needs to ground itself in the "corporeal" as well as the "discursive" register in order to acknowledge the "differences within and between particular groups" (Johnson 2005 132, 135). Adoption has different meanings for birth mothers than for adoptive mothers. Likewise, blood ties and cultural inheritance have different meanings for people (including children) of color than for whites and for those who live in the global North than for those who live in (or were born in) the global South. These different meanings are rooted in the ways in which different bodies are materially (as well as discursively) situated within the politics of reproduction—making it important, in quare theory's vernacular, to "throw shade" (in the many senses of that term) on the politics of adoption (Johnson 2005, 140).

Here, I take seriously the argument that adoption is a form of legal kidnapping potentially complicit, in the case of transracial and transnational adoption, with neocolonial processes of cultural genocide. Neoliberal practices of colorblindness combined with the privatization of family concerns may impede us, both as the consumers of adoption and as scholars who study it, from recognizing (and thus resisting) this complicity. The damage done by such blindness is far from negligible, however, and is most readily visible in its effects on transracially adopted children—children, I suggest, who are constructed queerly as orphans. As the narrative accounts of adult adoptees examined here illustrate, the ways in which white Westerners discursively construct adopted children as "orphans" discounts a child's familial origins and complex racial identity, leading to what Eng terms "racial melancholia." The autobiographical work of Deann Borshay Liem, Tracey Moffat, and others reveal that adoptive families may become sites of intimate colonization wherein people of color are rendered invisible.

These considerations suggest that we should not uncritically support adoption as a queer practice. At the same time, as I also argue here, we should be suspicious of the family preservation policies frequently advocated by adoption's opponents. Prioritizing family preservation (and family reunification)—at least as these terms are narrowly understood in the contemporary United States—poses a false choice between biological and other families. Privileging the "natural" family reinforces biocentrism, monomaternalism, and heteronormativity. To avoid *both* the racism of current transracial and transnational adoption policies *and* the biocentrism and heterosexism of current family preservation policies, we need to "interanimate" critical race studies and queer studies (Johnson and Henderson 2005, 1) as they each intersect with feminist studies of motherhood, thus reconfiguring our notions of kinship in ways that make room for two (or more) mothers.

Colorblindness in the Liberal Politics of Adoption

January 1992: As the academic that I am, I am preparing myself to become an adoptive parent by reading books on the subject. Somewhere along the way, I stumble upon a statement written two decades earlier by black social workers condemning the adoption of black children by white parents. This causes me considerable anxiety about my own motives for adopting transracially. I make an appointment with one of the caseworkers at the adoption agency who I trust to talk straight with me. I ask Jeannette, a gentle, but no-nonsense, African American caseworker, whether I'm just being a "white liberal do-gooder." She smiles wryly at me and says, "You obviously are white and yes, you are liberal and you want to do good." "But am I being naive in thinking myself capable of raising a child of color?" I ask. "Do you think such a child would be better off with parents of his or her own race?" Becoming more serious, Jeannette replies that she wishes she could locate more people of color to adopt children of color, but that—in the absence of this—she would rather place an ethnic minority child with a "good white liberal" than with a white family who lacks the do-gooder instinct. "Besides," she says, again smiling, "a child will cure you of your naiveté."

The era of the Civil Rights Movement witnessed a surge in transracial adoptions with the number of transracial adoptions more than tripling from 1968 to 1971. This trend alarmed communities of color, leading to opposition from Native Americans and African Americans and in subsequent years from Hispanic Americans and Asian Americans as well (Andujo 1988; Bartholet 1991; Simon, Alstein, & Melli 1994). The most vocal opposition to transracial adoption in the United States, however, came from the National Association of Black Social Workers (NABSW) who in 1972 publicly denounced the adoption of black children by white families as a form of "cultural genocide" detrimental to black children, as well as to black families and communities (NABSW 1972, 777). Affirming "the inviolable position of Black children in Black families where they belong," NABSW argued that the adoption of black children by white parents was "totally unnecessary" and nothing more than an "expedient for white folk" under circumstances wherein "the supply of white children for adoption [had] all but vanished" (1972, 778–79). Such adoptions, they argued, comprised a racist assault on black families and communities and was damaging to the well-being of black children.

In the wake of NABSW's opposition, the number of approved transracial adoptions in the United States dropped dramatically.[3] Yet NABSW's critique of transracial adoption as a practice of cultural genocide failed to restructure white desire. Instead, restrictions on domestic transracial adoption combined with domestic policies prohibiting adoption by unmarried persons and same-sex couples led to an exponential increase in transnational adoptions (Brodzinsky 2003).[4] The U.S. Child Citizenship Act of 2000 facilitated transnational adoption by promising immediate citizenship to foreign born children adopted by U.S. citizens; by 2004, the United States had become the largest transnational adoption industry consumer (Child Welfare Information, 2004; U.S. Dept. of State 2011).

Within the United States, supporters of transracial adoption worked to reverse the restrictions on the practice. Legal scholars argued that the equal protection clause of the Fourteenth Amendment disallowed the use of racial classifications except insofar as strong public policy reasons could be given for their utilization, thus placing the burden of proof on those (like NABSW) who would use racial criteria as a guide to adoptive placements.[5] Just as affirmative action had come under attack in the 1980s as "reverse racism," race-matching preferences in adoption came under attack in the 1990s as an allegedly discriminatory practice harmful both to white parents and to the children of color whom those parents wished to adopt. In both cases, critics of race-conscious policies contended that colorblindness was the only appropriate antidote to racism. Adopting children of color into white families was thus "promoted as race-neutral, altruistic, and advantageous to children of color" (Quiroz 2007, 19).

Attempting to balance the race-conscious concerns of NABSW and others with the concerns of critics of race-matching preferences in adoption, U.S. senators supporting the 1994 Multiethnic Placement Act (MEPA), prohibited agencies receiving federal funds from delaying or denying the adoptive placement of children *solely* on the basis of racial considerations, but nonetheless permitted consideration of race as *one of several factors* used to determine a child's best interests (U.S. Congress 1994). By 1996, however, the MEPA had been amended by an Interethnic Placement Act (IEPA) making consideration of race in adoptive placements *impermissible* (and punishable), unless such considerations could be documented as relevant to an *individual* child's particular needs (DCFS 1996). The arguments of NABSW and others concerning what was, in general, best for ethnic minority children were thus effectively blocked by prohibiting caseworkers from making any general assumptions concerning "what a child of a particular racial or ethnic background may need."[6] Within this prevailing climate, African American caseworkers—such as my own—could hardly be expected to be completely honest with prospective parents about the political and psychological complexities involved in practices of transracial adoption.

The insistence that adoptive placements should be colorblind was facilitated by a humanitarian rhetoric that positioned children up for adoption as "orphans," thereby positioning middle-class adoptive parents as the potential saviors for hoards of children "languishing in foster care" (see, e.g., Bartholet 1991; Kennedy 1994). These (allegedly) orphaned children are a species of what Kathryn Bond Stockton (2009) refers to as "the queer child." They are queered by their innocence, as captured in photographic portrayals of them on adoption websites and in the media, smiling gently and sadly, but also seductively, at the prospective parents who will protect and care for them. As Stockton notes, the child is simultaneously made "strange" (different from us) and yet also "appealing" (an object of our desire) by its "all-important 'innocence'" (30). The innocence of these "parentless" children (and the tenuousness of that innocence, which thus demands intervention to preserve it) is further highlighted by the notion that these are children who are "at risk." "At risk of what?" we might well ask. This is rarely specified by adoption agencies themselves, but a large body of social scientific research on the connections between being in long-term foster care and increased prevalence of juvenile (and adult) delinquency strongly suggests that what these "parentless" children are vulnerable to is precisely the danger of losing their innocence and thus their appeal. This accounts, in part, for the largely "unadoptable" status of older children and the high consumer demand for infants. "Experience," as Stockton suggests, is "hard to square with innocence, making depictions of streetwise children, who are often neither white nor middle-class, hard to square with 'children'" (32). A solution to this problem, she notes, is "to endow these children with abuse. As odd as it may seem, suffering certain kinds of abuse from which they need protection and to which they don't consent, working-class children or children of color may come to seem more innocent" (33). This is, of course, precisely the narrative by which older children on the adoption market are constructed. Traumatic histories of sexual, physical and/or emotional abuse inflicted by their previous (biological or foster) families—or failing this, simply the traumas associated with "being trapped in the limbo of foster care" as an "orphan of [racial] separatism" (Kennedy 1994, 38–39)—emphasize the urgency of saving these children and pull at the humanitarian impulses of white liberals.

As this suggests, within the discourse of transracial adoption, the children in foster care are further queered by their color. The child of color is peculiar, in part, because of its imagined suffering, oppression and courage—a representation that makes experience "intrude upon 'innocence'" (Stockton 2009 184). The peculiarity of the child of color is also due, however, to the ways in which this child enters the white family as "a kind of ghost" (192). Children of color are, Stockton suggests, like "gay" children—*as children* and thus *as innocent*, children cannot really be gay or other than white (pure). Hence, the adult child of color, like the adult gay child, is "unforeseen" by his (straight, white) family. Children of color are, thus, "strangers in the family"—strangers who wish, however, to "be acknowledged by the families they 'invade.'" As such, Stockton continues, children of color are tied to a "backward birth," as they (the children) birth their parents, forcing parents to reflect on their self-image as liberals. Here, "experience comes to sheltered whites through a black body seeking connection" (209).

The portrayal of children in domestic foster care as orphans—and thus as vulnerable innocents in need of protection—parallels a longstanding discourse portraying transnational adoptees as "orphans." Most histories of transnational adoption situate its beginnings in a humanitarian effort to rescue war orphans, first after World War II and subsequently at the end of the Korean and Vietnam wars. After the Korean War, in particular, the media carried "the plight of orphans into the homes and hearts of Middle America," fueling "rescue fantasies"; many U.S. parents' decisions to adopt were motivated, at that time, "by a religious or moral desire to 'save' orphans from an impoverished third-world country" (Bergquist 2004, 343–44). Rescue narratives continue to dominate transnational adoptions today. Legal scholar and adoption advocate Elizabeth Bartholet (2007a), for example, argues that transnational adoption "serves the fundamental need for family of some of the world's neediest children," children who would otherwise be "growing up or dying in horribly inadequate orphanages or in the streets" (154).

The drive to save orphans from an uncertain future abroad (even when the host country resists) is readily witnessed in the aftermath of natural disasters affecting countries in the global South. After the 2010 Haitian earthquake, for example, adoption agencies were bombarded with offers to care for Haitian children and the U.S. State Department waived visa requirements for children already "in the adoption pipeline"—including for some children whose adoptions had not yet been approved by Haitian officials—and began airlifting some of these 900 children out of Haiti. Some U.S. aid organizations urged the U.S. government to go beyond expediting those adoptions already in process and "bring thousands of earthquake orphans to the U.S. as soon as possible" (Jonsson 2010). As Karen Dubinsky (2010) notes in her study of child-lift operations in the Americas, whenever there is a disaster, our first instinct is to go in and get the babies.

Like the experience of queer political refugees who migrate from East to West and South to North, the experience of adopted children (described by one adoption advocate as "young refugees from destroyed families") has been largely been characterized by a "narrative of movement from repression to freedom" (Kennedy 1994, 38; Luibhéid and Cantú 2005, xxv). However, the Euro-American narrative that packages Western citizenship as a "gift" ignores the forms of structural and personal violence experienced by children who enter the adoption-immigration system, as well as the violence experienced by the parents, communities, and nations from whom these children have been "saved." Similarly the "savior" narrative characterizing the domestic adoption of children of color by white parents overlooks the possibility that adoption may be a "violent gift" whose contents include an assault on families and communities of color and the inhibition of a child's power of self-identification and belonging (Walker 1996). As Shani King (2009) notes, the idea that adoption saves needy children reflects "a narrow conception of children outside of the context of their family, community, and culture and through a narrow prism as the potential child of Western adults" (429). In reality, few children who are in domestic foster care or orphanages abroad are actually without kin.

Domestically, children who are orphaned (through the premature death of parents) are typically taken in and adopted by other remaining kin. The children of color who are depicted as "languishing in foster care" often are "parentless" only insofar as the State has terminated the custodial rights of their parents. Sometimes, as in the case of demonstrated physical or sexual abuse, these terminations of parental rights may be warranted. In many other cases, however, reasons for terminating parental rights are questionable. Children may be considered "abandoned" or "neglected" by social workers, for example, when they reside frequently outside the nuclear family—despite the fact that care of children by relatives in large extended families, communities, or tribes is not unusual within the child's ethnic community. Moreover, standards for "adequate care" based on middle-class values such as the square footage of a home, the availability of indoor plumbing, and family income has led to extraordinarily high rates of placing native and black children with white families (Fetzer 1999; Unger 1977). Indeed, "inadequacy of income, more than any factor, constitutes the reason that children are removed" from their parents' care against their parents' will (Lindsey 1994, 155).

In the United States (and other Western nations), there is little recognition that people of color continue to be disadvantaged in most areas of social life: housing, education, jobs, income levels, rates of imprisonment, health care, and child welfare. These disadvantages frequently stem from allegedly race-neutral government policies (in addition to the biases of bureaucratic institutions governing our everyday lives such as schools, banks, professional organizations, insurance systems, law enforcement, social welfare agencies, etc.). To understand why so many children of color are "languishing in foster care," one thus needs to understand the larger political context within which the humanitarian concern for these "parentless" children emerges—a context wherein affirmative action in employment and education was being rapidly dismantled, as was the safety net for poor women and children. In the late twentieth century, Aid to Families with Dependent Children (AFDC), a program that had been in effect since 1935, was blamed for enabling "welfare queens," incentivizing the economically and morally irresponsible breeding of illegitimate children, and promoting a culture of poverty. Thus, AFDC was replaced by Temporary Assistance for Needy Families (TANF) in 1997, as part of the Personal Responsibility and Work Opportunity Reconciliation Act (PRWORA). This federal law, which had the goal of putting putatively lazy welfare mothers (and others) back to work, supplanted the Job Opportunities and Basic Skills Training (JOBS) program of 1988 and practically eliminated federal assistance to working-class women.[7] Notably, in the very same year that AFDC was dismantled, President Clinton signed into law the Adoption and Safe Families Act, which provided tax incentives to those adopting ethnic minority or other special needs children—incentives that were further increased by the Economic Growth and Tax Relief Reconciliation Act of 2001. Viewed in this context, U.S. adoption reforms are plausibly viewed as part of a program to redistribute wealth—both monies and children—from poor families of color to middle-class, white families. "Combined with the 1980 federal Adoption Assistance and Child Welfare Act that provided subsidies to middle-class families adopting from foster care, the adoption tax credit meant that the federal government would provide upwards of a $13,000 bonus for middle-class white people to raise the same children taken from families for poverty-related neglect that it wouldn't pay to alleviate" (Briggs 2006, 85).

Similarly, transnational adoption is plausibly viewed as involving a redistribution of wealth (young, relatively healthy, children) from de-developed countries to industrialized nations. As King (2009) notes, "whether the exchange is viewed as one between birth parents with very few resources and families with resources, or as one between a country with an extensive (admittedly imperfect) social service infrastructure and a country with no social service infrastructure, the exchange bears a neo-colonialist hue" (425). Like "parentless" children in the United States, the "orphans" abroad who are the subject of humanitarian concern may find themselves "on the streets" only because government policies have actively destroyed their families. Sometimes the policies implicated in orphaning children are the murderous policies of a nation's own dictatorial regimes (e.g., the murder of political dissidents in Pinochet's Chile or Videla's Argentina). At other times, as in the case of so-called "war orphans" from Korea and Vietnam, the policies of the United States itself have caused children to lose their parents. Equally frequently, however, the children brought into the United States on "orphan" visas are not orphans at all. As we now know, not all "war orphans" brought here from Korea or Vietnam were truly abandoned or orphaned. In the aftermath of war, natural disasters, or political and economic crises, it is extremely difficult to determine who has or has not survived and thus who is or is not an orphan. Moreover, the mere fact that children have been placed in an orphanage or in the care of some other charitable organization for food, housing, and education that impoverished, struggling parents cannot provide, does not mean that they have permanently lost contact with their parents. As the Baptist missionaries attempting to transport children across the Haitian border into the Dominican Republic discovered in the wake of the 2010 Haitian earthquake, there is a fine line between "rescuing" children and "kidnapping" them. Many of the children discovered in orphanages or on the streets after the earthquake were not free for adoption. As one of the Haitian children who the missionaries attempted to smuggle across the Dominican border indicated, she believed she was going to a summer camp or boarding school and would be later reunited with her family who had, in fact, survived the earthquake ("Baptists in Haiti" 2010).

Making matters more complicated yet is the idiosyncratic way in which U.S. immigration law uses the term "orphan." Because law requires that all potential adoptees be classified as orphans, the term "orphan" gets defined as a child who has suffered "the death or disappearance of, abandonment or desertion by, or separation or loss from, both parents, *or for whom the sole or surviving parent is incapable of providing the proper care* and has in writing irrevocably released the child for emigration and adoption" (8 U.S.C. § 1101(b)(1) (F), italics added). Under such a definition, almost any child living in a de-developed country without an ideal family environment (one that is seen as "proper" through Western eyes) comes to be identified as an orphan. The "orphaned" transnational adoptee, like the "parentless" domestic adoptee, is any child who might be viewed as "abandoned," "lost," "living on the streets," "homeless" or simply "needy," that is, poor.

Just as there is a fine line between "rescuing" and "kidnapping" children, there is a fine—and rather blurry—line between "releasing" a child for adoption (as U.S. law requires) and "terminating" a parent's rights. The complexities of determining when a parent has "released" a child from his or her custody was highlighted during 2006 when a widowed Malawian peasant, Yohane Banda, who allowed his 13-month-old son to be adopted by U.S. pop star, Madonna, revealed he had not realized he was signing away custody "for good." Banda's wife had died in childbirth and it was his understanding that "the nice woman" (Madonna) would care for his child and then return him to his village. Those supervising the orphanage where his son resided—and where Banda continued to have ongoing contact with his son—had not explained to Banda that "adoption" meant David would cease to be his son or a member of his clan. The Human Rights Consultative Committee (an umbrella organization comprising 67 human rights groups) challenged the adoption on the grounds that Madonna's adoption would set a precedent for human trafficking ("Boy's Dad has Doubts" 2006). The challenge was unsuccessful, however, and Madonna's adoption of the boy was approved, allowing her to separate him from his father and bring him into the United States on an "orphan" visa. "Because all adoptees are classified as 'orphans' pursuant to statistics compiled by the U.S. Department of State," as King (2009) observes, "it is impossible to know how many children who are adopted have one birth parent, two birth parents, or can otherwise be cared for in their country of origin" (468).

Because of concerns about the international trafficking in children, the United Nations Children's Fund (UNICEF), emphasizing compliance with the 1993 Hague convention on international adoption, recently shut down international adoptions from Guatemala due to fraud and corruption, imposed new restrictions slowing down inter-country adoption processes from countries such as China and Russia and provided incentives for domestic families to adopt internally. These and other restrictions on intercountry adoptions significantly reduced the availability of children for transnational adoption. In 2011, Americans adopted only 9,319 children from abroad, representing a more than 50 percent drop in transnational adoptions to the United States from the peak of 22,990 adoptions in 2004 (U.S. Department of State, 2012). Not surprisingly, this left many Americans wishing to adopt, as well as adoption advocates, disgruntled.

Some complaints about the unfairness of tightened restrictions on transnational adoption reflect a concern with restrictions on the free market.[8] Most of the complaints, however, divert our attention from the commodification of children by reiterating the humanitarian rescue narratives that have long characterized U.S. attitudes toward both domestic and foreign adoptions. Stressing the urgency of loosening international adoption restrictions, Bartholet (2007b), for example, suggests the "[t]he real-world alternatives for the children at issue are life—or death—on the streets or in the types of institutions that a half-century of research has proved systematically destroy children's ability to grow up capable of functioning normally in society." Similarly viewing the situation as urgent, the National Council for Adoption in the United States pledged to "promote sound international adoption policy and practice, giving special attention to . . . [c]urbing nationalistic, anti-adoption sentiment that keeps children trapped in foreign orphanages" (Atwood et al. 2007). The subtexts of these humanitarian adoption narratives are significant from a postcolonial, queer perspective. NCFA's concern for the well-being of orphans is linked to criticisms of *foreign* nationalisms, thus raising the racialized specter of a primitive tribalism while simultaneously occluding the economic and military policies linked to Western nation-building that have made postcolonial resistance necessary. The notion that nationalism is a vice of struggling nations (rather than a feature of our own policies) should strike one as ironic. It is in keeping, however, with the rhetorical strategy of charging domestic communities of color who wish to retain children within their own communities with (reverse) racism.

Bartholet's humanitarian narrative, moreover, exposes a desire that exceeds the motivation to rescue children from poverty or death (which could, after all, be accomplished through forms of humanitarian aid which didn't involve removing children from their countries or families of origin). She wants to ensure that foreign children grow up to be "normal"—which we can only presume (since she does not clarify) means they will become well-aligned with Western expectations and values. Since the 1970s, a large body of social scientific literature has been devoted to showing that transracial and transcultural adoptive placements have positive effects for children of color. Much of this research, like the adoptions it facilitates, bears a neocolonialist hue (Park and Green 2000). Using Eurocentric standards of measurement and presuming white children are the standard bearers for cognitive and emotional development, most studies base their conclusions on evidence that ethnic minority children adopted by white families compare favorably to white adopted children on IQ tests and other white, Western measures of "success" and "well-being."[9] A Eurocentric standard of measurement is also implicit in claims that individual well-being and group well-being are separate issues. Much of the research on the well-being of transracially adopted black children, for example, focuses on individualistic conceptions of self-esteem (Goddard 1996; Juffer and van Ijzendoorn 2007). As such, it doesn't address the concerns of birth parents, cultural communities, and other nations that they are being robbed of their children in a process of cultural genocide. Nor does it address the concerns voiced by people of color that ethnic minority children reared in white homes or foreign-born children adopted into U.S. homes may be robbed of their cultural heritage and group identity.

The Racialization of Intimacy: Adopted Children Speak Out

October 1992: Attempting to be good adoptive parents of a biracial child, we have been responding to invitations from the Children's Home Society to attend educational and social gatherings of transracially adoptive families. On this evening, we attend a discussion panel featuring "experiential experts" on transracial adoption (namely adoptive parents, predominantly adoptive mothers). Notably, there are no birth mothers on this panel. Nor are there any adoptive parents of color. An audience member asks one white mother on the panel how she addressed her child's concerns about racial difference. The "expert" in question recalls telling her black son that "he tanned well" when, as a youngster, he had questioned their different skin colors. I stifle a giggle at the absurdity of this, waiting expectantly for the critical self-reflection that will surely follow this confession. But no critical analysis of this mother's erasure of her child's racial identity is forth-

coming. Noting the angry grimace of her now adolescent son, who is
seated silently beside her, I ask if we might hear from her son about
his experiences with racial difference. He mumbles, "it is hard some-
times," but says nothing more. The tension of the muscles in his body
and face, however, is readily visible.

It is easy for white adoptive parents to minimize the importance
of race and of a child's preadoptive history because race and historical
roots have fewer negative consequences if you are part of the dominant
group. People of color cannot afford to, nor are they permitted to,
ignore color. This is so even when (perhaps *especially* when) a person
of color is adopted by white parents. As Avery, the African-American
daughter of white Jewish lesbian parents reveals in the documentary
film, *Off and Running*, feeling Jewish because one is raised as Jewish,
doesn't mean that other people see her that way. "When you are adopted
by a white family, you see the whole world differently," she claims. It
isn't until she begins attending a majority black high school that she
recognizes that *both* whites and blacks "looked at me [as] a girl who
was different." It is at this juncture of her life that Avery reaches out
for her birth mother. Although her adoptive parents are supportive of
her desire to make contact, Avery's relationship with them deteriorates
as she explores her black identity. As Avery puts it, "I don't think they
understand who I am. . . . I'm beginning to identify with the African
American side of me and they don't really fit into that part of my life."

No parents, including white parents, can protect minority children
from the racial prejudice, discrimination, and oppression that exist outside of the family unit. And white parents, unlike parents who share
their child's racial identity, risk perpetuating racism and ethnocentrism
within the family itself. On the one hand, if white adoptive parents practice color blindness, they will fail to acknowledge, respect, and preserve
their child's racial and ethnic identity. On the other hand, white parents
who strive to preserve their child's racial and ethnic identity may risk
exoticizing the child as Other. Certainly, I have struggled with attempting to avoid both of these pitfalls in raising a biracial child who can—
and frequently does—pass as white. Allowing others to "whitewash"
her (especially when she was too young to speak for herself) seemed
inappropriate. At the same time, consistently pointing out to others
that she was "Guyanese-American, of Indian descent" seemed likewise
inappropriate—as though I was showcasing an object of exotic origins.

Choosing when to ignore racial difference and when to highlight
it is one of the many everyday (often unnoticed) privileges enjoyed by

those in the dominant group. White privilege also extends to the ability to choose when, where and how to fight racism and who to "invite" into the struggle. As mixed-race filmmaker Sasha Khokha notes, "[r]acism is made real to me by the Europeans in my family and in my life when they *choose to adopt* me into their world, either literally or figuratively. I have been officially 'adopted' as the daughter of a European patriarch and made 'legitimate' under his name" (Khokha 1995, 24). As Khokha's remarks, Avery's observations, and the nonverbal body language of a black teenage boy indicate, for children of color adopted into white families, transracial and transnational adoption may appear as simply the most recent in a long series of attempts to assimilate minority cultures into the white Eurocentric mainstream.

The artwork of Tracey Moffatt speaks piercingly of the racism and colonialism that formed the background of her experiences as part of the "lost generation" of Australian aboriginals forced to assimilate into white culture. Her print *Early Theft, Draw a Map* (2004), for example, depicts a photograph of herself at five years old, amidst classmates. The only dark-skinned child in the classroom portrait, she has obliterated the faces of surrounding white children with crayon drawings of a map of Australia and its native inhabitants (koalas and eucalyptus trees). While the visual elements of this print represent a child's attempt to reclaim her identity and centrality to indigenous Australia, the accompanying text suggests that such reclamation gives way to assimilation into white culture. In small print, to the left of the pictures, Moffat narrates her theft of a Grade 1 classmate's artwork, noting how proud it made her foster mother when she won an award for this (white boy's) artwork at a prestigious Queensland University competition. On the right-hand side of the print, a copy of the award letter that her mother would show to visitors is displayed.

Moffat's 1994 series, "Scarred for Life," also draws on memories from her childhood, including photographs that speak specifically to her ambivalent relationship to her foster mother. *Birth Certificate, 1962*, shows a young aboriginal girl clutching a piece of paper as she rests her head on a bathroom sink. The caption says: "During the fight, her mother threw her birth certificate at her. This is how she found out her real father's name." *Mother's Day, 1975*, is an image of a young aboriginal woman's head in rapid motion as if she has been slapped; the caption reads: "On Mother's Day, as the family watched, she copped a backhander from her mother." These photos depict "the consequences of colonial benevolent love for the colonized subject," as does Moffat's

1989 short film *Night Cries—A Rural Tragedy* (Secomb 2007, 90). As the adult aboriginal daughter depicted in this film cares for her dying white mother, it is apparent that this care is the result of both genuine tenderness and resented obligation. While gently washing her mother's feet, she hums (together with her mother) "Onward Christian soldiers." As the foot washing takes place, the daughter remembers a childhood simultaneously joyful and terrifying and she dreams of an escape from her isolation, alienation, and confinement. Such escape is not possible, however, as the daughter is trapped in "the exchange economy of reciprocal colonial love"— an economy of intimacy that obligates her to care for her mother who, in caring for her, isolated her from the other life of which she dreams (Secomb 2006, 92).

The adult children of Western adoptions with Native, African, Asian and Latin American ancestries whose narratives and analyses are collected in the anthology *Outsiders Within: Writing on Transracial Adoption* give further voice to the themes of displacement, assimilation, and self-sacrifice expressed in Moffat's artwork. Like Moffatt, First Nations' author Shandra Spears (2006) speaks poetically of having "no future and no past, only a long, isolated now" as a "pet" or "companion" to "fill in missing pieces in people's lives, to be a bandage over the wound in adoptive parents' hearts" (117). African American Kim Fardy (2006) speaks of the "brutally silencing reality" of "growing up Black with white parents in white suburbia," likening adoption to being "posted up like a modern-day slave on the block" (57). El Salvadoran Patrick McDermott (2006) recounts being literally stolen from his mother at three months old and sold to a couple in Massachusetts (105). Korean-born Jae Ran Kim (2006) talks about "baptizing" herself "with holy tears" and becoming "a sacrificial lamb of God and an American family" (151). Vietnamese-born Rachel Quy Collier (2007) discusses the "tragedy" of "children caught in an invisible yet strong net of denial and nonacceptance, dying, yet forced to play out a fictive role in order to enable those upon whom they depend for life . . . to enjoy their self-appointed role as caregivers"—a fiction that turns the child into the self-sacrificing caregiver of the parent (207).

Collectively, the voices (and silences) of adopted children reveal transracial and transnational adoption as "the intimate face of colonization, racism, militarism, imperialism, and globalization" (Oparah et al. 2006, 7). In particular, they make visible "the affective labor" that Eng describes as accompanying "the gendered movement of bodies from the global South to the global North" (98). Situating the transnational adoptee on a spectrum of the exploited labor of intimacy including mail order brides, domestic servants, and sex workers, Eng argues that transnational adoptees support first-world middle-class families by consolidating their social and psychic boundaries (20, 97):

> [T]he consumption of the transnational adoptee by parents in the global North completes the ideal of newly emergent multicultural families as a supplement to capital precisely through the exploitation of the child's affective, rather than wage, labor. . . . [W]hile Third World women from the global South have traditionally been exploited for the wage labor in the manufacturing sector, their emotional labor in the domestic sphere, and now their reproductive labor as birth mothers, the exploitation of the transnational adoptee is largely an emotional affair. She helps to consolidate the *affective* boundaries of the white, heteronormative middle-class nuclear family. (108–09)

To illustrate the affective labor of the transnational adoptee, Eng examines Deann Borshay Liem's (2000) documentary film, *First Person Plural*. Borshay Liem's documentary explores her life as a Korean adoptee through the integration of family photographs, her adoptive father's home movies, news reel footage and photographs of Korea during the time she was adopted, and footage she shoots thirty years later of her American parents and siblings reflecting on their life together, as well as footage of their first visit to Korea to meet her newly discovered Korean birth family. Borhshay Liem's 2010 film, *In the Matter of Cha Jung Hee*, uses a similar technique, broadening the montage to provide the historical context of her personal past and her present search for her Korean identity. Both films document what Eng describes as "the racialization of intimacy," a phenomenon wherein racial subjects are "reinscribed into a discourse of colorblindness" as race (and racism) are "occluded within the private domain of private family and kinship" (10). They do so by exploring several interrelated themes including: adoption as a consumptive choice that employs the language of ownership, the production of the adoptee as both same and other, the overwriting of histories of militarization and suffering by narratives of family and kinship, the erasure of the adoptee's identity and past as engendered by colorblindness and the temporal containment of familial history, and the emotional struggles of the transnational adoptee.

Adoption as a consumptive choice for adoptive families—yet a disorienting experience for the adoptee—is illustrated in the early scenes of *First Person Plural,* which document the first meeting of the Borshays and their adoptive daughter. As a small, lost, and frightened girl arrives at the airport (amidst several other small Korean girls), the Borshays greet her with enthusiasm. Watching this footage later, Denise Borshay (Borshay Liem's adoptive sister) recollects her mother approaching "the wrong person," indicating that they didn't know which child belonged to them until they checked nametags. That the various Korean children who had arrived were interchangeable commodities is revealed by Denise's claim that the initial confusion "didn't matter" because they knew "one of them was ours."

"Over time, I became one of them," Borshay Liem suggests in *In the Matter of Cha Jung Hee.* "I learned to change the way I smiled, carried my body to match theirs. So I no longer saw a difference between us. When I looked in the mirror, it was no longer my face I saw, but their beauty, their bodies reflected back at me." That Borshay Liem's attempts to become "one of them" were doomed to failure, however, is made painfully clear in the montage of photographs and home movie clips collected in *First Person Plural.* Documenting both the assimilation and the exoticization of the transnational adoptee, pictures of Borshay Liem as a small child amidst beloved white dolls are juxtaposed with a picture of her dressed up as a Korean doll. An image of Borshay Liem and her sister with "twin" hairdos documents Borshay Liem's assimilation into the white family, while simultaneously demonstrating the impossibility of such assimilation (the perm she sports is laughable). An image of Borshay Liem as the high school prom queen demonstrates her success at "fitting in." Yet a photo of her with her high school sweetheart starkly emphasizes her otherness; his height emphasizes her small stature; his pale white skin and white tuxedo accentuate her dark complexion. A photo of Borshay Liem wearing a hat bearing images of the American flag is followed by her adoptive sister recollecting how everyone used to think they "looked alike." However, the notion that she could be just like other white Americans is immediately undermined by a high school class photo in which she, as the only brown-skinned member of the class, is clearly Other.

Throughout the film, Borshay Liem's adoptive siblings alternate between othering her and assimilating her into their (white) family. Denise, for example, notes that "even though we look different—different nationality or whatever—we were your family." National, cultural, and physical difference are acknowledged here, but as the words "or whatever" signify, a narrative of familial belonging ultimately elides these differences. Borshay Liem's brother, Duncan (a self-professed American nationalist and xenophobe), informs her authoritatively that "You didn't come from my mommy's womb. You don't have the family eyes, but you've got the family smile. Color and look doesn't make any difference. It's who you are. You're my sister." Both of Borshay Liem's adoptive siblings acknowledge her origins as different from their own—her origination in a different womb and a different nation—but deny that these differences (along with their visible traces in their different skin colors, the shape and color of their eyes, the shape of their ears, and the color and texture of their hair) "make any difference" to Deann's identity. Through these and other scenes, *First Person Plural* reveals adoption as implicated in the processes of what bell hooks (1990) terms "consumer cannibalism," processes of the commodification and consumption of difference wherein difference is eradicated through an exchange that "not only displaces the Other but denies the significance of that other's history through a process of decontextualization" (31).

As Borshay Liem's story unfolds in her two documentaries, she tells us the history of her origins to which her family is indifferent, providing the backstory to her complicated threefold identity, introduced at the start of *First Person Plural*.

> My name is Kang Ok Jin. I was born on 14 June, 1957. I feel like I've been several different people in one life. My name is Cha Jung Hee. I was born on 5 November 1956. I've had three names, three different sets of histories. My name is Deann Borshay. I was born 3 March 1966, the moment I stepped off the airplane in San Francisco. I've spoken different languages, and I've had different families.

Deann Borshay, as she was named by her white adoptive family and is identified on her U.S. birth certificate, was originally born—or so she was led to believe for many years—Cha Jung Hee, a Korean war orphan. Alveen Borshay, the adoptive mother, explains the humanitarian impulse that led her to sponsor Cha Jung Hee through a "Foster Parents Plan:" "Daddy had gone into real estate and was doing really well and I said we should do something for somebody because life has been really good for us." Watching television, Alveen saw a commercial indicating the need for foreign sponsors of war orphans and began sending $15 a month to the orphanage in which Cha Jung Hee resided. A nurse sent updates to the Borshays on the health and well-being of the child they were sponsoring, letters that depicted Cha Jung Hee as a child (and stereotypical Asian girl) who was "obedient," "calm," and "smiles all the time." When the Borshays decide to adopt her and she arrives in San Francisco, however, she is not smiling. Indeed, her sorrow and fear (no doubt combined with the strangeness of American food) interfere with her ability to enjoy a family dinner with the Borshays during her first night in their home. As Donald Borshay, the adoptive father, recollects: "Mother prepared you something that was very nice. And we were sitting at the table and you just kind of dropped your head and the tears started to come down. No words were spoken. Mother could see what was happening, and she simply took you away from the table and you were excused and from then on it was perfect."

Commenting on this scene, Eng notes that the adoptive father's claim that "from then on it was perfect" effaces Borshay Liem's Korean past, starting "history proper" at the moment of the Korean child's arrival in the Borshay home (113). Even if we were to accept this starting date for Borshay Liem's history, however, it is clear that not everything was perfect. Interspersed with happy family photos and home movies are her mother's recollection that she "didn't sleep very well at first," her father's recollection that she was so "eager to please" that she "became ill," her sister's recollection that she "freaked out" on her first day of school and Borshay Liem's own recollections of early childhood yearnings for Korea and the deep depression that overtook her during her college years, as forgotten memories of Korea returned to her.

The repression of Borshay Liem's past by her family, as Eng observes, is facilitated by managing her affect: "the silent tears that mark her traumatic arrival and the negation of her past . . . cannot have symbolic life or recognition. [They] must necessarily be refused, as Donald Borshay does indeed first deny and then excuse them, such that Borshay Liem has little psychic recourse to work through her considerable losses" (114). The repression of Borshay Liem's past is also facilitated by her mother's rewriting of her memories as dreams. In *First Person Plural*, Borshay Liem recalls making a decision, as a child, that she "would not forget" Korea: "Every day I would close my eyes and remember the road from my home to the orphanage." In both of her films, however, Borshay Liem recounts an episode with her mother in which her certitude about her past was undermined.

When I had learned enough English to talk to my parents, I decided that I should tell them who I really was. I remember going up to her and saying "I'm not who you think I am, I'm not Cha Jung Hee and I think I have a mother and sisters and brothers living in Korea still." And she turned to me and said "Oh honey, you've just been dreaming. You don't have a mother. . . . Look at these adoption documents. They say that you are Cha Jung Hee and that your mother died giving birth to you. . . . This is just a natural part of you getting used to us. Don't worry about it. These are just bad dreams and they are going to go away soon.

As time goes on, Borshay Liem loses her memory of her childhood, of her Korean family, her Korean landscape, and her Korean language. It is only after she moves away from her American family and starts living on her own that her "dreams" return. Over the course of "a year or so," she recollects, as the dreams became more frequent and intrusive, she realized that these images were images of her life in Korea, "that they weren't just dreams, that they were real." In an attempt to put together her past, Borshay Liem searches through her adoption papers and discovers two different pictures, each of which is identified as "Cha Jung Hee," but only one of which looks like her. In order to discern her identity and her real past, Borshay Liem writes to the orphanage from which she was adopted and they put her in touch with her Korean family. In a letter, her Korean brother informs her she is Kang Ok Jin and has four siblings and a mother "who thinks of you day and night is so happy to read the letter you wrote."

Both of Borshay Liem's films challenge Western understandings that, as Alveen remarks, "[being in] an orphanage meant that you had no family." As we learn, Cha Jung Hee (like Kang Ok Jin) was not a war orphan. Discovered to be at the orphanage by a searching father, Cha Jung Hee was surreptitiously removed and taken to her familial home during the time of the Borshays' sponsorship. Thus, when the Borshays indicated their desire to adopt Cha Jung Hee, the orphanage sent another child, Kang Ok Jin, in her place. Here we also witness how the racialization of intimacy is aided and abetted by social institutions that count on the inability of the white Westerner to "see" difference. One may speculate that the Korean adoption agency facilitating the fraudulent transaction with the Borshays counted on the inability of Westerners to detect the difference between one Korean child and another. As Borshay Liem observes in *In the Matter of Cha Jung Hee*, the Korean economy in the wake of the war depended almost exclusively on the United States; even after the Korean economy improved and few war orphans remained, "thousands of children whose parents could not support them were sent overseas. What began as a humanitarian effort, turned into an industry that brought millions of dollars into the Korean economy." Given this historical context, the fact that Korea might exchange one desirable export for another similar-yet-different one (an impoverished child for a war orphan, Kang Ok Jin for Cha Jung Hee) is not altogether surprising—although it does highlight in discomforting ways the commodification of adopted children.

Whether these speculations are correct or not, the inability of the Borshays to distinguish between Cha Jung Hee and Kang Ok Jin is quite stunning when considering the different photos displayed side by side in *In the Matter of Cha Jung Hee*. How could they "have no idea" that the girl they adopted was not the girl they sponsored? Borshay Liem clearly sees the distinction between the photos, as do various Korean social workers and the many women named Cha Jung Hee who Borshay Liem visits during her search for "the girl whose place she took in America." Through their eyes, we too learn to notice the difference in their eyebrows, in the slant of their eyes, and in the shape of their jaws. We learn, in other words, to become less colorblind—which is to say, less blinded to the variations within, as well as the variations among, people of different colors.

It is not clear when Alveen and Donald Borshay discovered Cha Jung Hee had been replaced with Kang Ok Jin, but it does not appear to matter to them. As Alveen tells her daughter in *First Person Plural*, once again illustrating the effacement of difference by narratives of family belonging, "I didn't care that they had switched a child on us. You couldn't be loved more and just because suddenly you weren't Cha Jung Hee but you were Kang, Kong or whatever, it didn't matter to me. You were still Deann and you were my daughter." *Or whatever*. As Borshay Liem recounts in *In the Matter of Cha Jung Hee*, "after my parents found out I was not Cha Jung Hee, they behaved as if nothing had happened. For a while, I too pretended that nothing had changed. Then everything fell apart." For Borshay Liem, the discovery that she is not Cha Jung Hee prompts an identity crisis. "I became obsessed with home movies and kept going backwards in time, searching for the exact moment when I forgot who I really was, but I couldn't see myself in these images. I saw a stranger."

Boshay Liem's identity crisis, combined with the discovery of her Korean family and the related discovery that her adoptive parents had lied to her leads her to distance herself from her American parents. In *First Person Plural*, Borshay Liem notes, through her tears, that "as a child I accepted them as my parents because I was dependent on them, but as an adult I think I've had difficulty accepting them as my parents. . . . Sometimes I look at them and I see two white American people that are so different from me that I can't fathom how we are related to each other and how it could be possible that they are my parents." In not revealing to her their own discovery that she was not Cha Jung Hee, the Borshays have broken what Borshay Liem refers to as "an unspoken contract" between her and her adoptive family: "we had all agreed . . . that I was an orphan with no family ties to Korea. I belonged only to my American parents. It meant I didn't have a Korean history or Korean identity."

Borshay Liem's depression during her college years illustrates what Eng describes as the unresolved "racial melancholia" of transnational adoptees. Noting that racial melancholia is a common (not pathological) experience of immigrants who are forced to relinquish cultural ideals but who cannot attain an "idealized whiteness," Eng argues that the transnational adoptee, however, lacks the intergenerational and collective context within which such losses—and thus the passage from melancholia to mourning—are typically negotiated by the immigrant. As Borshay Liem notes, "I was never able to mourn what I had lost with my American parents." The adoptee's inability to mourn losses within their adoptive familial context is overdetermined. Not only does the adoptee's family fail to share in her losses, her sorrow actively contradicts the adoptive family's idealized happiness. There is thus "an emotional cleaving of great consequence in the intimate space of the [adoptive] family" (Eng 2010, 122). Further complicating the affective geography of the adoptive family is the rescue narrative that frequently accompanies motivations for adopting. If adoptive parents believe that they have offered a child a better life than the one she would otherwise have had (and what adoptive parent does not?), the adoptee's mourning for what she has lost may be interpreted as (shameful) ingratitude. That Borshay Liem struggles with feelings of shame in attempting to speak to her adoptive parents about her losses is clear: she characterizes her inability to talk to her American parents about her Korean family and, in particular, her inability to talk to her American mother about her Korean mother, as stemming from feelings of "disloyalty," noting that "it was like putting dirt in my mouth somehow" *(In the Matter of Cha Jung Hee)*.

The "affective embargo" under which Borshay Liem functions makes it difficult for her to transform her melancholia into mourning (Eng 2010, 123). Forced to "negotiate her losses in silence and isolation," Borshay Liem's racial melancholia is "redoubled": In being unable to speak about the loss of her original family with her adopted family, Borshay Liem's adoptive family becomes a further site of loss as their relations too become severed (122). This situation is not, of course, unique to Borshay Liem. It is a common experience of transnational adoptees and also of domestically adopted children of color placed in white families under neoliberal ideologies of colorblindness. Any child who is forced to relinquish the ideals of the ethnic culture into which they were born but who cannot (by virtue of their visible racial difference) or who (despite their ability to pass) does not desire to attain an "idealized whiteness" is apt to experience racial melancholia.

Reconfiguring Family:
Making Room for Two (or More) Mothers

In light of the critiques and portrayals of adoption by adopted children, it becomes increasingly implausible to claim that transracial adoption and transnational adoption uphold the best interests of children. The racial melancholia of the transracial and/or transnational adoptee, considered together with the grief of birth mothers (and others) who are too often coerced or manipulated into relinquishing their children, strongly suggest that the involuntary separation of children from their mothers (and other kin) is harmful. Moreover, it is clear that these harms, as perpetuated by current adoption practices, fall disproportionately onto mothers and children of color, making this a matter of racial injustice, both nationally and internationally.

In response to such racialized harms and injustice, both NABSW and UNICEF have advocated policies of family preservation. In closing this chapter, I critically examine this position. Should family preservation be the primary goal of both domestic and international child welfare agencies, as NABSW and UNICEF suggest? Or might family preservation be a conservative and reactionary goal? This depends, I think, on what is meant by "family." It also depends on the methods by which families are to be preserved.

In its 1994 position paper, "Preserving African American families," NABSW explicitly advocates for "the rights of families to raise their children in a loving, safe, and supportive environment," "the right of kinship to raise their relative child in a loving, safe, and supportive environment" and for the "fair and equitable treatment of families of African ancestry who wish to adopt" (9). Prioritizing (a) "stopping unnecessary out-of-home placements" and (b) "reunification of children with parents" where such placements have been made, NABSW establishes a clear preference for preserving the nuclear black family, followed by (c) preserving a child's extended family ("placing children of African ancestry with relatives") and (d) same-race adoptive placements ("placing children with unrelated families of the same race and culture"), arguing that transracial adoption of African American children should be a last resort considered only when compelling evidence of the inability to make a same race placement has been reviewed and supported by representatives of the African American community (4). The United Nations has established a parallel set of priorities affirming its belief that "every child has the right to know and be cared for by his or her own parents, whenever possible," advocating kinship care where parental care is not possible, intracountry adoptions when "living relatives to care for the child cannot be found" and "suggesting that intercountry adoptions should only be permitted when these are not possible" (UNICEF 2007, 2010).

I do not question NABSW's claim that unnecessary out of home placements should be stopped. Nor do I question UNICEF's claim that all children have the right to know and be cared for by their parents where this is possible. Except in cases of documented and ongoing abuse, separating children from their parents and/or other kin who have raised them is both unwarranted and harmful. It would be much preferable to provide financial and social support to parents in crisis that enables them to care for their children. Similarly, I do not wish to question the claim that children of color are best served by color- and community-conscious placements that enable children of color to retain connections with their ethnic communities and nations of origin. As Eng suggests, "at a time when race appears in official U.S. political discourse as only ever disappearing, it becomes increasingly urgent to contest such . . . pronouncements" (10). From a queer perspective, however, family preservation policies that privilege biological, heteronormative nuclear families over other forms of kinship are questionable. From this perspective, it is troublesome to privilege parents over grandparents, aunts, uncles, or other extended kin who may have played a central role in a child's life. Similarly, it is troublesome to privilege (perhaps distant) living biological relations over nonrelated caregivers with whom the child may already have a relationship. If we are truly interested in child welfare policies that prioritize the best interests of a child, we need a notion of "family" that is child-centric, rather than biocentric—one that seeks to preserve the bonds already established between a child and those who have cared for that child, *whether or not* those bonds are grounded in a genetic connection.

Moving away from biocentric notions of family need not and should not render a child's birthmother invisible. Insofar as a birth mother has cared for and established a connection with her child during the gestational period and often much longer, preserving the bond between that mother and her child would typically be among the connections a child-centric policy would want to preserve. Preserving this connection, however, doesn't necessitate that her birth mother must be her *only* caregiver or, indeed, her only mother. Foster families, adoptive families that are open, and "orphanages" or other caregiving structures that provide for a child's short- or long-term socioeconomic or other needs provide examples of how a child's connections with her birth mother (and other kin) may be preserved while also permitting a child to develop bonds with one or more additional caregivers. Unfortunately, a focus on "permanency planning" for children combined with the assumption that a nuclear, two- (heterosexual) parent family best serves a child's needs has led to a forced choice between the legal, social, and political preservation of birth parents' bonds with their child and the establishment of new bonds that also may need legal, social, and political recognition.

The erasure of a child's birth mother in current adoption policies is rooted not in the practice of adoption itself (informal adoptions have been practiced in many cultures over many centuries in ways that did not sever a mother–child bond). The difficulty resides, rather, in legal policies (and social and political practices) surrounding formal adoption practices evolving over the past several decades—policies that, as anthropologist Judith Modell (1994) notes, redescribe the adopted child "as-if-begotten" and the adoptive parent "as-if-geneological" (2). The most obvious symbol of these policies and practices is the birth certificate that is produced upon the adoption of a child—a public record that rewrites a child's history by recording the adoptive parents as the birth parents. In listing the mother (and, in most cases, the father) who received the child as the "real" parents, the reality of the birth mother is literally obliterated; she does not exist, her parenthood "vaporizes" (Modell 1994, 2).

Two important aspects of our notion of family are revealed by this transaction. First, the "as-if" fiction of adoption presumes that "real kinship" is based on a genealogical connection. Hence, this is the connection that adoption is supposed to simulate as closely as possible—even as the child's actual genealogical connections are denied. It is, in part, by means of this recuperation of adoption into a practice that mimics the biocentric family (rather than resisting it) that transracial and transnational adoptions become problematic. In particular, the attempt to model the adoptive family on a genealogical family lends itself to practices of colorblindness that render not only the birth mother, but also the adopted child, invisible. The reissuing of a (false) birth certificate in the case of adoption further reveals the presumption that a child can only have one mother. Why, we might ask, can't a birth certificate—or other official document—record both the mother who gave birth to and the mother who has become legal guardian to the child? Moreover, why is a "transfer" of the child from one mother to another necessary in the first place? Why is it not possible for women of privilege (such as myself and other middle-class, white women) to "adopt" or "foster" or otherwise help to support a child (and/or the child's mother) without demanding that the birth mother relinquish all rights and legible connection to her child?

Closely tied to the assumption that a child can only have one mother (and hence must be separated from one in order to "belong" to another) is a heternormative ideal of the family we wish to preserve. In the United States, this heteronormative family ideal has been largely responsible for a shift away from child welfare policies that, during the 1960s and 1970s, focused on early childhood education and federal aid to single mothers and poor communities as a means of "breaking the cycle of poverty" and improving the lives of struggling families (Katz 2001; Rose 1995) to policies that, during the 1980s and 1990s, pathologized single motherhood (especially black single motherhood) as the *source* of poverty and other social ills such as juvenile delinquency (Katz 2001; Peck 2001; Pierson 1994). Under the ascendancy of neoliberalism in the United States (and other industrialized countries), responsibilities that were once shouldered by the State were transferred to the private sector, including the privatized family. An emphasis on self-sufficient families and welfare reform—including child welfare reform—began to focus on the production and maintenance of two-parent, heterosexual, nuclear families. The opening paragraph of Title I of the PRWORA (which replaced AFDC by TANF) states Congress's "findings" as follows:

1. Marriage is the foundation of a successful society.

2. Marriage is an essential institution of a successful society which promotes the interests of children.

3. Promotion of responsible fatherhood and motherhood is integral to successful child rearing and the well-being of children. . . . (U.S. Congress, 1996, H.R. 3734)

Attempting to reduce out-of-wedlock births (for the putative sake of children's well-being), TANF authorized the use of funds for prevention of teen pregnancy, abstinence education, and marriage promotion (Levin-Epstein et al. 2002). When President George W. Bush reauthorized TANF in 2002, he encouraged further "strengthening the American family" by marriage promotion and responsible fatherhood initiatives. Thus, in 2002, Congress passed the newly named Personal Responsibility, Work, and Family Promotion Act (PRWFPA) intended to fund such initiatives. Although neither this bill nor its amended version (the PRWFPA of 2003) was signed into law, its intended promotion of the heterosexual, nuclear family was accomplished by the Deficit Reduction Act of 2005 (DRA) wherein Congress established a five-year, $150 million per-year grant program for Healthy Marriage and Responsible Fatherhood while making deep cuts to Medicaid and other services for needy families. Under President Obama, the U.S. Department of Health and Human Services (DHHS) continues to fund such initiatives, affirming its belief that "[c]hildren who live with their biological fathers are, on average, at least two to three times more likely not to be poor, less likely to use drugs, less likely to experience educational, health, emotional and behavioral problems, less likely to be victims of child abuse, and less likely to engage in criminal behavior than their peers who live without their married, biological (or adoptive) parents" (U.S. DHHS 2011c; see also DHHS 2011b). Among the programs funded are several major projects specifically aimed at improving child well-being by promoting healthy marriages and nuclear families in Native American and African American communities (U.S. DHHS 2011b; U.S. DHHS, ANA and HMI 2011).

Internationally, the United Nations has advocated that developing countries foster family initiatives and agencies "analogous to" U.S. government programs and the AID's Family in Development initiative (an initiative wherein the spread of AIDS in Africa and other regions is to be stemmed by the promotion of family development). Tying the effects of modernization to a deterioration of family values in which "the young generation hardly believes anymore in values that call for the constitution and the preservation of family units," in the late 1980s, the United Nations associated the emerging lack of cohesion in families across the globe with "high levels of criminality, violence, and widespread abuse of alcohol and drugs" (United Nations 1987, 10).

Within this context, "family preservation" appears a conservative and reactionary goal. Despite the fact that NABSW claims that its 1994 position on family preservation is simply an extension of its earlier 1972 position, a comparison of the two documents reveals a significant shift from the radical rhetoric and goals of Black empowerment to a much more conservative rhetoric embracing the heteronormative portrait of family values championed by neoliberals. The "vehement stand against the placement of black children in white homes for any reason," that NABSW controversially proclaimed in 1972 becomes softened in 1994 to an emphasis on "documenting evidence of unsuccessful same race placements" prior to permitting transracial adoption. The 1972 assertion of the black child's "inviolable" position in a black family where they will receive "the total sense of themselves" by developing "positive identification with significant black others" and be taught to navigate a society "characterized by white racism at every level" shifts notably in 1994 to the race neutral language of "advocating for the rights of families" to rear their children "in a loving, safe, and supportive environment," along with advocacy for the "fair and equitable treatment" of African-American families who wish to adopt. The earlier scathing critique of transracial adoption as an "expedient for white folk" facilitated by the redefinition of black children as biracial in order to assign them "chattel status" disappears in 1994 as does the biting critique of white adoptive families who engage in "superficial" attempts to accommodate the black child, who is ultimately othered. Most significantly, perhaps, the stated commitment of NABSW in 1972 to reorientating the social work profession to viewing extended black families as a source of strength appears to shift in 1994 and beyond to a commitment to strengthening the black family by reshaping it in the image of the self-sufficient, two-parent, nuclear family. Thus the

2007 report of NABSW's Family Preservation Task Force, for example, "champions . . . the reauthorization and increase of funding" for the 2001 Promoting Safe and Stable Families Program—a program that funds state initiatives for the promotion of healthy marriages in addition to other family preservation services (Oliver and Freeman 2007). Similarly, the Institute for Black Parenting and many other organizations committed to preserving ethnic minority families have taken on the neoliberal commitment to "strengthening" their families, highlighting this goal with promotional materials that frequently depict happy family portraits of sons and daughters together with their biological mothers and fathers.

Borshay Liem's first documentary, *First Person Plural*, concludes with a similar, surprisingly conventional, family portrait depicting her marriage to a Korean American man with whom she gives birth to a son. The image with which the film closes is a sentimental photograph of mother, father, and child embracing one another and smiling happily into the camera. That the creation of the nuclear heteronormative family is ultimately an unsatisfactory resolution to the adoptee's predicament is nonetheless clear in the overall context of Borshay Liem's two films. Thus, it is instructive to return to her story.

Despite the "happy ending" of Borshay Liem's first film, ten years later, in *In the Matter of Cha Jung Hee*, Borshay Liem continues to be haunted by ghosts (both living and dead) from her past. It is only by directly confronting these ghosts (her dead Korean father, her living Korean mother, her aging American parents, and Cha Jung Hee herself) that Borshay Liem is enabled to move from the past into the present.[10]

Arguably, a major impediment to Borshay Liem's ability to move through her melancholia is her inability to perceive the complex, non-nuclear family she inhabits as the child of two mothers and two cultures as a potential source of strength. Instead, she struggles for years with the question of who is her "real" mother and her "real" family. "Emotionally," as Borshay Liem acknowledges in *First Person Plural*, "there wasn't room in my mind for two mothers." Feeling that she must choose one mother, and thus one family and one identity, over the other, Borshay Liem struggles with the desire to reclaim her Korean mother and feelings of disloyalty to the family who has adopted her. Attempting to resolve her struggle, Borshay Liem asks her adoptive parents to accompany her on a trip to Korea to meet her birth mother and family: "I felt if I could actually see them come together in real life that somehow both families could then live within myself." At the first meeting of her families, however, the psychic integration desired fails to be achieved. The family patriarchs (Borshay Liem's adoptive father and her eldest Korean brother), while mutually respectful, seem not to understand Borshay Liem's damaged psychic geography or the purpose of the visit. And while both mothers do recognize her pain and assume responsibility for it, neither understands "the need to move beyond the singular notion of the real mother" (Eng 2010, 128). Thus, each graciously relinquishes Borshay Liem to her other mother. "You look like your mother," Alveen tells Borshay Liem upon their arrival at her Korean family's home. Through a translator, the Korean mother acknowledges the familial resemblance but insists that she "only" gave birth to Borshay Liem (Kang Ok Jin) and that she should love her adoptive parents. Thus rejected by both mothers (and feeling like a "visitor" in both the United States and Korea), Borshay Liem remains psychically stuck. It is only during the next decade of her life that Borshay Liem resolves her dilemma of two mothers by moving beyond the desire for a traditional Oedipal, nuclear family.

Eng analyzes Borshay Liem's claim that she doesn't have psychic room for two mothers as not quite true, arguing "while she cannot have room in her mind for two good mothers, she does indeed have ample room in her mind for two bad ones" (130). A decade later, however, Borshay Liem forgives her Korean birth mother for "abandoning" her and her American mother for being unable to empathize with "her emotional and racial predicaments" (Eng 130). In *In the Matter of Cha Jung Hee* (2010), Borshay Liem recollects that when her birth mother came to visit her in California a few years previous, "an unexpected anger welled up in me. There was a mutual betrayal. She gave me up for adoption and I'd betrayed my family by forgetting about them." Upon learning her mother's history during several visits to Korea, however, Borshay Liem could see that her birth mother's decision "fit into a life long struggle to survive. Also, she'd looked for me. Believing it was addressed to the wrong person [Kang Ok Jin], I'd destroyed the letter." Borshay Liem also learns to forgive her adoptive mother for not telling her that she was Kang Ok Jin and not a war orphan. After discovering paperwork indicating that her Korean father committed suicide, Borshay Liem "suddenly [understands] why [her] parents had insisted [her] father had died during the war:" "They were protecting me."

In finally connecting emotionally with her two mothers, Borshay Liem is able to accept both her Korean and American identities and homes. An important part of this journey, however, is traveling to Korea to attempt to uncover the "real" Cha Jung Hee who haunts Borshay Liem. "Because I wasn't the child my parents had originally fallen in love with, part of me always questioned whether I belonged and whether I had a right to accept my family's love." Borshay Liem's search for the "real" Cha Jung Hee fails to uncover with certitude the specific child whose "place" she took in America (there are hundreds of Cha Jung Hees) but, importantly, it "connects" her to a "generation of [Korean] women," leaving her "grateful to all the Cha Jung Hees [she has] met." Noting that "the facts [she] thought were important don't match [the] history" of the woman she hopes is "the one [she has] been looking for," Borshay Liem reflects that this woman "was replaced after her father got her by another Cha Jung Hee. Then I became the Cha Jung Hee. Cha Jung Hee became the template for any orphan. Once the template existed any girl could step into it."[11] It is by learning that "Cha Jung Hee" marks a functional place in a complex Korean history and not necessarily a specific person that Borshay Liem reconciles herself with her Korean past and moves beyond feeling like an imposter. After trying (unsuccessfully) to return the shoes her adoptive mother had sent to Cha Jung Hee to the woman she believes may have been the girl she replaced, the second documentary concludes with Borshay Liem's realization that "they don't belong to her, they belong to me. The path I've taken has always been my own. And if I look closely, I can see a glimpse of the girl I used to be and I can picture her stepping out of the past and into the present." Borshay Liem's present is finally one in which she can be a transnational (postcolonial) subject—a subject who travels back and forth across borders and learns to feel "at home" in multiple locations, a subject who has origins in two worlds, a subject who has two mothers.

4

Making Room for Two Mothers

Queering Children's Literature

Unlike conservative narratives of family preservation, I believe that a child's interests are best served by "maintain[ing] as many . . . parental connections with adults who wish to maintain these bonds as is . . . feasible in any given case" (Narayan 1999, 85).[1] Protecting a child's best interests thus requires a serious adjustment of child custody laws to allow for multiple, simultaneously occurring, parenting relationships. Legal approaches that "[allow] for a wider range of parental relationships to be preserved" would be preferable to, for example, the "all-or-nothing" approach that currently characterizes adoption law. Present laws provide a biological mother with an exclusive maternal claim prior to giving her child for adoption, and no parental claims after a statutory change-of-mind period has passed. The adoptive parents have no parental claims prior to the cessation of the biological mother's rights and all parental claims thereafter. In contrast to this all-or-nothing approach, Uma Narayan (1999) suggests legal reforms that would recognize biological mothers who wish neither to assume full responsibility for a child, nor to surrender all ties to that child. Such reforms would better preserve the interests of mothers, while also having "the virtue of privileging a child's interests above those of competing parents, treating children more as ends-in-themselves than as objects of property-like disputes between contending parents" (85).

Maintaining as many child–mother (and other) bonds as possible also will require solidarity among a child's various parents (e.g., genetic parents, birth parents, foster parents, adoptive parents, stepparents, etc.). As I subsequently argue, complex families require coalitional strategies in order to build solidarity among their different members. In the present chapter, however, I do not debate legal policy or even informal custodial arrangements. Instead, I direct my attention to the ways in which a child's affective psychology might be queered to allow "room in her mind" for two (or more) mothers. In Borshay Liem's story of coming to terms with having multiple mothers and multiple homes, the question of whether Alveen Borshay and/or widow Kang are Deann's "real mother," in the sense of *real-for-her*, is a separate question from who did or should have had legal custody of her. It is also a separate question from whether or not these women have participated or do participate in certain sorts of mother work—although as I suggest here, certain forms of mother work may detract from or contribute to a mother's becoming real to her child.

Although Borshay Liem eventually finds a way to make "room in her mind for two mothers" as an adult, her journey—like the journey of many adoptees—to this reformed affective geography is an arduous and painful one. My focus here is on developing an alternative to the ideology of monomaternalism that would permit *young* children to recognize multiple mothers (and thus re-cognize motherhood) for themselves—inside or outside of the context of legal or political reforms. To this end, I interrogate the social constructions of motherhood that, when taught to young children, give rise to a child's sense of divided loyalties, arguing for a conception of "real mother" that is more fluid and inclusive than found in most childhood narratives about motherhood.

Serial Motherhood and Children's Literature

A fluid metaphysics of maternity would allow that maternal status is not static. Traditional conceptions of motherhood treat genetic, gestational, and social mothering as indivisible, imagining motherhood as a stable concept and institution. Such a conception of motherhood ignores the historical realities of genetic families divided by poverty, war, and slavery. It is further contested by the now common forms of family created by adoption, divorce, and remarriage, and new reproductive technologies such as surrogacy and in vitro fertilization (IVF). Thus, we need a concept of family in general and motherhood in particular that allows for change over time.

Unfortunately, the normative assumption of monomaternalism has largely responded to shifting family forms by allowing for what I call *serial mothering*. Here again the analogy between monomaternalism and monogamy is telling. As Laura Kipnis (2003) notes in her polemic against modern coupledom, the way in which the Western ideal of lifelong monogamy has yielded to serial monogamy through revamped divorce laws demonstrates that "social institutions can develop elasticity when threatened with their demise" (172–73). Just as adultery and divorce have threatened the nuclear family in recent decades, so too have a proliferation of new reproductive technologies and the inability (or unwillingness) of women to live up to the ever higher ideals of good motherhood.[2] Medical interventions into pregnancy (e.g., IVF, surrogacy) combined with government interventions into family forms (e.g., the removal of children from homes deemed to be neglectful or abusive) and a general lack of citizen cooperation in maintaining fixed families (e.g., divorce and remarriage) have placed pressure on social and legal conventions to recognize that children may have more than one mother during the course of their lifetime. Yet, as our continued discourse of "real" mothers indicates and continued barriers to legal recognition of stepmothers and lesbian co-mothers demonstrates,[3] social and legal conventions are reticent to recognize *simultaneously existing* multiple mothers for a child. Serial mothering, like serial monogamy is one thing; polymaternalism, like polyamory or polygamy, is quite another.

Serial motherhood, like serial monogamy, is based on the notion that one relational dyad must be "dissolved" in order to make room to embark on another relationship. As Serena Petrella (2005) notes in her genealogical account of serial monogamy, the underlying ontology of monogamy remains intact in serial monogamy insofar as the "ideal of emotional and erotic fulfillment" continues to be "fashioned *out of the pair*" in ways that "effectively fuse self-actualization to the ability to successfully commune with another [one and only one other]" (176). Similarly, in serial mothering, the underlying presumption of monomaternalism remains intact. Serial mothering, like serial monogamy, follows a teleological script (what Petrella refers to as a "mythological life-script") that assumes a dyadic coupling is the route to both human fulfillment and ethical propriety (176–77). In both cases, a politics of "conservative containment" continues to dominate (170). Kipnis's description of serial monogamy as "liberal reformism writ familial" can be applied to practices of serial mothering; in both cases, "the players change but the institution remains the same" (Kipnis 2003, 176).

In serial monogamy, the institution of monogamy is unques-
tioned; the breakdown of a marriage or other monogamous relationship is blamed on the individual participants rather than the institution
itself. Similarly, serial motherhood denies that there is anything wrong
with the institution of motherhood or the premise of monomaternalism. When motherhood, like marriage, goes wrong (when, for example,
a mother neglects or abuses or abandons her child or—for whatever
reason—chooses or is forced to relinquish her parental role), we are to
assume the problem resides in the flawed character of the individual
occupying the maternal role. Conversely, we are to assume that when
a woman is a good mother, there is no need for other women to participate in the rearing of this ("her") child.

There is an important difference underlying our treatment of
serial monogamy and serial monomaternality, however. When erotic
dyads fall apart, blame does not automatically or irrevocably accrue to
one of the separating parties. Except in cases of documented abuse, the
assumption is—regardless of who left who—that each partner is worthy
of another chance at love and simply needs to find a partner with whom
they are "better fit" or more compatible. In contrast, when a mother
leaves her child (regardless of how necessary a temporary or permanent departure might be to her own or to her child's physical, mental,
or economic well-being), the presumption is that "[i]t is the *mother*
who . . . is actively in the wrong" and thus must be "ostracise[d] and
reviled[d]" (Jackson 1994, 39). The assumption that motherhood is a
good (socially useful and personally fulfilling) institution coupled with
the assumption that all children are innocent (regardless of how many
challenges they may present), leave only one party to blame, namely
the mother.[4] If a woman leaves a dyadic husband–wife coupling, she is
not (usually) assumed to be a bad woman or even a bad wife, but if a
mother seeks to free herself from the dyadic mother–child coupling, the
assumption is "you cannot be a good woman, let alone a good mother"
(43). Moreover, the dominant ideology of monomaternalism encourages
us to see "staying with" or "leaving" a child to be an all-or-nothing
matter. As Rosie Jackson (1994) notes in her study of "mothers who
leave," this is not always the case; many noncustodial mothers struggle
to maintain regular and ongoing contact with their children (37–49).
In other words, they continue to mother even under circumstances
where they are presumed to have "abandoned" their child.

An inclusive metaphysics of motherhood—unlike monomaternalism in either its lifelong or serial forms—would permit a child to rec-

ognize more than one real mother (and more than two real parents), an option preferable to the notion that a child must lose one mother in order to gain another. Although this might be more easily achieved within a reformed legal, social, or political environment, it also can be achieved, I argue, by a child who develops the ability to epistemically and ethically reorientate herself toward (m)others.

As Robinson, Nelson, and Nelson (1997) note, within the sentimental family, the power to name reality typically accrues to parents, rather than children (91). This does violence to a child's ability to develop a sense of him or herself as a moral agent, as a person "with the power to shape reality" (95). Here, I explore how mothers might respect and nurture a child's potential to shape his or her own familial reality without sacrificing the mother's own perspectives on that reality. My hope here—and throughout this book—is that we might queer our conceptions of motherhood in ways that respect *both* maternal reality as experienced by mothers *and* maternal reality as experienced by children, without violating the perspective of either those who are caregivers or those to whom care is given. Indeed, addressing the challenges of these sometimes conflicting and sometimes intersecting viewpoints is, I argue, a central project for both those (caregivers) who would mother queerly and those (scholars) who would queer motherhood.

The social and cultural meanings of motherhood as transmitted to, negotiated with, and potentially resisted by, children are embodied in children's popular culture—especially, although not exclusively, the stories told to young children. Thus, I frame my analysis of "real" mothering, in this chapter, against the backdrop of children's literature. As critical legal theorist Barbara Bennett Woodhouse (1995) suggests, stories written about and for children "provide a window on children's experience" from which we may draw conclusions about meaning (5). To read children's stories from a child's point of view, however, requires that we imagine what these texts say to the listening child (rather than what is intended by the author or narrator), and also what they "fail to say, and what they suggest by innuendo" (Rosenau 1992, 36–37). Sometimes, of course, children may uncritically digest the adult-centered narratives proposed by storytellers. At other times, however, children, including even very young children, may develop "counternarratives" as they listen to (or read) these stories (Cloud 1992, 6). In imagining what the texts here examined might mean to children, I am aided by the counternarratives offered me, both implicitly and explicitly, by my own children during their elementary school years.

The specific stories I use as examples of narratives (and potential counternarratives) of "real" motherhood include *Are You My Mother?*, *A Mother for Choco*, *Stellaluna*, *Horton Hatches the Egg*, and *The Velveteen Rabbit*. Collectively, these stories exemplify constructions of motherhood common in American children's literature, much of which functions as a series of (sometimes competing) parables of family relationships and children's belonging. The first two stories take up alternate sides of the nature/nurture debate over children's needs and parental rights. Similar to those who advocate identity politics and policies of family preservation, *Are You My Mother?* depicts motherhood as a static biological identity, assuming that a child's birth mother is, and always will be, a child's real mother. In direct opposition to this claim and paralleling the claims of many adoptive mothers, *A Mother for Choco* portrays motherhood as a social identity that can transcend significant biological difference. From an adopted child's perspective, these two frameworks are irreconcilable; loyalty to either script requires the child to be disloyal to someone in her life. Hence, as I suggest here, neither script's notion of "real" mother is adequate and the adopted child—indeed all children with multiple mothers, including children of divorce and remarriage, children of lesbian partners, and children birthed with the aid of new reproductive technologies and relationships—need to learn to deconstruct the nature/culture dichotomy that gives rise to these notions.

Stellaluna and *Horton Hatches the Egg* provide more complex narratives that begin to queer familial relationships by deconstructing the natural mother/social mother dichotomy and by rejecting the notion of motherhood as a unified process. Although advocating a more fluid conception of motherhood, however, *Stellaluna* and *Horton* resist an inclusive notion of motherhood that would allow a child to make psychic room for two mothers. Indeed, taken together, these stories illustrate the *competing* claims to motherhood that inform discussions about adoption, as well as nonadoptive custody disputes.[5] In these stories, the notion of "real mother" is a contested notion that requires evaluation of several facets of maternal fitness. Serious questions arise in these narratives concerning how other a mothering figure can be while still claiming fitness as a mother. In defining "real mother" as an issue of maternal fitness, these stories, I suggest, erect the problematic good mother/bad mother dichotomy that grounds both our practices of maternal profiling and the ideology of serial mothering.

I conclude my reflections on "real" mothering by exploring themes in the *The Velveteen Rabbit*. Despite the fact that (or perhaps because) this story is not about motherhood, it provides a glimpse of how children might resist adult perceptions of reality and, through their own agency, construct an alternate reality. The central notion of this children's story is that we can make others real by loving them. Using feminist accounts of ontology and epistemology to elaborate on this idea, I develop an existential notion of motherhood that allows a child room for multiple mothers, constructed in relation to, rather than opposition to, each other.

Mothers and Non-Mothers: The Nature/Culture Dichotomy

Fall 2000: "You are not my REAL mother!" she screams from behind a locked bathroom door. She is seven. Although all adoptive mothers anticipate this moment, I'm not ready for this yet. What is a real mother? Am I one? What would it mean to claim this? And how do I defend my status as real without implying that her birth mom is somehow unreal, or at any rate less real than I am? Clearly my daughter's current metaphysical schema will not readily permit the notion of multiple mothers. One of us must, according to her, be an imposter—someone who, like Descartes' evil genius, has subjected her to an illusory construction of reality.

As I sit in a stupor outside the locked door contemplating the metaphysics of maternity, my younger daughter saunters over and plops herself in my lap. "You're MY real mother," she confidently claims while giving me a big hug. I'm not sure whether she says this to comfort me or to further annoy her sister. Probably both. And although the hug does help, her possessive metaphysical claim further confounds me. I have never used the phrase "real mom" to describe either my elder daughter's birth mother or myself. Nor have I ever used (or even thought) the phrase "real daughter" to privilege my birth daughter over my adopted daughter. Yet here these phrases are in my home, functioning to exclude and include, to marginalize and privilege, to separate and bind together.

My elder daughter's insistence, during her elementary school years, that I was not her "real" mother stemmed from two sources: first, that she was not borne to me and second, that she does not look like me. My younger daughter's proprietary embrace of me as *her* real mother likewise drew on a notion of family belonging as a factor of birth and genetic mirroring, reflecting her internalization of a traditional kinship narrative.

The notion that family membership is a function of biological origins and genetic inheritance is a theme both accepted and contested in children's literature. In the 1960 story, *Are You My Mother?*, a book in the beginner's reading series still widely reproduced and distributed, a baby bird hatches from his egg while his mother is off in search of worms for him. Looking up, down, and all around in search of his mother, but not finding her, the newborn bird leaves his nest and goes off in search of his mother. Along the way, the bird encounters many creatures—chickens, dogs, cats, and cows, as well as cars, planes, and boats—asking each in turn "Are you my mother?" Each creature encountered either ignores him ("the kitten just looked and looked. It did not say a thing") or responds negatively, highlighting the differences between themselves and the baby bird. ("'How could I be your mother?' said the cow. 'I am a cow.'") In the end, however, a rather frightening earth-moving machine returns the baby bird to his nest where he is happily united with his "natural" (i.e., species) mother. Although the hatchling is oblivious to the importance of genetic mirroring at the start of the story—walking right by his bird mother and failing to see her, by the story's end, he has successfully learned the politics of identity. Encounters with the indifference and hostility of the Other, including a potential predator (the "Snort," i.e., the earth-moving machine, whom he fears will "do something" to him and from whom he cannot escape), the baby bird learns to appreciate the safety and security of home where he is embraced by his species appropriate mother.

In direct contrast to the privileging of biological connection in *Are You My Mother?*, the 1992 story *A Mother for Choco* tells the story of a little bird who lives all alone, wishes he had a mother, and eventually finds a mother bear. Like the baby bird in the earlier adventure, Choco encounters all kinds of creatures who have, at best, a marginal family resemblance to him—for example, a giraffe who is yellow, penguins who have wings, a walrus that has big, round cheeks—and who uniformly reject his request for a mother.

> "Oh, Mrs. Walrus!" he cried. "You have big, round cheeks just like me. Are you my mother?" "Now look," grumped Mrs. Walrus. "I don't have striped feet like you, so don't bother me!" (Kasza 1992)

Dismayed by his inability to find anyone who looks just like him, Choco cries, eliciting a maternal response from nearby Mrs. Bear who comforts him with hugs, kisses, singing, dancing, and apple pie and adopts him into her family—a family already including a baby alligator, a pig, and a hippo. The moral of this story is clear: When Choco quits looking for someone who *looks* like him and begins thinking instead about all the things that his mother would *do*, if he had one, he finally finds the mother he needs.

> "If you had a mommy, what would she do?" asks Mrs. Bear.
> "Oh, I'm sure she would hold me," sobbed Choco.
> "Like this?" asked Mrs. Bear. And she held Choco very tight.
> "Yes . . . and I'm sure she would kiss me, too!" said Choco.
> "Like this?" asked Mrs. Bear. And she lifted Choco and gave him a big kiss.
> "Yes, and I'm sure she would sing and dance with me to cheer me up," said Choco.
> "Like this?" asked Mrs. Bear. And they sang and danced together.

Illustrating the reverse narrative arc of *Are You My Mother?*, *A Mother for Choco* traces the journey of a lost child who can only find his way home by *un*learning his (misplaced) emphasis on genetic similarity. It is the creature he encounters who is *most* different from him (who is not yellow, has no wings, lacks big round cheeks or striped feet like his own) who makes him feel at home—and in the end, "Choco was very happy that his new mommy looked just the way she did."

The contrasting depictions of mothers found in these stories parallel two traditional (straight) lines of thought about motherhood. The first line of thought assumes motherhood to be a natural state, assuming that genetic, gestational, and social mothering are one and the same. Thus, a woman's biological connection to her offspring automatically gives her (and only her) the rights and responsibilities of a mother. It is this concept of motherhood as a natural and unified process that makes it difficult for many persons, including many children, to understand why a pregnant woman could decide not to mother, choosing instead to abort her fetus, place her child for adoption, or even abandon her child. Like the mother bird with her nesting and worm-gathering instinct in *Are You My Mother?*, adult women are supposed to have a natural bond with their offspring that guarantees they (and only they) will have both the desire and the ability to engage in responsible mothering activities.

As the phrase "maternal instinct" connotes, a mother's work is viewed as a natural, not a learned, ability or skill.

If we assume that biological and social mothering are one and the same, questions concerning children's identity formation and sense of belonging within the family are rendered unproblematic. Like the baby bird in *Are You My Mother?*, children who remain in their family of biological origin can easily see themselves in their parents. They look like and, it is often assumed, act like their parents due to genetic connections. Hence, their "fit" in the family unit is uninterrogated. Idiosyncratic differences may be tolerated to a greater or lesser degree, but the homogeneity of the family unit is largely taken for granted. As I suggested earlier, however, the assumption that families are homogenous and unified is highly questionable, even where family members bear genetic resemblances; certainly family likeness cannot be presumed in adoptive families (or in other families based on nonbiological bonds).

As Elizabeth Bartholet (1993) notes, because the assumption of family homogeneity underlies the tale *Are You My Mother?*, the story is profoundly anti-adoption. In contrast, *A Mother for Choco* is a positive tale of adoption. Its underlying theory of familial belonging depicts motherhood in terms of social labor rather than biological connection. Moreover, its happy depiction of the nonhomogenous family opens the possibility of building affectionate familial ties between those who are different in quite significant ways. A much loved story of adoptive parents—especially those who have, like myself, adopted transracially, *A Mother for Choco* depicts families as chosen, not given and mothering as an activity that can be successfully extended to children in need, regardless of those children's natural origins. The happy heterogeneous family with which the story ends is also quite queer. As mother bear embraces her alligator, pig, hippo and bird babies, we are provided a portrait of family that resists biocentrism, reprosexuality, and repronarrativity.

A Mother for Choco thus seems a radical departure from the dominant ideology surrounding motherhood that for centuries has deemed a women's destiny to be a function of her biology. And indeed, it is. Nonetheless, as Fineman (1995a) notes, "in examining discourses about motherhood . . . underlying symbols and values are more uniformly shared than differences in discourse would superficially indicate" (220). On the surface, *A Mother for Choco* embraces an understanding of motherhood that combines norms of choice and caregiving in ways compatible with feminist and queer values. However, a closer reading of the story reveals a conservative counternarrative in tension with those feminist values. The story line is rendered plausible by the fact that it is a *female* bear who embraces the abandoned, vulnerable Choco, thus alleviating any concerns that this large and potentially dangerous creature (like the predatory big bad wolf whom Red Riding Hood encounters or the frightening bears that Goldilocks encounters in their solitary travels through the woods) might put Choco at risk. (If the storyline were to involve a male protagonist who hugged and kissed the babies and enticed them home with him, it would read *much* differently.) Moreover, although father bear never appears in this story, the moniker *"Mrs.* Bear" assures us of mother bear's "fitness" as a (heterosexual, married) mother. The singing, dancing Mrs. Bear bakes an apple pie (a trope of both gendered homemaking and American nationalism) as a token of her caregiving. This act, in combination with a textual failure to develop Mrs. Bear's character in even minimal ways, gives rise to a stereotypical depiction of the caregiving mother as perpetually happy and instinctively nurturing. This stereotype of mothering could be potentially undermined here by including in the narrative a depiction of Choco's birth mother relinquishing her child as an act of care. By omitting such story elements from the narrative, however, *A Mother for Choco*'s redefinition of motherhood falls short of radicalizing the concept. Instead, its redefinition of motherhood as the gendered act of nurturing ultimately channels a potentially radical idea into what Fineman (1995a) describes as "set categories approved by the existing conceptual system," thus "domesticating" a rhetoric of motherhood by choice into a rhetoric of mothering as caregiving (219–20). This is problematic for both mothers and children.

My initial response to my elder daughter's insistence that I was not her real mother was to attempt to undermine her claim by pointing out all of the maternal activities I engaged in for and with her. After all who had fed, diapered, and bathed her as an infant? Who had walked the floors with her each night when she had colic? Who encouraged her to take her first steps, say her first words, and make her first friends? Who has played, sang, and danced with her? Who has consoled her when she is hurt and applauded her many achievements? In short, who has lived with her and cared for her since she was 3 days old? Downplaying the role of biology and focusing on social aspects of mothering also seemed a satisfactory solution to avoiding my younger daughter's one-upmanship in the form of a claim to biological connection with me that her sister lacked. Seeking to reconnect sisters, as well as adoptive daughter and mother, it was expedient to force a redefinition of mother that made me equally real to both of them; and made them equally real to me. I thus positioned myself as Mrs. Bear. Strangely, however, only my younger, biological daughter was receptive to my bear hugs.

To understand why my adopted daughter resisted my attempts to redefine mothering as a social activity, I had to read the social mothering narrative from her, rather than my own, perspective. When I did so, I recognized that from an adopted child's perspective, A Mother for Choco oversimplifies the concepts of mothering and family in important ways.

First, in this narrative, as in many classic and contemporary children's parables,[6] a child's birth mother is notably absent. "Choco was a little bird, who lived all alone." Why? Where did he come from? And how did he manage to survive at all in the absence of any nurturing creature? From a child's perspective, the narrative erasure of the birth mother is both implausible and ethically suspect. The erasure of Choco's bird mother, combined with the notion that a non-bird is his real mother negates the possibility of genuine competing grounds for claims to motherhood. By positioning myself within this narrative context, I had implicitly erased my daughter's past, starting "history proper" (like Donald Borshay) at the moment of my daughter's arrival in my own home. In so doing, I had devalued my daughter's own narrative context, a context within which her birth mother figured prominently as a key to her own identity.

Second, A Mother for Choco falsifies the experience of the adopted child by suggesting that the child voluntarily chooses her adopted family. In reality, adopted children rarely exercise any influence over such decisions. Women who adopt, in an important sense, choose motherhood; moreover they exercise the right to accept or reject any particular child offered them for adoption. Adopted children, on the other hand, are "placed" within a home deemed suitable for them. Indeed, my daughter's anger (like Borshay Liem's anger at her adoptive mother) could be explained, in part, as stemming from her inability to choose her home and family, and by virtue of this, her inability to know what has been lost to her. Although no child is able to choose the circumstances into which they are born, a special sense of frustration and loss attends the experience of adopted children (and stepchildren) insofar as they know that choices *were* available; they were simply unable to intervene.

Finally, *A Mother for Choco* devalues the fears and anxieties that may be related to an adopted child's sense of difference within her adopted family. This adoption parable minimizes the potential effect on children of the truly heterogeneous family. Can bears, alligators, hippos, pigs, and birds truly live together harmoniously? Can they all eat the same meals? Enjoy the same games? Speak the same verbal, emotional, or physical language? Real family relationships are complex; even in the most homogenous families tensions may arise. These tensions are exacerbated as the family becomes more heterogenous. In families where racial or ability differences exist, for example, ordinary sibling rivalries may become intensified and, as I have often noted, motherwork becomes more intense.

From my adopted daughter's perspective, however, the situation is no doubt more anxiety provoking than even this suggests. Her experience is the experience not of a truly heterogeneous family, but is perhaps the experience of being a bird among bears. It is the experience thus of being "other" among those who are (or at least appear) alike; related to this, it is the experience of being small and vulnerable. Like Choco, my daughter is relatively powerless among bears (or alligators, hippos, or even pigs). Noting this, it becomes less surprising that she resists my overtures of comfort. Even a well-intentioned bear hug may appear risky to receive; in order to refrain from crushing her spirit or her potential to fly, I must ensure that I am not overbearing.

Real Mothers and Other Mothers:
The Good Mother/Bad Mother Dichotomy

Spring 2001: "My REAL mother wouldn't make me do this!" Tomeka is doing her homework. More accurately, she is supposed to be doing her homework. She hates homework; she especially hates having to write vocabulary definitions. She has difficulty sitting still and difficulty concentrating. She is hungry. She needs a glass of water. She wants to phone a friend. She wants to watch TV. Her younger sister is watching TV, as her homework was long ago completed.

I am tired. Tired of the nightly homework wars. Tired of being unfavorably compared to her "real" mother. "You can do this. Just sit down and concentrate," is the best response I can conjure up. Of course, concentrating is precisely what she seems unable to do. "I want to live with my birth mom! She'd be nicer to me!" she retorts. "Sit back in that chair and finish your vocabulary definitions!," I respond, still refusing to take the bait, but raising my voice enough to live up to her accusation of my unkindness.

Later, as I tuck my daughter into bed, trying to recoup my losses, I explain patiently that I am quite certain that her birth mother would also want her to do her homework. "All mothers want their children to do well at school, so that they can grow up to be whatever they would like to be." At my request, Trish sends a letter confirming my hypothesis and urging our child to do her homework. In separate correspondence, however, she reveals that she too had childhood difficulties in school. I begin to wonder if I am mistaken in believing that my elder daughter can succeed in school simply by internalizing the work ethic on which I was raised. I wonder also about the value our family places on academic success—a success that has come more or less easily to my husband, my younger daughter, and myself, but that is a struggle for my elder child. Perhaps, because of her similar experiences, my daughter's birth mother would be better able to empathize with our child's struggles.

In the contemporary children's story *Stellaluna*, a mother bat loses her child during an encounter with an eagle. Subsequently adopted by a family of birds, the young bat is well cared for but has difficulty assimilating to her new environment—an environment that requires eating worms and insects, sleeping upright, and giving up her nocturnal ways. The ways of birds are strange to Stellaluna and she becomes the queer Other in her new home. Although her bird siblings are open to learning bat ways, mama bird is less flexible. Coming home one day to find all of her children hanging upside down, mother bird panics, sending all of the baby birds back to the nest, but stopping Stellaluna:

> "You are teaching my children to do bad things. I will not let you back into the nest unless you promise to obey all the rules of this house." Stellaluna promised. She ate bugs without making faces. She slept in the nest at night. And she didn't hang by her feet. She behaved as a good bird should. (Cannon 1993)

Importantly, Mama bird does care for Stellaluna. Yet her care is inappropriate for a bat, indicating her failure to understand that

Stellaluna's needs differ from those of her bird siblings. Mama bird's care for Stellaluna thus instantiates a colonial love, a love that is (like Alveen and Donald Borshay's love for Deann) benevolent but that denies the importance and value of identities that differ from one's own. In denying difference, Mama bird's care may be seen as what Sara Ahmed (2006) terms a "straightening device," wherein one is perceived according to normative orientations that bring one into alignment with normative others (66). By telling Stellaluna to literally "straighten *up*," that is, to perch atop the tree branch in vertical alignment with her bird siblings, rather than to hang by her feet below it (encouraging similar queer, "upside-down," behavior in her siblings), mama bird circumscribes Stellaluna's movements in ways intended to de-queer her. In contrast, Stellaluna's "real" mother understands her offspring's queer (to birds) perspectives and needs; she knows the value (to bats) of forbidden fruit, night escapades, and hanging out. Thus the story ends happily when bat mother and child are reunited and "upside-down" becomes "right side up."

Like *Are You My Mother?*, *Stellaluna* is a story that ultimately resolves the question "who is the real mother?" by identifying the biological mother as real. Unlike the earlier story, however, the resolution of this question results from a more complex narrative that depicts Stellaluna's bat mother as possessing caregiving and relational skills relevant to mothering—skills that Stellaluna's other (bird) mother lacks. From the beginning, we are assured that Stellaluna's bat mother is a good mother, who "loved her soft tiny baby," crooning to her and clutching her to her breast each evening, as she went in search of food (Cannon 1993). Stellaluna is lost to her originary mother through bad fortune, not through a failure of good mothering. This is what makes this story of serial mothering—wherein Stellaluna moves from the care of her genetic mother into the (foster) care of her bird mother and then back to the care of her genetic mother—a story that ends happily through the eyes of the child.

Unlike the essentialist narrative in *Are You My Mother?* that reduces motherhood to a biological connection, biology and identity here are depicted as *instrumental*, rather than intrinsic, to mothering. Biological identity is important insofar as it gives rise to similar needs and experiences which in turn ground empathy. The story opens the possibility, however, of empathic connection across difference. Whereas mama bird, having no previous experience with bats, seems unwilling to accommodate Stellaluna's difference, the baby birds are more playful and willing to try new things. Even after Stellaluna is reunited with her natural mother, she and the younger birds continue to explore one another's worlds, learning both the possibilities and the limitations of their boundary crossings. Visiting Stellaluna's rediscovered bat family, the birds—not wanting to feel "upside-down" in the bat world—hang by their feet (which they manage) and accompany Stellaluna on a night flight (leading to catastrophe from which Stellaluna must rescue them). As the story ends with a hanging bat embracing the perched birds she has brought to safety, they contemplate how they can "be so different and feel so much alike" as well as how they can "feel so different and be so much alike," concluding that this is "quite a mystery" but affirming resolutely that they are "friends."

By deconstructing the notion of the "bad child," the story of *Stellaluna* is comforting for children and educational for parents. Stellaluna's story suggests that children's nonconformist (queer) behavior may be neither good nor bad but simply an expression of their needs and abilities (a lesson I will have to relearn many times in subsequent years). It suggests that parents need to be flexible; children's active resistance to and/or inability to follow household rules may indicate a difficulty with the rules rather than a difficulty with the child. Unfortunately, the story deconstructs the good child/bad child dichotomy by erecting the good mother/bad mother dichotomy. Although Stellaluna continues her relationship with her bird siblings, solidifying a kinship across difference, mama bird disappears from the story as soon as Stellaluna's bat mother reappears. We might question this. Why does Stellaluna not invite her bird mother, along with her bird siblings, to visit her bat family? Is she, perhaps, an ungrateful and narcissistic child? Such questions do not arise however—and perhaps cannot arise—given the positioning of the young bat (and young birds) as creatures innocent of prejudice. Here, as elsewhere, the assumption of childhood innocence leads to blaming mothers for any rupture in the mother–child dyad. Thus, we do not question Mama bird's disappearance from Stellaluna's life story, because it is clear that she was—however well intentioned—a bad mother to Stellaluna, a mother who was unable to accommodate, much less respect, Stellaluna's differences from herself and her own genetic offspring. Innocent of prejudice, the baby bat and baby birds are able to bond affectively across differences but Mama bird cannot, demanding that Stellaluna be "the same" as her in order to gain entrance to their home. Thus, we conjecture, Mama bird would be unable or unwilling to "fit in" to the extended bat family as she cannot or will not try out ways unfamiliar to herself.

The good mother/bad mother dichotomy also features prominently in the Dr. Seuss classic, *Horton Hatches the Egg*. In *Horton Hatches the Egg*, Horton the elephant is charged with caring for the egg of a Lazy-Mayzie bird who flies south to frolic for the winter. Horton suffers many trials and much ridicule for his troubles but is ultimately rewarded when an elephant-bird that hatches from the egg identifies him (and not Lazy-Mayzie) as her mother. In contrast to *Stellaluna*, *Horton Hatches the Egg* advances the notion that real mothering can transcend significant differences. Although it requires extraordinary care and Horton is belittled, ostracized, and exoticized for it, Horton learns the skills necessary to faithfully nurture the egg that he promised to care for. In exchange for his willingness to become bird-like, the hatchling emerges with elephant traits. As the bird with "ears and a tail and a trunk just like his" flies toward Horton, an astonished crowd cheers in approval (Seuss 1940).

As Mahoney (1995) suggests in discussing legal rights to frozen embryos, and as Horton exemplifies, such cases are "not . . . about who is a [natural] parent," but are instead about "who has a right to become, or not become a parent" (41). The crowd surrounding Horton cheers precisely because Horton has earned the right to become a parent. As the book concludes:

And it should be, it should be, it SHOULD be like that.
Because Horton was faithful. He sat and he sat. (Seuss 1940)

This seems right. And yet the obvious distinction between good and bad mothers underlying the Horton parable is troubling. Unlike Stellaluna's loving, caring, genetic mother, the elephant-bird's genetic mother is, as her name clearly indicates, a lazy, neglectful, untrustworthy, irresponsible Other with no legitimate claim to her offspring. After all, she abandoned her maternal responsibilities for no apparent reason other than the desire for an extended vacation, and she broke her promise to Horton that she would "be back in no time at all." This depiction parallels our social and legal constructions of women who neglect or abuse their children. No context for their behaviors is provided; they are simply "bad" mothers (Ashe 1995; Kline 1995).

Nonetheless, such mothers may claim a proprietary right to their children based on a biological connection. Echoing, but also satirizing, birthmothers' claims that adoption is kidnapping, Lazy-Mayzie claims such a proprietary right to her egg and its contents:

"But it's MINE!" screamed the bird, when she heard the
    egg crack.
(The work was all done. Now she wanted it back.)
"It's my egg!" she sputtered. "You stole it from me!
Get off of my nest and get out of my tree!" (Seuss 1940)

In direct contrast to what is portrayed as Lazy-Mayzie's selfish-
ness, Horton is self-sacrificing to a fault, willing to give up his friends,
his natural environment, his freedom, and ultimately "his" child as well.

Poor Horton backed down
With a sad, heavy heart (Seuss 1940)

Indeed, like the "real" mother in the story of Solomon, it is Horton's willingness to give up the child that proves, in part, his status
as the mother.

On a surface level, the story of Horton is both funny and heart-
warming. Yet, from a foster or adopted child's perspective, this tale
has disturbing underlying messages. It suggests that those who grant
others temporary or permanent custody of their offspring do not care
about them while simultaneously raising the child's hope that a birthmother may return for them and the fear that if she does, the child's
connection to her foster or adoptive family will be severed.

Horton also raises completely unrealistic expectations regarding
a child's adoptive parents. As Kline (1995) notes about expectations
for female caregiving, "the caring is never sufficient" (152). Am I, like
Horton, willing to suppress all of my wants, desires, and abilities for
my children? At what price do I become "real?" Frankly, sometimes
like so-called Lazy-Mayzie, I too feel I need a vacation.

In her essay, "A Different Reality," Caroline Whitbeck (1989)
develops a feminist ontology that "has at its core a conception of the
self-other *relation* that is significantly different from the self–other
opposition that underlies much of so-called 'western thought'" (51).
The self–other opposition, she argues, is closely aligned with other
dualistic oppositions such as culture/nature, productive/reproductive,
knower/known, lover/beloved, and theory/practice. These dualisms, she
suggests, are rooted in the hierarchical practices of patriarchy and the
competitive practices of individualism that ignore human vulnerability
and human development. They can be undone, however, by engender-

ing practices that entail the "(mutual) realization of people," practices exemplified by the rearing and education of children.

At the core of Whitbeck's proposal for an interactive model of reality is a "self–other relation that is assumed to be a relation between beings who are in some respects analogous" (62). In such relationships, we do not see the other as a mirror image of us, although we may have commonalities. Nor do we see the other as opposite, although we may be distinct and different in some respects (60). Horton's elephant-bird metaphorically captures this self–other relation in ways readily understandable by children, depicting Horton and "his" hatchling as similar enough to mutually recognize one another despite their equally obvious differences. This mutual recognition is made possible by Horton's responsible maternal practices.

Whereas the self/other dualism between Horton and the hatchling is transcended, however, the self/other dualism between Horton and Mayzie is not. Starkly contrasted as responsible (good) and lazy (bad) mothers, Horton and Mayzie have no basis for mutual recognition. The result is that the hatchling must choose one and only one mother, rendering the self–other relation in this story a dyadic one. *Horton* thus occludes the possibility of polymaternalism by following the serial mothering script. (The hatchling *was* Mayzie's child, but is *now* Horton's child.) As Whitbeck notes, however, the dyadic relation of self and other may undermine a truly interactive model of reality. The relation sought "is better expressed as a self–*others* relation, because relationships, past and present, realized and sought, are constitutive of the self, and so the actions of a person reflect the more-or-less successful attempt to respond to the whole configuration of relationships" (62, emphasis mine).

If we take Whitbeck's understanding of self–others relations seriously (as I think we should), two important considerations emerge. The first is an understanding of the self as constituted by, rather than preceding, its relationships with others. This postmodernist conception of the self relinquishes the modernist notion of subjective autonomy in favor of a notion of subjectivity as dialogically produced. As Charles Taylor (1994) claims, our identity is always defined "in dialogue with, sometimes in struggle against, the things our significant others want to see in us" (33).[7] In *Horton*, the hatchling appears to forge its identity (as elephant-like) in dialogue with Horton, while resisting Mayzie's perception of it as belonging to her (i.e., as bird-like).

The second consideration that emerges from Whitbeck's proposal, however, is an understanding of the self as fundamentally plural, rather than singular and unified. Insofar as the self is constituted by a variety of relationships (and not merely a single self–other relationship), the self becomes a plurality and identity becomes, in Maria Lugones' (2003) terminology, "multiplicitous" (62). As Lugones observes, although no self is unified, "bicultural people" (those who, of necessity, must travel back and forth across cultural borders) are more likely to *experience* the self as "more than one" (57). Horton's elephant-bird is clearly a bicultural person in the making. Like a biracial child, the hatchling is analogous, in some respects, to both her birth mother (who has wings and can fly) and to her adoptive mother (who has elephant ears and a trunk). Why, then, does the hatchling not *experience* its identity as complexly related to two mothers (and two species communities)?

On one reading—a reading wherein elephants are stronger and more powerful than birds—the hatchling's identification with Horton (and erasure of its birth mother) might be viewed as a form of false consciousness that is tied to the desire to view itself as a member of the dominant group. On this reading, the elephant-bird's queer bispecies nature creates "the desire and need for recognition by the dominant culture" and, in so doing, "reinforces the dominance of the oppressor and the subordination of the oppressed" (Oliver 2001, 26; see also Fanon 1968). Many elements of the Horton story undermine this reading, however. As a newborn, the hatchling elephant-bird has yet to be acquainted with relations of domination and oppression (although she will surely encounter them in the not too distant future). Moreover, in Dr. Seuss's narrative, Horton does not represent power or dominance. Indeed, Horton's story entrances us precisely because Horton is the underdog (to mix species' metaphors). In a reversal of the class dynamics that characterize most transracial adoptions, here it is the birth mother who represents the dominant class (she flies away from her maternal duties to vacation at Palm Beach), while the adoptive parent represents the subordinate class (poor Horton is literally left out in the cold):

So Horton kept sitting there, day after day.
And soon it was Autumn. The leaves blew away.
And then came the Winter . . . the snow and the sleet!
The icicles hung
From his trunk and his feet.

> But Horton kept sitting, and said with a sneeze,
> "I'll stay on the egg and I won't let it freeze . . ." (Seuss
>   1940)

The adoptive parent (Horton), in this narrative of adoption, cannot be accused of kidnapping Mayzie's offspring. Far from the privileged subject who can "buy" a child, Horton occupies the position of exploited labor; the arduous task of caring for Mayzie's egg is foist on Horton without his informed consent. Moreover, in a reversal of the racial structures that characterize most transracial and international adoptions, here the adoptive parent (Horton) is the colonized (African) other who faces (white) men with guns seeking to contain (as well as exploit) his otherness by capturing him and exporting him (along with the egg for which he cares) elsewhere. Horton attempts to resist such colonization (facing his captors, "[h]e held his head high [a]nd he threw out his chest") but is unsuccessful. The armed men capture Horton, remove him from his jungle and take him across the ocean to New York where they sell him to a circus.

As the "thousands of folks [who flock] to see [a]nd laugh at the elephant up in a tree" demonstrate, Horton is considered queer as well as exotic. The difficult unpaid labor (women's work) that Horton (a male elephant) performs effects a reversal of traditional gender roles. In addition to transgressing gender roles, Horton transgresses species norms. And it is this queerness (of a male elephant perched daintily atop an egg) that clearly leads to Horton's social ostracization. His friends

> . . . taunted [and] teased him.
> They yelled, "How absurd!"
> "Old Horton the Elephant
> Thinks he's a bird!" (Seuss 1940)

Left alone without any friends, taken from his home and transported to another continent where he is placed in a circus freak show, Horton (the adoptive parent) is here cast as a gentle, queer, and vulnerable creature, deserving of our sympathy.

It is helpful to understanding the complexity of adoptive mothering to read this form of mothering as a queer practice, as I earlier argued. Viewing adoptive mothers as simultaneously embedded within matrices of classism, racism, and colonialism (as bearers of privilege) *and* as queer resistors to dominant heteronormative narratives of mothering illuminates the multiplicitous identity of adoptive mothers. To understand the hatchling's (adopted child's) point of view, however, it is also necessary to understand the queer identity that is borne from a *combination* of Horton's *and* Mayzie's defiance of gender roles. The story of Horton concludes at the moment Horton's egg hatches and he is recognized by "his" child. Much like fairy tales wherein kind and self-sacrificing women rise above circumstances of injustice and are rewarded by the loving gaze of a prince, Horton's story ends prematurely. What we need to know—but is occluded from view in these tales of "happily ever after"—is what occurs *after* the pivotal moment of mutual realization. Horton's transgressions of normative elephant behavior combined with Mayzie's transgressions of maternal instinct give birth to further queerness in the form of the "elephant-bird" who hatches from the (their) egg. It is unlikely that this queer product of two mothers and two species will be able to sustain a unitary self-concept as it grows and develops within a dialogic context including colonialism, ethnocentrism, and species normativity. The elephant-bird's desires, character, personality traits, actions, thoughts, feelings, and embodiments will be interpreted differently in the elephant-world than in the bird-world and the ways in which it is marked (as same, as different, as queer) in each of these worlds will differ from the interpretations of its identity within human reality. It will be necessary thus for the elephant-bird, like the bicultural person, to become "fluent in several 'cultures,' 'worlds,' realities" (Lugones 2003, 58). But this will only be possible insofar as the hatchling can come to understand his bird mother, as well as his elephant mother, as an analogous being.

In adoptive relationships, as well as in parent–child relationships in queer and blended families, a complex configuration of relationships is essential to a child's developing identity. Thus maternal practices must be aimed at ensuring children acquire the "virtues necessary to engage in the key practices of mutual recognition" with a variety of others (Whitbeck 1989 67). However, as Whitbeck suggests, following Jean Baker Miller (1976), developing these skills in others doesn't entail self-sacrifice for those engaged in this practice (68). The erasure of self (as practiced by Horton) is as destructive to self–other relations as the erasure of others (as practiced by both Mayzie and the hatchling). In my own case, this means that I would be ill advised to be as self-sacrificing as Horton. At the same time, neither my daughter's birth mother nor I can or should erase one another's existence. Our daughter's multiplicitous identity (as an elephant-bird) depends on maternal practices that enable our daughter to see both of us—in addition to a variety of others—as real, even when (like Lazie-Mayzie) one or both of us fails to live up to the socially constructed ideal of good mothers.

Becoming Real: To Love and Be Loved

Summer 2001: "Mom, when I said I hated you earlier, I didn't really mean it. Sometimes words just come out of my mouth before my brain thinks." This is comforting. I am glad to hear she doesn't hate me; I am also glad for her developing ability to engage in candid self-observation. I reassure her that I know she doesn't mean such things, at the same time gently cautioning her that, just like her, I am capable of having my feelings hurt. "I don't want to hurt your feelings, Mom, but I really want to live with my real mom." Here it is again. I'm not hurt this time; the words aren't spoken in anger. Yet, it is not a straightforward statement of desire either. It is a test and I'm not sure how to respond because I'm not sure precisely what the question is. Would I give her up? (No.) Would I let her visit her birth mom for a weekend or a few weeks? (Yes, but this is not solely my decision.) Will I allow her to love her birth mom without retracting my own love for her? (Yes.)

I decide to choose the last question, as it is the easiest to answer. "I know that you miss your birth mom and you would like to spend more time with her. That's OK. I know you love me too." "I do love you, but you're not my real mom," she explains. I try a different angle. "Am I fictional?" I inquire playfully. She giggles. So do I. And on this evening, she initiates the bear hug.

In the classic children's story, *The Velveteen Rabbit*, a young boy loves a stuffed bunny into being real. The bunny, who loves the boy very much, nonetheless yearns to be like real rabbits. Having encountered real rabbits on an outing with the boy and having been made to feel inadequate because of his obvious stitching and inability to hop, he inquires of his friend the skin-horse, how he might become real. The skin-horse, the nursery stable philosopher of the story, explains:

> Real isn't how you are made . . . It's a thing that happens to you. When a child loves you for a long, long time, not just to play with, but REALLY loves you, then you become

Real . . . It doesn't happen all at once . . . You become. It takes a long time. That's why it doesn't often happen to people who break easily or have sharp edges, or who have to be carefully kept. (M.Williams, 1922)

On this theory, reality is a function of being seen lovingly by another. As Marilyn Frye (1983) reminds us, love is too often equated with servitude (73). This is not the sort of love I have in mind nor is it the sort of love that the boy has for the bunny. From an adult's perspective, a stuffed toy is just an object to be put on a shelf and admired or to be exploited for one's own enjoyment until it is no longer good for either. Certainly, this is the point of view of the boy's nanny who throws the threadbare bunny in a cupboard and the boy's doctor who demands the bunny be thrown into the trash because it may carry scarlet fever germs. From the child's point of view, however, the bunny is, or more accurately *becomes*, beloved. The boy imagines the bunny as having its own desires and powers, as a being capable of exploration and adventure, indeed, as a being capable of independent existence. And in perceiving the bunny as real, he makes it so.

The loving eye both recognizes and enables the other's independence, both sees the other as real and contributes to the other's reality (Frye 1983). Such recognition is rarely immediate; it requires, as the skin-horse suggests, considerable time and patience. Indeed, as Lugones and Spelman (1983) suggest, receiving recognition from another, especially where that other is significantly different from you, may require us to "be patient to the point of tears." We also need to learn to accept criticism from the other(s) whose recognition we seek (26). This is why those who are brittle, sharp-edged, or fragile may never become real.

Unlike accounts of maternal love as instinctive (the biocentric narrative) and accounts of love as something that happens "at first sight" (a frequent narrative of adoptive parents as well as romantic monogamists), here love is portrayed as a *practice* that is sustained over time. Both the giving and the receiving of love require patience, openness, and generosity toward the other. The sort of love that can bring another into being for us cannot absorb, dominate, or constrain the other. Loving perception is incompatible with colonial love. It does not attempt to uplift, civilize, or assimilate the beloved; instead it attempts to see the other on her own terms as a potentially independent subject. Such loving perception has much in common with the maternal practice described by Sara Ruddick (1995) as "attentive love," a *discipline* developed through *training* ourselves to "really look at" and thus love a "real child" (123). Distinguishing this practice from that of empathy ("the ability to suffer or celebrate with another as if in the other's experience you know and find yourself"), Ruddick emphasizes the importance of knowing one's child "without finding yourself in her" (121). Quoting Iris Murdoch (1971), Ruddick explains:

> A mother really looks at her child, tries to see him accurately rather than herself in him. "The difficulty is to keep the attention fixed on the real situation"—or the real children. Attention to real children, children seen by the "patient eye of love," "teaches us how real things [real children] can be looked at and loved without being seized and used, without being appropriated into the greedy organisms of the self." (121)

Ruddick's discussion of maternal love highlights two connections between love and reality. First, love is connected to the cognitive capacity to see another as she "really is." Secondly, this capacity (or epistemic virtue) depends on our willingness to see the other as non-analogous to ourselves. I partially agree and partially disagree with each of these claims. My areas of disagreement are as follows: Ruddick's account seems to suggest that the other (one's child) has a "nature" or "reality" that precedes its relationships with others. Insofar as Ruddick is presuming a modernist notion of the self as a unified subject, I part ways with her. As Judith Butler (2005) suggests, the significant others who are primary to our dialogical development are those who care for us: "the ego is not an entity or a substance, but an array of relations and processes, implicated in the world of primary caregivers in ways that constitute its very definition" (59; see also Winnicott 1986). This leads to my second area of departure from Ruddick's conception of attentive love. If we are subjects formed *through* our relations with and internalizations of other subjects, then we should *expect* to find ourselves in others (and them in us)—especially if they have been intimately involved in our processes of dialogical formation (as are primary caregivers).[8] This said, I do agree with Ruddick that loving perception is a practice that includes an epistemic and ethical commitment to avoiding fantasy. Fantasy (understood here not as daydreaming or imaginative play, but instead as a "self-induced blindness" designed to "protect the psyche from pain" and insight) leads us to project our own needs and desires onto others. For example:

> Fantasy creates children to meet a mother's desires; creates an abstract plan for their lives that will fulfill a family's or nation's aims; creates a mind for the child that embraces a mother's world and a will that satisfies her desire. A mother whose vision of herself or her children was primarily a fantasy would manipulate realities in the service of that fantasy, would act capriciously, and would strike out at herself or her children when the fantasy failed. (Ruddick 1995, 121)

Such fantasy is incompatible with the loving perception that confers reality on another person. In order to perceive another lovingly, we need to understand her in her "own world," not merely as a character in our world (Lugones 2003, 85). Doing this is compatible with seeing the other as an analogous being (as someone neither "just like," nor "entirely different" than, ourselves). But it is incompatible with what Lugones (following Spelman 1988) terms "boomerang perception," namely, a way of looking at another (our child, our mother, our friend, our lover, or a stranger) that "comes right back to myself" (Lugones 2003, 157). Loving perception will not attempt to draw analogies (connections) or disanalogies (disconnections) between the lover and the beloved, the knower and the known, *prior* to knowing them on their own terms, in their own world.

Ruddick's focus is on how a mother views (or should view) her child in order to ascertain her child's reality. It is equally important, however, to see how children can ascertain their mother's (or mothers') reality. If we take seriously the notion that reality, in the sense of reality-for-others, is a function of being seen lovingly by others, it follows that a real mother is one whose child does not see her primarily with reference to his interests. A primary task for a mother who would be real-for-her-child is thus to nurture non-arrogating perception in her child. The arrogant perceiver sees the world as revolving around him. As Frye notes, his vision organizes everything as either "for him" or "against him" (67). Just as a mother who engages in narcissistic fantasies about her child constructs a child subservient to her own desires, a child who sees with an arrogant eye will see a "real" mother as one who serves him and his wishes exclusively and expediently. Any blood relative or guardian who does not provide such service is apt to be cast out of the arrogant child's world as a non-mother or "bad" mother. The sad irony here is that a real mother, on this arrogant conception, fails to be a real person; she is merely an appendage of the perceiver who cannot imagine her as having separate interests from his own. "Being taught to perceive arrogantly," as a child, Lugones notes:

> I . . . learned to graft my mother's substance to my own . . . I thought that to love her was consistent with my abusing her: using, taking for granted, and demanding her services in a far reaching way that, since four other people engaged in the same grafting of her substance onto themselves, left her little of herself to herself. (78–80)

As Lugones suggests, a child needs to learn the skills of a "world-traveler," in order to see others, including her own mother, through "loving eyes."

> It was not possible for me to love my mother while I retained a sense that it was fine for me and others to see her arrogantly. Loving my mother also required that I see with her eyes, that I go into my mother's "world," that I see both of us as we are constructed in her "world," that I witness her own sense of herself from within her "world." (85–86)

Traveling, as an adult, with her mother to her mother's "world," Lugones finally sees her mother as "a creative being" (98). Thus seeing her, Lugones is able to identify with her, to see her, in Whitbeck's terms, as an "analogous being," thus overcoming the self-other divide that previously separated them.[9]

Lugones suggests that "world"-traveling must be a mutual activity in order for both self and other to become real. Distinguishing her notion of loving perception from Frye's notion that loving requires seeing the other as an independent being, Lugones claims that she and her mother cannot love one another in this independence: "We are fully dependent on each other for the possibility of being understood and without this understanding, we are not intelligible, we do not make sense, we are not solid, visible, integrated; we are lacking. So traveling to each other's 'worlds' would enable us to be through loving each other" (86).

I am skeptical that the mutuality demanded by Lugones and by Whitbeck is always possible, although it certainly is desirable. Thus, I think that we need to countenance the possibility that in daughter–mother (or daughter–mothers) relationships, as in any self–other (or self–others) relationships, loving may not occur in all directions. You may be more willing or more able to travel to my world than I am willing or able to travel to yours (or vice-versa). When this happens, as I think it frequently does, you know and love me better than I know and love you. Thus, I become more real (or become real more rapidly and/or fully) in the context of this particular relationship than do you. In extreme cases of asymmetrical loving—for example, the love of a mother for a severely autistic child or the love of an adult child for a mother with advanced Alzheimer's disease—the beloved may be real, while unable to confer any reality whatsoever onto those who love her.

In saying that you are not real if I fail to love and know you well, I am not advocating a social constructionism run amok. My claim is simply that our reality, as social beings, is always within a given *context*. Someone may be very real as so-and-so's friend, or mother, or lover, yet fail to be real within another relational context (e.g., as a secretary to a CEO). There is no such thing, I am suggesting, as unsituated reality. To say that reality is situated, however, is not to say that it is merely a matter of perspective. As philosopher Sally Haslanger (1996) notes, "a change in my thinking, *by itself*, cannot make my body, my friends, or my neighborhood go out of existence, nor thankfully can a change in anyone else's" (85). However, my thinking (or failures to think) in conjunction with the actions (or omissions) intimately linked with such thinking can bring (or fail to bring) someone or something into existence insofar as that being is defined in terms of its relation to me. "Mother" and "daughter" are examples of such relationally defined entities that depend on the embodied thinking of the participants to such a relation, as are "lover," "friend," and so forth.

There is, nonetheless, a ring of paradox to the claim that you may not be real, even when you know and love me. Ordinarily, we speak of someone as a "real friend," for example, when we feel they know us and love us well. On the account I am suggesting, someone may possess these epistemic and moral virtues while failing to be a real friend; their reality does not depend on their own actions so much as it depends on ours. Thus, if we fail to possess the skills and virtues necessary to perceiving our friend lovingly, they cannot become real. To reduce this air of paradox, however, we need to note that when we speak of someone as a "real friend" what we ordinarily mean is that they are a *good* friend; they do the sorts of things that we expect of friends.

If, however, I do not reciprocate—I fail to travel to your "world" by listening to your stories, visiting your home, meeting your family and friends, discovering your hopes and fears and dreams, and responding to your needs as appropriate—then, as Lugones suggests, I am alone in your presence (97). You are not real at all. Like the woman who remains in an abusive relationship, your acts of self-sacrifice, while marked as virtuous within the phallocratic moral scheme, result in a literal sacrifice of the (your) self.

This asymmetry of loving is common in mother–child relationships and is another reason that some feminists have rejected motherhood as both an institution and a practice.[10] Certainly, in mother–infant relations, caregiving is largely nonreciprocal because abilities to know and to love and to act based on this knowing and loving are radically unequal. On the other hand, as Whitbeck notes, infants can and do initiate relationship and, in limited ways, attempt to know their mothers. Moreover, young children's play indicates a capacity for imaginative "world" travel that brings others into reality-for-themselves. Like the young boy who makes the velveteen rabbit real by loving it, most children's worlds are rich with companions and possibilities. Indeed, it is the adult world that instructs them that the dolls and animals they cherish "are just toys," and that the friends whom we can neither see nor hear "are just imaginary." We also teach them that animals "are just pets (or meat)," that unknown others "are just strangers," and that people who can't distinguish between imaginative play and reality "are just crazy." Once they have internalized *our* truths about reality, we then criticize them for their self-centeredness, wondering why they insist on believing that the whole world should bend to their wishes. Often, it is we, however, who have diminished their world by teaching them to see with an arrogant eye.[11]

As this suggests, the difficulty in achieving the epistemological and moral maturity required for bringing others into being-for-ourselves may be a result of a particular sort of social acculturation prevalent in, although not exclusive to, the post-industrial, Western world. Given this social conditioning, many children may fail (as did Lugones as a child) to reach the level of epistemic and moral maturity necessary to a practice of loving perception that confers reality on others. In addition to teaching children to internalize our own frameworks of arrogant perception, practices of generational segregation may lead to nonreciprocal loving and knowing between mothers and children. In post-industrialized, urban cultures (unlike in many rural and agricultural economies), children are frequently kept isolated from both the joys and struggles of the adult world, making it difficult for our children to travel to our world(s).

As hooks (1984) notes, children of post-industrial cultures are rarely exposed to the occupational world of parents and other adults (143). Similar points apply to the non-work worlds typically inhabited by adults only. Contemporary western parents frequently isolate ("shelter" or "protect") their children from the adult worlds of politics, finances, law, culture, sex, and even spirituality. In many churches, for example, children are ushered into nurseries or Sunday school while the adults participate in more solemn rituals; similar practices of adult–child segregation also may take place at weddings and especially funerals. Under such circumstances, it should come as no surprise that our children might know little about us. To be real to our children, we need to resist such isolationary practices.

In addition to excluding children from adult activities, parents may also be reluctant to reveal their affective lives to their children. This too has unfortunate results. As a mother claims in Amy Tan's novel, *The Joy Luck Club*:

> For all these years, I kept my mouth closed so that selfish desires would not fall out. And because I remained quiet for so long, now my daughter does not hear me . . . All these years, I kept my true nature hidden, running along like a small shadow so nobody could catch me. And because I moved so secretly, now my daughter does not see me. (67)

In contrast, the mother in Tan's novel, *The Kitchen God's Wife*, does share her stories with her daughter. Here reciprocal caring is achieved. Similarly, a reciprocal relationship between Deann Borshay Liem and each of her mothers is achieved through Borshay Liem's continual traveling to their physical and affective worlds. By inviting and encouraging them to share their stories with her, Borshay Liem comes to know them as they really are.

As Borshay Liem's documentaries reveal, the reality of an adoptive mother (or foster mother, or stepmother, or other mother) is not in opposition to a child's recognition of her birthmother as also real. Why then did it take Borshay Liem so long to "make room in her mind for two mothers?" In part, the answer appears to lie in the inability of her two mothers to see one another lovingly. A small child cannot engage in either literal or metaphorical "world"-traveling on her own. Maternal work is needed in order to develop the non-arrogating perception in a child that provides the foundation for a child's ability to bring multiple others into reality. This collaborative mother work may take a variety of forms from the exchange of letters, photographs, phone calls and emails to invitations and efforts to travel to one another's physical homes to imaginative "world"-traveling where other means are not available (i.e., in cases where the possibility of open relations, and thus mutuality, is foreclosed by law or by the choice, death, or disability of one or more parents).

However it takes place, traveling between and among worlds is necessary in order to bring multiple mothers into reality for a child—such as my own—whose complex identity can only be grounded in a non-dyadic self–others relationship. Respecting such a complex—in Lugones' terms, "multiplicitous"—identity requires (when possible) mutual collaboration and cooperation among two (or more) mothers who not only see their child lovingly, but *also see one another lovingly*—as beings analogous to, albeit different from, one another. Such collaboration and co-operation requires a willingness to abandon the nature/nurture dichotomy that separates biological mothers from other mothers and a resistance to the good mother/bad mother dichotomy that underwrites the "all-or-nothing" approach associated with serial mothering. It also requires the willingness to queerly invert the lines of generational transmission, encouraging the child to give birth to her mother(s) rather than the other way round.

PART II

Resisting Domestinormativity

Queer Assemblages

The Domestic Geography of Postmodern Families

[P]art of what has made queerness compelling as a form of self-description . . . has to do with the way it has the potential to open up new life narratives and alternative relations to time and space.

—Judith (Jack) Halberstam (2005)

To this point, I have focused largely on the triangulated mother–child–mother relationship within adoptive and other nonbiocentric families and the queer affective geographies to which it gives rise. The domestic geographies of postmodern families—whether created through open adoption or through separation and repartnerings of parents or by some other means of chosen kinship—require equal attention, however. Except for the homonormative lesbian family and the heteronormative adoptive family that attempts to pass as a nuclear genealogical unit, polymaternal families typically reside outside of what Kathleen Franke (2004) calls "domestinormativity." In polymaternal families, the boundaries of "home" blur the distinction between the private and the public.

In *A Queer Time and Place*, Halberstam (2005) suggests that queer perspectives on and uses of time and space are negatively linked to the normative ways in which families inhabit time and space as a naturalized, heterosexual unit "upheld by a middle-class logic of reproductive temporality" (4). Thus notions of queer time and space develop, in part, "in opposition to the institutions of family, heterosexuality, and reproduction" (1). Here I use the notion of queer time and space, as developed by Halberstam, to interrogate how queer uses of time and space may develop *within the institution of family itself*. This may seem an odd (even perverse) project, given that Halberstam's work is aimed at examining how queer subcultures develop as *alternatives* to kinship-based notions of community (154). "At a moment when so many middle-class gays and lesbians are choosing to raise children in conventional family settings," she notes, "it is important to study queer life modes that offer alternatives to family time and family life" (153). I agree this is an important project, but believe it also is important to examine how children may be raised within nonconventional familial settings—settings that may, at least sometimes and in some ways, depart from the temporal and spatial structures of domestinormative life.

Halberstam acknowledges that "not all people who have children keep or even are able to keep reproductive time," but contends that "many and possibly most people believe that the scheduling of repro-time is natural and desirable" (5). Indeed, the (Western) norms of good families suggest that we *should* all live in the same place (a nuclear family household) and follow the same schedule (one premised on the alleged needs of children). Yet the "conventional family setting" to which Halberstam alludes is a relatively recent (post-World War II) invention that is rapidly becoming extinct—even among the middle-class families for whom it was invented. For this reason, I argue here that the alternative "logics of location, movement and identification" to which Halberstam alludes may breach the divide between queer forms of life, on the one hand, and familial forms of life, on the other. My focus here, like Halberstam's own, is on the queer time and place-making practices that emerge within postmodernism (6).

If we think about queerness, as Halberstam does, as an "outcome of strange temporalities, imaginative life schedules, and eccentric economic practices," we "detach queerness from sexual identity" (1). For Halberstam (and other queer theorists), the unmooring of queerness from issues of sexual identity better enables us to understand Foucault's (1996) claim that "homosexuality threatens people as a 'way of life' rather than as a way of having sex" (310). The ways in which queer friendships and alliances inhabit space and time, Halberstam argues, "mark out . . . the perceived menace of homosexual life" (1). In contrast—but also using a distinctly Foucauldian form of argument—

Cheshire Calhoun (2000) suggests that "gay men and lesbians have become family outlaws not because *their* relationships and families were distinctively queer, but because *heterosexuals'* relationships and families queered the gender, sexual, and family composition norms" (159). In *Feminism, the Family and the Politics of the Closet*, Calhoun argues that a combination of technological, social, and economic factors combined during the late twentieth century "to produce an explosion of new family and household forms that undermine the nuclear, biology-based family's claim to be *the* natural, normative social unit" (148). New technologies enabled reproduction outside of the heterosexual pairing; for-profit child-care providers took childrearing outside of the private household; soaring divorce rates led to single-parent families, divorce-extended families (with shared custody of children), and blended families (created through remarriage or repartnerings); and poverty gave rise to extended "fictive kin" networks who pooled resources and/or relied on social welfare agencies for family survival. In this age of the postmodern family, "marriage and its biological relations have ceased to determine family composition" and the "rule of one-mother, one-father per child" that has dominated both social policy and juridical reasoning about families has ceased to be adequate. (149).

Conservative anxieties about family values have centered, in large part, on the non-normative configurations of heterosexual kinship in recent decades (e.g., the choice not to marry or to divorce or to have an abortion or to become an unwed mother—all of which disrupt normative reproductive time and space). That conservative arguments against same-sex families are rooted in anxieties about heterosexual (mis)behavior was made evident during the 2010 trial over California's Proposition 8. In his closing argument, attorney Charles Cooper argued that Proposition 8 (the ballot initiative prohibiting same-sex marriage) must be sustained *in order to regulate heterosexual behavior*. Opposite-sex couples, he argued, present a "unique threat" to social interests that marriage is supposed to neutralize, namely, "the threat of irresponsible procreation:" when "procreative sexual relationships between men and women are not channeled into marriage and these stable unions with these binding vows," then the state has to "cope with the adverse social ramifications and consequences of irresponsible procreation." According to Cooper, marriage is not intended for same-sex couples because the purpose of marriage is to "channel" heterosexual, procreative conduct into its approved forms. The explicit message of those opposed to same-sex families reveals itself here, as Calhoun presciently suggested a decade earlier, to be the message that "misbehaving heterosexuals are responsible for . . . undermining family values. . . . To avoid being like lesbian and gay pretend families, heterosexuals need to increase their compliance with traditional marital norms" (152).

The failure of many heterosexual families to comply with traditional norms of marriage and childrearing and the ways in which they have queered our notions of home and family—and along with this, our practices of mothering—is the subject of this chapter. Here, I consider Rosi Braidotti's figurations of the "migrant" and the "nomad" to explicate the shifts from fixity to mobility that accompany the shift from living within a nuclear family to living within a family that is geographically dispersed. Resisting both the romanticization of nomadism (inhabiting queer domestic space and time may be challenging and even traumatic) and the pathologizing of postdivorce families as "broken" homes, I suggest that divorce-extended (and other postmodern) families might be understood, following Deleuze and Guattari, as "assemblages." In the second half of this chapter, I turn my attention to a particular assemblage within the postmodern family, namely the cyborg mother. Drawing on the work of theorists of cyberspace such as Donna Haraway, Mark Poster, and Allucquére Rosanne Stone, I explore the importance of communication technologies as extensions and modifications of maternal bodies within postmodern (decentered), queer (non-normative) families that transform our inhabitance of space and time. Borrowing feminist philosopher Kelly Oliver's notion of "response-ability" in the final section of this chapter, I suggest that communication technologies (or, as I term them, *technologies of co-presence*) enhance the subjectivity of both mothers and children by virtue of increasing their mutual ability to respond to one another—especially, although not exclusively, in queer time and space. The mother as a hybrid assemblage of human and machine is, thus, an important component of the contemporary assemblage of family commonly known as the extended, blended family.

Familial Assemblages

```
I am here. Where are you? [04:28:52 PM]
On my way home. [4:30:15 PM]
Which home? [4:31:23 PM]
```

—Text message between Dakota
(fourteen years old) and me, October 2008

Home is a notion that has become increasingly complicated for me, as well as for my children, as the spaces we inhabit have become increasingly complex. Whether speaking about my academic home, my homeland, or the physical structure (house) in which my family lives, "home" is a term with no fixed geographical referent. As a philosopher who became an interdisciplinary humanities scholar, I travel back and forth between and among feminist, postmodernist, postcolonial, and queer theories and artifacts. As an ex-administrator who now works at a satellite campus, I commute between cities and campuses on a regular basis. As a Canadian citizen who lives and works in the United States, I refer to both nations as home and frequently travel between them. As the member of a divorced-extended family, I live in and travel between multiple domiciles, as do my children.

After we separated several years ago, my husband and I agreed to an unorthodox custody arrangement wherein we timeshared two homes: the suburban family home in which my daughters had been raised and a small two-bedroom apartment at the coast, approximately sixty miles away (but near my second office). For five years after our separation, our daughters remained consistently in the "family home" (except for occasional vacations at the beach or sleepovers elsewhere) while my husband and I moved in and out of that home on a rotating basis. During our noncustodial weeks, we alternated use of the apartment where we shared common public spaces but each had our own bedroom. On some of my noncustodial weeks, I lived not in the coastal apartment but with my new partner at her downtown city home. The situation was similar for my husband who spent some of his noncustodial time at his new partner's home. Hence, we had four homes between us (one shared between us and our children) and our lived domestic reality consisted of regularly commuting between homes.

Although some might suggest (and, indeed, my husband did) that this queer lifestyle emanated from a shift in (or disclosure of) my sexual orientation, such a suggestion occludes several important truths. First, as a phenomenological matter, I do not think of myself (and hence, do not write of myself) as either bisexual or lesbian; nor does my current partner self-identify as a lesbian (hers is a gender-queer practice of female masculinity). My narrative is not a "coming out" story that can be neatly captured by essentialist or even fluid categories of sexual identity, but simply the narrative of someone who grew out of one relationship (that happened to be with a biological man) and subsequently entered another (that happened to be with a biological woman). Second, as a factual matter, the queer lifestyle that resulted from the separation between my husband and me is one shared—to some degree or other—by all separated and divorced couples who share children (whether these couples are heterosexual or gay or lesbian or other less gender-identifiable pairings). Indeed, as I emphasize here, encounters with queer familial space and time are a feature of many postmodern families who are geographically distended (sometimes for reasons of divorce and sometimes for other reasons) and thus (by choice or by chance) live outside of conventional family forms. Finally, projecting a coming out narrative onto my story mischaracterizes my experience (and that of most separated and divorced couples) as a "migration" from one home to another. When I left the nuclear domestic family I previously inhabited, I did not do so with any clear destination in mind.

In her book, *Nomadic Subjects*, feminist philosopher Rosi Braidotti (1994) describes herself as "a migrant who turned nomad" (1). I would describe myself as somewhere in between a migrant and a nomad. A migrant, as defined by Braidotti is "a woman with a clear destination, who goes from one point in space to another for a clear purpose" (23). She is "caught in an in-between state whereby the narrative of origin has the effect of destablilizing the present" (24). The nomad, in contrast, is "the kind of subject who has relinquished all idea, desire, or nostalgia for fixity." Her identity is "made of transitions, successive shifts, and coordinated changes, without and against an essential unity" (22–23). Unlike the migrant woman, I am not nostalgic for the past. I was happily married for many years. It was a good and loving (and sexually satisfying) relationship and the domestic, nuclear family within which I lived was a simpler place than where I currently find myself, to be sure. However, I do not yearn to return to the nuclear family. As an unmarried woman, I have greater legal, economic, social, and erotic freedom. As a part-time custodial parent, I enjoy the occasional freedom to live according to a schedule not regulated by children's activities and needs. I have more time to write and engage in other solitary or adult-centered activities. At the same time, my origins—both as a child and later as a married woman—in a single- and fixed-family home—destabilize my present. I have worried also that it may destabilize my children's present—which was why, for several years, my husband and I opted to commute while keeping our children in a fixed environment. In contrast to Halberstam's claim that queer subcultures produce alternative temporalities and geographies (whereas families reproduce normative time and space), in our case it was the "straight" act of childrearing (and concerns about what was best for our children) that provided a portal into inhabiting time and space queerly. We lived as nomads in order that our children could develop a stable sense of place and self.

The figure of the nomad, for Braidotti, is a metaphor for a critical self-consciousness that is fluid and mobile rather than fixed and stagnant. A nomadic consciousness is not easily achieved, however; thus it is, as Braidotti suggests, a "minority position" (29). Although not nostalgic for the past, during the years of incessant commuting I frequently desired greater fixity than my life then had. For this—and other reasons related to the economic recession and our children's age and increased independence from home—my husband and I formally divorced and split property five years after our original separation. For the next two years, he and I each had a house and address of our own. This was a shift to which our daughters responded quite differently. Tomeka—a rather nomadic teenager who would stay at friends' homes as frequently as with her dad or me—embraced the shift, indicating "it was about time." Dakota, in contrast, resisted the requirement for greater nomadism on her part, opining the fact that she would now "have to be like a kid in a *normal* divorced family."

Although the burden (or freedom) of commuting shifted, in part, to our teenaged daughters, our own fixity as parents was only marginally increased as we continued to navigate multiple overlapping domestic spaces. My ex-husband and I continued to alternate custody on a biweekly basis (with flexibility as needed), maintained a joint bank account for basic children's needs, consulted one another on parenting issues, shared keys, a dog, and two stray kittens as well as parenting responsibilities, and maintained a fluidity between and amidst homes. Our homes still numbered four—now his, mine, his partner's and my partner's. Because neither of us immediately recreated a nuclear family home (I still have not), we too continued to commute back and forth between our own homes and those of our partners. Navigating multiple homes and diverse styles of caregiving and domesticity continued to be an intentional, cooperative effort between all of us.

If queerness is less a matter of sexual identity than it is an outcome of "strange temporalities, imaginative life schedules, and eccentric economic practices," as Halberstam suggests, then our postmodern, nomadic family—like other extended, blended, and commuting families who live domesticity outside of traditional nuclear family spaces and routines—may be considered queer. Such queerness is not, of course, without its challenges. Some of the difficulties with which a decentered life is fraught, and with which others who have engaged in commuting and/or joint custodial relationships may be familiar, are the following: being unable to find one's clothes or other needed material possessions, high gas or other travel costs, not being at (the right) home to pay one's bills or collect one's mail, increased time and money spent maintaining multiple residences, and the ongoing need to coordinate one's schedule in accordance with one's geographical placement.

I often do not have the right color socks or shoes to go with the clothing available at my current residence. As I move from one residence and one office to another, I have to fill large bags with all of the books and papers I need in the upcoming days for teaching and writing projects and cannot always foresee every tome that it might be useful to have handy. Prior to regaining a "home of my own," family and friends from out of town frequently were required to travel from residence to residence with me, and I or my husband or my partner needed to ensure there were clean towels, adequate food, and other amenities for guests in each home. Even postdivorce, there remain multiple homes to be cleaned and maintained and paid for and multiple lawns to mow and gardens to plant and weed. Moreover, it remains difficult to establish stable communities and a regular routine as "home" remains fragmented across different counties. Friends don't just drop in at one's home for coffee. Social engagements, as well as doctor's appointments and haircuts, must be carefully scheduled with reference to where, as well as when, I am available. Similar difficulties (although not those associated with home maintenance) were faced by my children who, during their commuting years, would frequently forget something essential or desired at their other home and find certain friends and activities (not to mention parents), but not others, within reach at a given home.

As this suggests, neither nomadism nor the queer relationship to time and space that accompanies it should be romanticized. Both the migrant and the nomad, as travelers and border-crossers, have become celebrated figures within contemporary critical theory. This is particularly problematic when, as Ahmed (2000) notes, the figure of the migrant and nomad are used as metaphors for a style of thinking that is predicated on the erasure of the diversity of migratory experiences and the often difficult—even traumatic—histories that accompany real experiences of migration, exile, and homelessness. "To say 'we are all exiles,' is to conceal the substantive difference it makes when one is forced to cross borders, or when one cannot return home" (81). For this reason, the naming of theory as nomadic, Ahmed argues, is a "violent gesture" that betrays the liberal humanism of a privileged subject "who chooses homelessness and a nomadic lifestyle, or a nomadic way of thinking, one that can do so, *because the world is already constructed as its home*" (83).

I agree with Ahmed that, insofar as we are privileged subjects, we need to take care with our appropriation of notions of migration and nomadism in describing transgressive ways of thinking and living. When I describe myself, my children and other members of extended, blended, and commuting families as nomadic, I mean this in a some-what literal sense—which is to say that by choice or by circumstance we find ourselves in perpetual motion across geographical (and not simply metaphorical) spaces. And this can be quite disorienting (not to mention exhausting). At the same time, the Western commuter such as myself who packs a suitcase and moves amidst different suburban, urban, or rural homes is quite different from the nomad who must move with the seasons from place to place in search of food, water, or grazing land. The nomadism of the privileged subject also is quite different than the nomadic life of less privileged Western subjects for whom home fails to be fixed or stable because of the economic neces-sity of moving from place to place in search of employment. This is the situation of the migrant farm worker or any seasonal worker; it is also an apt description of certain white-collar workers such as the adjunct or "visiting" instructor who moves from job to job and place to place in order to eke out a living. These may be queer lives—lives that inhabit non-normative space and time—but it would be a mistake to simply celebrate such queerness as a (or even *the*) model for politi-cal transgression (Puar 2007, 22–23). Queer lives, just like normative ones, may be caught in the nexus of privilege or of exploitation and oppression (or, frequently, both). As Saba Mahmood (2004) suggests, we cannot identify a universal category of acts of resistance "outside of the ethical and political conditions within which such acts acquire their particular meaning" (9).

These considerations also apply to the notion of the extended, blended family, a category that also may conceal important differences if understood in abstraction from particular life histories and contexts. Although divorce, for example, and the subsequent reconfiguration of one's home into a geographically dispersed space may be liberating for some, it may be traumatic for others. We would do well to remember here, for example, the fact that standards of living postdivorce are frequently gendered and that living in separate homes may be a significant hardship—or even an impossibility—for those who are poor. Thus, to simply celebrate the dissolution of the nuclear family as a queer act also may be violent in its erasure of the substantive difference it makes when one is *forced* out of one's home and cannot return. To avoid a universalizing narrative premised on a privileged queer subject, one must take seriously the differences between those who choose to leave the nuclear family and those who are given little choice in their exile. This may be a difference between the spouse who leaves and the spouse who is left in cases of nonmutual decision making about family reconfigurations. And it is frequently the difference between parents who choose to divorce and the children of divorce. It is in recognition of the potentially traumatic effects of divorce on children that divorced families are often referred to as "broken homes."

Throughout much of the twentieth century, sociological studies of broken homes have studied the effects of divorce on child development and teenage delinquency, suggesting that homes affected by separation and divorce are toxic to children and to the larger social fabric.[1] The difficulties of a broken home are often thought to be remedied through remarriage. Thus, as the nuclear family is recreated (with different players), the "broken" family is transformed into the "blended" family. Both metaphors are problematic. Although the notion of a broken home may capture the difficulties for children of unexpected and unwelcome changes in family configurations, the assumption that divorce is *always* damaging to kinship relations (like the contrary assumption that it is always liberating) obscures different experiences of divorce. Divorces, like marriages themselves, may be orthodox or unorthodox, amiable or hostile, functional or dysfunctional. Thus, the notion that a family spread across two or more households is necessarily and irretrievably fractured, damaged or incapable of functioning well (broken) betrays a serious lack of imagination about the possible ways of "doing" family.[2]

The metaphor of the blended family, in contrast to the notion of a family that is broken, suggests a happy unity in which no fissions or fractures exist. Although I have used this term here in accordance with common parlance, the terminology requires deconstruction. To blend two or more substances together implies they can be combined or mixed in ways that eradicate difference as they become merged into one unity. This fails to capture the very real struggles of many stepparents, stepchildren, and stepsiblings who—like adopted children—may struggle with feelings of divided loyalties and belonging. Like Deann Borshay and other adopted children, for example, the stepchild may find it difficult to "make room in her mind" for two mothers, making the connection between a stepchild and stepmother a tenuous or even hostile one. Moreover, the eradication of differences through assimilation into a unity is questionable even as an *ideal* or goal for familial relations. Children of divorce, like adopted children, need room to mourn their losses and the politics of family assimilation, like the politics of colorblindness, may render their mourning melancholic. What we need, then, is a model of kinship that embraces *both* the connections *and* the differences between and among kin, as well as *both* the opportunities *and* the challenges posed by inhabiting queer familial time and space.

The (queer) assemblage, described by Puar (2007) as "a series of dispersed but mutually implicated and messy networks," is useful for thinking about postmodern families (211). An "assemblage," as originally defined by Deleuze and Guattari (1987), is a collection of multiplicities including both organic and nonorganic forces that can be neither divided (broken) nor unified (blended), but only transformed: "a multiplicity is defined not by its elements, nor by a center of unification or comprehension. It is defined by the number of dimensions it has; it is not divisible, it cannot lose or gain a dimension *without changing its nature* (275). The postmodern family—in its queer extensions of kinship relations and its dispersion across various spaces or "territories"—shares important characteristics with an assemblage as articulated by Deleuze and Guatarri. In addition to being aptly described as an indivisible multiplicity that undergoes transformation, its form is rhizomatic, it relies on connectivity rather than reproduction, and it is a site of territorialization, deterritorialization, and reterritorialization.

Deleuze and Guattari's contrast between a rhizome and a tree is useful for rethinking families as sites of affective energies, rather than as sites of genealogical origin:

> Unlike trees or their roots, the rhizome connects any point to any other point and its traits are not necessarily linked to traits of the same nature. . . . Unlike the tree, the rhizome is not the object of reproduction: neither external reproduction as image-tree nor internal reproduction as tree-structure. The rhizome is anti-geneology. . . . In contrast to centered (even polycentric) systems with hierarchical modes of communication and pre-established paths, the

rhizome is an acentered, nonhierarchical, nonsignifying system . . . defined solely by a circulation of states. (23)

Postmodern families—including stepfamilies and families created
through the adoption of children or the inclusion of "fictive" kin—are
rhizomatic in this sense. There are no unifying traits that necessarily
link family members. This is true whether we are talking about physical traits, intellectual abilities, aesthetic styles, or modes and objects
of desire. Nor can postmodern families be mapped onto a genealogical
family tree. My adopted daughter confronted this head on when she
found herself perplexed by an elementary school homework project
that asked her to glue photos of her family onto the template of a
tree with a single unifying trunk from which all other family members were supposed to emerge as branches and leaves (a project whose
difficulty would have increased exponentially after her father and I
divorced and repartnered). After many attempts to modify the tree diagram to allow for photos of her Guyanese American birth family and
her Jewish grandparents, aunts, uncles, and cousins, in addition to the
family members with whom she lived (at that time, her sister, father,
and me), she took a clean piece of construction paper on which she
pasted various photographs drawing a series of arrows to signify lines
of relationship between these family members. It was a messy reproduction (image) of her family that failed to capture the complexity of our
familial assemblage—except perhaps in its messiness itself. Her family
could not be organized into a centered (even a polycentric) diagram.
What her visual assemblage did capture, through its multiple arrows
and connecting lines, was that her family was "composed not of units
but of dimensions, or rather directions in motion" (23). This was a
diagram of connectivity rather than reproduction.

It is because the postmodern (rhizomatic) family is perpetually
in motion that it cannot be captured by any static image. Assemblages
create territories (e.g., my home, my family) but these territories are
not fixed. They are made and unmade, reterritorialized, and deterrito-
rialized. Territorialization has a literal interpretation. Family gatherings
and events (the family dinner, birthday celebrations, etc.) take place
in a physical locale with clearly delineated spatial boundaries—most
typically the familial home. Territorialization refers also, however, to
"non-spatial processes which increase the internal homogeneity of an
assemblage" (De Landa 2006, 13). In the case of a familial assemblage
such nonspatial processes may include, for example, shared genealogi-

cal origins, shared histories, shared surnames, and clearly demarcated lines of legal relationships and responsibility. These forces of territorialization that stabilize the familial assemblage by delineating its physical and social boundaries are countered by forces of deterritorialization in the postmodern family as a shifting family structure that exceeds or escapes the very norms of place and kinship that have been used to order the nuclear family (88). As homes are multiplied and the people inhabiting these diverse familial places become increasingly heterogeneous, the nuclear family once marked by strict boundaries of marriage, reproduction, and a shared household transforms into a less recognizable (queer) form of kinship.

Another deterritorializing process that destabilizes spatial boundaries and allows for increased heterogeneity within a familial assemblage is the use of communication technologies. From writing and the advent of a reliable postal service to more recent digital technologies, communication technologies have blurred the spatial boundaries of social assemblages such as the family by reducing the need for physical proximity (13). With this in mind, I explore in the remainder of this chapter a specific queer figuration of embodiment within the postmodern family, namely the cyborg mother.

Technomoms and Cyborg Mothers:
The Mother as Assemblage

Families are becoming cyborgian; their very forms are mediated or determined by technoscience. Just as different types of cyborgs are now proliferating, so are cyborg families.

—Chris Hables Gray (2002)

As I exited the nuclear family I had previously inhabited, I needed to develop practices of loving my adolescent daughters consistently while only occupying shared material space with them half of the time. An important way in which my daughters and I retain contact while living apart is to inhabit virtual space together. We talk on the cell phone; we text and email, instant message and Skype one another; we play games together, share photos, and are updated on one another's lives via social networking sites. Indeed, given the proclivity of my daughters to be permanently attached to a cell phone or computer, we may meet in virtual space even during the weeks we are living under the same roof. Sometimes technology enables a mutual presence that physical proximity does not.

Given the number of commuting parents, divorced parents, and wired teenagers, I think it unlikely that I am the only mother who relies on technology to care for her children. Reading the feminist literature on mothering, however, one would not suspect that mothers use technology as an integral part of their mothering activities. Conversely, reading the cultural studies literature on communication technologies, one would not suspect that technology users engaged in mothering. Indeed, the scholarly literature in these two fields largely embodies a strangely traditional division of labor wherein women have children and boys have toys and each engages in their respective labors in their respective spheres. This is not to say that feminists have ignored technological developments. Indeed, postmodernist feminists such as Donna Haraway (1991), Anne Balsamo (1996), and Katherine Hayles (1999) have been instrumental in bringing to our attention the ways in which the hybridization of human bodies with technology disrupts the nature/culture dichotomy and, in so doing, thrusts us forward into a potentially post-human and post-gender world. However, even in the cyberfeminist literature—infused as it is with gender analyses of technological issues, mothers and mothering are notably absent. Cyberfeminist theorists, like other cultural analysts of technology, can be found exploring, using, celebrating, and critiquing military, scientific, entertainment, communication, and medical technologies. Cyberfeminist practitioners work in laboratories, construct websites, play video games, have cybersex, surgically reconstruct their bodies, and play with gender online. They also conceive babies via "artificial" reproductive techniques (the one notable point of intersection between the literatures on mothering and the scholarship on technology). And yet, like their male counterparts, cyberfeminists appear not to care for children (or other dependents). For those of us interested in both mothering and technology, an important question arises: How is caregiving—specifically mothering—in the postmodern world transformed by technology?

Can technology liberate us from the patriarchal institution of motherhood? Can it be used to subvert the heteronormative paradigm of family? Or does it simply reinforce gendered relations of oppression? Legitimate feminist concerns have been raised about the ways in which technology may reproduce relations of oppression under heteropatriarchal capitalism. Many of these concerns focus on the invasiveness and health risks of reproductive technologies and the ways in which such technologies reinforce compulsory motherhood (see, e.g., Lubin 1998; Rapp 2000; Spar 2006). That reproductive technologies can, indeed, be damaging to both the well-being of mothers and of their children was highlighted by media outrage at the physician-assisted predicament of Nadya Suleman, more commonly known as "octomom." The media's demonization of Suleman for her reproductive choices was unquestionably tinged with sexist, racist, and classist overtones (she is the daughter of an Iraqi citizen, a single mother, and was not gainfully employed, thus raising the racialized specter of the much-maligned welfare queen). Yet, the fact remains that bearing octuplets carries a significant health risk and raising fourteen children carries with it significant psychological, social, and economic challenges for any woman. Moreover, as feminists have rightly noted, Suleman is but one example of a "competitive natality" that has been fostered by patriarchal backlash aided and abetted by reproductive technologies (P. Williams 2009). Suleman's story thus needs to be understood in the broader social context of a renewed compulsory motherhood that links technologically assisted breeding to celebrity status (consider the U.S. reality television show, *Kate Plus Eight*) and celebrates technology's ability to satisfy maternal desire (consider the "baby boom" among women aged forty-plus and lesbian women).

Feminist concerns about technology go beyond the dangers of technologically assisted reproduction, however. Feminist concerns also have focused, for example, on the ways in which so-called "labor-saving" devices in homes and offices enslave women. As Friedan (1963) noted, the advent of washing machines, vacuums, and other domestic machinery expanded, rather than decreased, the time women spent housekeeping as the expectations for homemaking were raised. Moreover, the mechanization of housework meant that women were "often kept busy buying, using, and repairing the devices and their attachments which are theoretically geared toward saving her more time" (Altbach 2007, 265; see also Leonard 2002; Wajcman 1991). Similar concerns have been raised about the longer hours in the office necessitated by technology (see, e.g., Potter 2011).

Feminists also have been wary of the ways in which communication technologies increase men's and children's access to women's time and services. In particular, feminist explorations of the marketing and use of communication technologies have remarked on the gender ideologies intertwined with technological innovation and application. Margaret Honey (1994), for example, examines the diverse goals of men and women as producers of such technologies, noting that men focus on solving technical problems, whereas women focus on enhancing communications. Lana Rakow and Vija Navarro (1993) explore gender differences among consumers of cell phones, noting that men are more likely to use the technology for business purposes, whereas women use cellular technology for safety purposes and/or to manage their responsibilities for home and children. Thus, this technology as others, they argue, serves to "represent and enact gender ideology," including an extension of the male role as "protector," and a gendered division of labor between the public and private spheres. Paige Edley (2001) argues that corporations have used communication technologies to seduce employed women into believing that they can have it all, re-establishing the myth of "supermom" and gaining women's "consent to be controlled through the illusion of removing spatial and temporal constraints" (29). More recently, feminists have argued that technology (of all sorts) is gendered—and potentially reinforces existing gender constructs—in both its design and its use (see, e.g., Lerman et al. 2003; Wajcman 2004).

I do not wish to dismiss these feminist critiques of technology, including communications technologies. Indeed, I have voiced many of them myself. I recall, for example, resisting my husband's suggestion, more than a decade ago, that I purchase a cell phone. He worried about how to reach me when I was away. I, on the other hand, wanted to be alone sometimes—to sit in the park and read a book, to go for a walk and just think, to attend conferences without familial interruptions, to be unreachable. Like several of the "remote mothers" interviewed by Rakow and Navarro (1993), my resistance to carrying a cell phone was a resistance to additional responsibility. I emphatically did not want to be accessible to others—at work or at home—all of the time. In retrospect, however, this stance manifested a particular standpoint of privilege—namely, the standpoint of someone who, at that time, was an administrator with staff who could competently handle matters in my absence and take messages for me and the standpoint of a primary breadwinner in a family that included a husband with flexible work who accommodated my children's needs during the weekdays. My stance also reflected my ability to respond in physically embodied ways to the needs of others (colleagues and children) who might need my reply. It was permissible to be out of (virtual) touch sometimes because most of the time I was within (physical) reach: as a department chair, I was in the office for extended periods of time every weekday and as the member of an intact nuclear family, I was at home with my children almost every night and weekend.

Subsequent shifts from a single, regularly occupied office to multiple workplaces and from a single, regularly occupied home to multiple domiciles created lived divisions within my public sphere and especially within my private sphere, however. In light of these reconfigurations of the public and private spaces I inhabited, I learned to embrace a cyborg identity and, in particular, the identity of a cyborg mother as a way of bridging these divisions. In the days and months after I exited my nuclear family, I began to refer to my cell phone and laptop as "my electronic umbilical cords" and, years later, this is how I continue to experience them—as extensions of my body that sustain and nourish my relationship with my daughters. Sometimes my cyborgian extensions have been a frustrating part of my maternal identity—for example, when I have been awoken from sleep by the phone's ring in the middle of the night because one of my children is frightened by nightmares or angered by frustrations, or when I have been called away from my work because a child missed her school bus or forgot a needed item. Like the breastfeeding mother, at these moments I resented feeling like the only parent to sustain my children and thus, the only parent deprived of time to sleep or work. On the other hand, the umbilical cord, unlike perhaps the mother's breast, is a two-directional connection for which I am grateful. Yes, my daughters have greater access to me than they would have without such electronic and digital extensions of my body. But I too have greater access to my daughters. A greater responsibility to be available, yes; but also a greater knowledge of their lives, a stronger and more consistent connection to them than I would otherwise enjoy.

When my elder daughter received her first cell phone at twelve, she would regularly call me from the school bus on her way home to tell me about her day. This was not a mere substitution for the conversation we might have had when we both arrived home; Tomeka was considerably more enthusiastic and informative regarding her day in a cell phone conversation than in a face-to-face dinner conversation. (In a face-to-face conversation, the typical response to an inquiry such as "how was your day?" was a perfunctory and often sullen, "fine.") Our cell phones thus enlivened our relationship during Tomeka's middle school years. My younger daughter, in contrast—a real chatterbox in a face-to-face context—would largely ignore (or forget) her cell phone, until she got texting privileges at age fifteen. An avid writer and keyboarder,

Dakota now contacts me regularly to let me know where she is and what she doing. My electronic connections to each of them—via cell phone, texting, emailing, and social networking—has become crucial during recent years, in part because I am not always in physical proximity to them, but also in part because, as my daughters have become teenagers, the traditional family meal no longer functions as a regular mechanism for keeping in touch with one another, even when we are living together. Immersed in a wide variety of extracurricular activities, by her high school years, my younger daughter rarely had time for a languorous dinner conversation, and my older daughter frequently refused to join us for a meal even when we were all home. A true cyberteen, Tomeka, throughout much of her adolescence, remained locked in her room glued to her computer, listening to music and chatting with friends in virtual space. Although I fought this behavior in its early years, I subsequently learned to give her (physical) space and meet her on her own ground (cyberspace).

Kelly Oliver (2001) comments on the connection between responsibility and what she terms "response-ability" (the ability to respond) as the foundation of personal subjectivity. She says:

> We are obligated to respond to our environment and other people in ways that open up rather than close off the possibility of response. This obligation is an obligation to life itself. . . . Subjectivity is founded on the ability to respond to, and address, others. . . . Insofar as subjectivity is made possible by the ability to respond, response-ability is its founding possibility. The responsibility inherent in subjectivity has the double sense of the condition of possibility of response, response-ability, on the one hand, and the ethical obligation to respond and to enable response-ability from others born out of that founding possibility, on the other. (15)[3]

If, as Oliver contends, subjectivity is response-ability—the ability to respond and to enable responsiveness from others (91), then my subjectivity is enhanced (as is the subjectivity of my daughters) by means of the various electronic umbilical cords without which it would be difficult for me to respond to and enable response from my daughters. As Clark (2004) indicates, cyborg technologies "impact what we feel capable of doing, where we feel we are located, and what kinds of problems we find ourselves capable of solving" (34). By virtue of communication technologies, I become potentially capable of mothering, of feeling—indeed being—close to my daughters, despite the physical distance created by multiple domiciles or locked doors. Over the past decade, I have used my cell phone and laptop to sing lullabies to my daughters, kiss them goodnight, play games with them, empathize with them about romantic break-ups, remind them and be reminded about important tasks and events, hear or read about the highlights and low moments of their days, and share with them my important moments and daily routines as well. I can—regardless of where I am physically located—be present in their lives and they in mine. Technologies of co-presence allow me to open up the possibility of responses delivered in both directions and my identity as a cyborg is thus essential to my maternal subjectivity and not merely an adjunct to it.

In order to capture both the legitimate feminist critiques of technology and the ways in which technologies enhance our capacities as mothers, it is important to reconfigure our discussions of technology to emphasize the importance of women's agency in using technology. To do so, we need to distinguish between different sorts of technology use by women. This can be done by distinguishing between what I call *technomoms* and *cyborg mothers*. Technomoms are assemblages of the organic and nonorganic that *reproduce* existing gender and domestic relationships. As technomoms, we may indeed be complicit in our own oppression by using new technologies as tools that extend and magnify traditional heteropatriarchal practices of mothering. Cyborg mothers, in contrast, are assemblages of the organic and nonorganic that may disrupt and transform such traditional practices, creating new spaces for new social practices. As cyborg mothers, we are not uncritical consumers of technology, but instead use it selectively to modify our maternal embodiment in ways that transform our experiences of intimacy and extend our ability to create, maintain and transform our relationships with others. Transformations in those relationships, in turn, engender new uses and conceptions of technologies.

To be clear: I am not suggesting here that there are two distinct sets of mothers—those who do and those who do not use technologically critically. We are all capable, at certain moments, of behaving as technomoms and, at other moments, as cyborg mothers. Indeed, I frequently find myself—as I suspect do many women—fluctuating between critical and uncritical uses of technology as I mother. Sometimes I do and sometimes I do not automatically answer my daughters' electronic and digital calls on my time. Sometimes I use communications technologies in creative ways that playfully enhance and transform my relationships with my daughters (a cyborgian version of Lugones' playful "world"-traveling) and, at other times, I use such technologies to nag or berate my daughters into obedience (a strategy that, by the way, rarely succeeds). Thus, in distinguishing between technomoms and cyborg mothers, I do not deny that we are frequently both—sometimes within the course of a single day. What the distinction emphasizes is that the mother–machine–child assemblage—like all assemblages—is unstable (i.e., subject to the forces of both territorialization and deterritorialization). Viewed as assemblages, technomoms and cyborg mothers are not static types of beings; they are better understood as contingent forms of "doing." These terms thus name not some essential attributes of subjects but instead "events, actions, and encounters between bodies" (Puar 2011).

In *Simians, Cyborgs and Women*, Donna Haraway (1991) re-imagines our bodies as "hybrids of machine and organism" or, in other words, as "cyborgs." Cyborgs, Haraway suggests, live intimacy in ways that embody an oppositional politics, that transgress the boundaries of mind and body, culture and nature, and abandon "the polarity of public and private," in part, by reconfiguring "social relations in the . . . household" (151). Urging us to embrace "the skillful task of reconstructing the boundaries of daily life, in partial connection with others, in communication with all of our parts," including those parts that find pleasure in reason and technology, Haraway (1991) concludes her famous "Cyborg manifesto" with a rejection of cultural feminism's celebration of an idealized femininity, claiming that she would (and we should) "rather be a cyborg than a goddess" (181).

In an essay contemplating technology and gender, Halberstam (1998) concurs with Haraway's recommendation, rejecting a feminism predicated on a "goddess-given right to birth children" as ultimately rooted in a patriarchal story about women's essential connection to nature and moral superiority to men (478). Disparaging the notion that there is "some 'natural' or 'organic' essence of woman that is either corrupted or contained by any association with the artificial," Halberstam claims that "femininity is always mechanical and artificial—as is masculinity" (478). The female cyborg, a fusion of femininity and intelligence as described by Halberstam, "thinks gender, processes power, and converts a binary system of logic into a more intricate network. As a metaphor, she challenges correspondences such as maternity and femininity or female and emotion. As a metonym, she embodies the impossibility of distinguishing between gender and its representation" (479).

Although I am less optimistic than Haraway (1991) about the cyborg as "a creature in a post-gender world" (150), I agree with Halberstam (1998) that "gender is a technology" irreducible to "natural" bodies and that "[g]ender emerges within the cyborg as no longer a binary but as a multiple construction dependent upon random formations beyond masculine and feminine" (480). By denaturalizing gender, a view of ourselves as cyborgs also complicates and multiplies our notions of mothering by rejecting any residual essentialist ideas about mothering as rooted in "natural" or "instinctual" female practices of caregiving performed in particular bodily ways or in particular material spaces. Mothering, like gender itself, is a technology (a social artifice produced by shifting power relations), not an essential identity tied to natural bodies. One way to see this is to recognize the ways in which technologies (machines) are integrated into the practices of mothering in ways that transform the maternal body, its location in time and space, and its engagement with others, making possible resistant forms of maternal agency.

Haraway claims that "communications technologies and biotechnologies are the crucial tools for recrafting our bodies," tools that "embody and enforce new social relations" (164). I have misgivings about Haraway's suggestion that technological tools (in the sense of machines) are *the* crucial tools with which we can recraft our bodies. To privilege such technologies as the only (or the best, or a necessary) form of resistance to oppressive social relations is to privilege forms of resistance often more readily accessible to those in post-industrialized nations who are financially advantaged. A perspective that privileges technological modes of resistance may thus devalue forms of resistance by those who may be technologically marginalized, for example, hooks' (1988) "talking back" or Lugones' (2003) "streetwalking." Nonetheless, I agree with Haraway that communications technologies and biotechnologies are *a* tool for re-embodying ourselves and our social relations that we should take seriously.

Among the social relations transformed by these new technologies are the relations of sexuality and of reproduction (168–69). Sexuality, as conceived by sociobiology, Haraway notes, becomes an instrumental activity emphasizing a genetic calculus as well as desire-satisfaction (1991, 169). Haraway's description of instrumental sexuality is akin to Warner's description of "repro-sexuality." The straight personal identity

supported by sociobiological accounts is closely interwoven with biological reproduction; it is, as Warner contends, a "breeder identity"
(1991, 9). Breeder identities combine with medical technologies in the
postmodern era, however, in ways that transform reproductive relations, making clear the social nature of such relations. As Haraway
observes, these technologies—sonograms, amniocentesis, IVF, and so
forth—permeate the boundaries of women's bodies via photographic
and biochemical means, undermining claims about the "naturalness"
of reproductive bodies and identities (Haraway 1991, 169).

By denaturalizing the reproductive body, reproductive technologies challenge us to redefine families. Like adoptive families and
stepfamilies, the families produced by IVF, surrogacy, and other technological means can no longer assume bonds based on common biological
roots. Artificial reproduction, like adoption and the nongeneological
family assemblages created through divorce and remarriage also allows
us—indeed forces us—to make sense of a multiplicity of "real" mothers. As Kathleen Biddick (1993) observes, multiple women may now
contribute to procreation:

> It is possible now for one female to provide an egg for pro-
> creation, another female to provide her uterus for nourish-
> ing a fetus and birthing, yet other females (and even males),
> including child-care workers, may act as social mothers to
> the growing infant. The acts of conception, pregnancy, and
> birthing, which had once unified the dominant cultural
> notion of the maternal and connected it as a "natural"
> sequence to social mothering, are distributed across differ-
> ent procedures in reproductive technology. (169)

By the late twentieth century, stories such as *Horton Hatches the
Egg* were no longer mere fiction but a metaphor for lived relations of
real mothering. Because reproductive technologies radically challenge
notions of "natural" motherhood, such technologies have been the primary focus of feminist investigations into the connections between
mothering and technology. Biomedical technologies are not, however,
the only technologies that reveal mothering as artifice. The wide variety
of domestic technologies producing and satisfying maternal desires also
requires feminist attention. As both feminists and queer theorists have
suggested, "reprosexuality involves more than reproducing. . . . [I]t

involves a relation to self that finds its proper temporality and fulfillment in generational transmission" (M. Warner 1991, 9).

Generational succession requires us to feed, clothe, teach, and
nurture our offspring in order that they can, in turn, reproduce our
values as well as our genes. As Ruddick (1995) suggests in her account
of mothering, mothers engage in protective efforts to preserve the children they have borne, nurture their children's self-esteem and identity,
and train their children to develop values and habits consistent with a
mother's own. Such maternal activities are closely linked to the temporal norms of "bourgeois families" as critiqued by Halberstam (2005). In
A Queer Time and Place, Halberstam suggests that the temporal norms
governing traditional families include not only the "time of reproduction" (women's "biological clock"), but also the "normative scheduling
of daily life (early to bed, early to rise) that accompanies the practice
of childrearing" ("family time") and "generational time within which
values, wealth, goods, and morals are passed through family ties from
one generation to the next" ("the time of inheritance") (Halberstam
2005, 5). These cultural processes of reproduction—and with them
the normative temporal and spatial structures of mothering—may be,
in part, resisted. Many of us are nighthawks (working or playing during the night hours after our children are asleep) and may awaken
long after our children's morning departure times—expecting them
to walk, bike, ride a bus or, if old enough, drive themselves to school
(Pafunda 2010). Moreover, many of us fail to have college savings funds
or inheritance monies to pass on to our children, either because we
are unable to do so or because we choose to enjoy the present rather
than enmesh ourselves in an economy of futurity. Nonetheless, most
of us do make efforts to protect, feed, and clothe our children and to
provide a reasonably sanitary and loving home, in which they (and we)
might grow and thrive. Like biological reproduction itself, these cultural processes of reproduction are also intertwined with technologies
(machines) that reveal mothering, as a specific gendered identity, as a
hybrid assemblage of organism and machine.

In *The Cyborg Mommy User's Manual*, performance artist Pattie
Belle Hastings focuses on the postpartum technologizing of mother
and child. In the introduction to her multimedia work, Hastings suggests that in contrast to "movies and fiction that depict the cyborg as
a futuristic, superhuman, or technological monster . . . it is actually
your average mother and housewife that are among the first so-called

cyborgs" (Hastings 2006b). The machine, she observes, has "extended the body of the mother for centuries"; mothers have "tended the stove, cranked the washer, peddled the sewing machine and vacuumed the house" (Hastings 2006b). Today, mothering occurs in an environment in which "microchips are embedded in everything from toys and greeting cards to thermometers and baby monitors" leading to a situation in which mothering relationships are increasingly "mediated, complicated and enhanced by machine" (Hastings 2002, 79).

As Hastings observes, the cyborg mommy is liberated and not merely oppressed: "as machines and bodies increasingly become fused, cyborg theory celebrates" as well as "criticizes and condemns the process—the machine/body relationship is at once liberating and oppressive" (Hastings 2002, 79). To see how we can use technology to transgress the oppressive social norms of motherhood, my primary focus in the remainder of this chapter is on a particular type of technology, namely, communication technologies such as cell phones, texting, email, instant messaging, and social networking sites such as MySpace and Facebook. I call these *technologies of co-presence* in order to emphasize that they allow us to be present to and with others in ways not tied to the physical facticity of the body. These technologies thus permit us, as mothers, to inhabit space and time differently—in ways that enable resistance to bourgeois family norms (especially self-sacrificial forms of mothering) and suggest different forms of intimacy between family members. Unlike the self-sacrificing Horton and much like Lazy-Mayzie, I have frequently flown (or driven) away from my nest (my physical home and my children), leaving my children in the care of their father or other mothers. However, unlike the bird-mother (and others) who are characterized as abandoning their children by such flight, I have the advantage of technological mechanisms that allow me to stay "in touch" with my offspring while I am away.

Technologies of Co-presence: Queering Spaces and Bodies

MOM, CHECK IT OUT! I'M AN ANAGRAM CYBORG!!!!!!
Wow, you certainly are! How is that score even
   possible? I'm still a mere "professor." Guess
   I'm going to have to practice more, in order
   to catch you.
You'll NEVER catch me xD

Hmmmm. Sounds like a dare to me. Now I'll HAVE
to play until I am a cyborg too!

> —Facebook communications between Dakota
> (fifteen years old) and me, while competing at the
> "Word Challenge" game application. September 2008.

I grew up in a game-playing family; rarely did a holiday or visit from
relatives pass without a game of cards, a word game, or a board game.
Playing games with my own daughters also has been a primary place
of connection for us. While living apart, my younger daughter and I
have frequently used the Internet as a space in which we can playfully
engage. Given the wide array of role-playing games on the Internet,
this space—unlike the card table—allows us to engage playfully with
identities other than that of mother and daughter. In the case of our
"word challenge," for example, my fifteen-year-old and I successfully
worked through the identities of such personas as "bankers," "teachers,"
"professors," and (the ultimate identity category) "cyborgs."

Cultural theorist Mark Poster (2001) distinguishes between a
modernist (enlightenment) understanding of machines as tools or pros-
thetic devices providing humans greater control over (natural) reality
and postmodern understandings of machines as, instead, reconfiguring
our reality and transforming who we are. Speaking specifically of the
Internet, he suggests:

> The Internet is more like a social space than a thing, so
> that its effects are more like those of Germany than those
> of hammers: the effect of Germany upon the people within
> it is to make them Germans (at least for the most part); the
> effect of hammers is not to make people hammers . . . but
> to force metal spikes into wood. . . . The problem is that
> modern perspectives tend to reduce the Internet to a ham-
> mer. In this grand narrative of modernity, the Internet is an
> efficient tool of communication, advancing the goals of its
> users, who are understood as preconstituted instrumental
> identities. (177)

Poster's analogy is useful for thinking about the distinctions
between two paradigms of technology. Indeed, his analogy can be
used to further explicate the distinction between what I have named

technomoms and *cyborg mothers*. Technomoms view technology—including communication technology—merely as a tool with which to carry out their preassigned domestic and familial duties. Cyborg mothers, on the other hand, are aware of technology's potential to open new social spaces that help reconstitute our maternal subjectivity. Nonetheless, Poster's distinction between social spaces and tools may underplay the ways in which tools themselves are misunderstood as mere extensions of the human will. It is no more a "preconstituted instrumental identity" that uses a hammer than it is a preconstituted subjectivity that uses the Internet. Technological tools—including the bottle washers, vacuums, and washing machines used by Hastings' cyborg mommy, as well as Poster's hammers—do not merely extend the embodied will of their users. They also mediate and transform human agency and social norms. As Betty Friedan (1963) argued, the domestic gadgetry imported into suburban U.S. households in the mid-twentieth century produced (in addition to being produced by) new norms of good housekeeping and good mothering. As such, these tools played an important role in transforming (bourgeois) women's desires, goals, and identities. In this sense, Hastings is right: Cyborg mothers—mothers whose agency can only be understood as inextricably intertwined with domestic technologies—have been around a long time.

One could argue that computers are simply a new form of domestic technology insofar as women use them to organize accounts and schedules, find and record recipes, and research parenting techniques. This would be a mistake, however. As Madge and Connor (2005) report in their study of first-time mothers visiting the Internet site "Babyworld," new mothers used the Internet not only as an "information source," but also as a form of "social support" wherein friendships were formed and new identities were "tried out" (84, 91). Although Madge and Connor refer to the Internet as "a new 'tool' in the armory of new parents" (94), the considerations they raise exemplify Poster's emphasis on the Internet as a *space* rather than a *thing* and suggest that there is something qualitatively new about the ways in which communication technologies, such as the Internet, transform our human subjectivity.

Reflecting on what is "special" about cyberspace, Madge and Connor suggest that "Babyworld" was significant because it provided the dialogical process necessary to the development of a maternal subjectivity. By enabling women to "try out different versions of themselves in the rapidly changing time/space of motherhood[,] . . . virtual space provided the possibility of competing, contradictory and sometimes transgressive performances of motherhood to occur" (91). Experimenting with different identities as mothers is important because "becoming a mother is an ongoing process" (91). As Stern et al. (1998) note, "the birth of a mother does not take place in one dramatic, defining moment, but gradually emerges from the cumulative work of the many months that precede and follow the actual birth of the baby" (3). Indeed, a mother's reality may shift and change *during her entire life*. The process of becoming a mother is not a process with a definitive temporal (or instrumental) end. Because motherhood is a relational identity (as all assemblages are), the identity of a mother shifts as children grow from infants to toddlers to teenagers to adults and as our family configurations and life circumstances change—sometimes in response to our children's changing needs and sometimes for independent reasons. This means that "trying out" different identities in various social spaces—including cyberspaces—continues well beyond the reality of "Babyworld." Moreover, as our children themselves become technologically skilled (sometimes more so than ourselves), the social spaces in which we may play with various technologically mediated maternal identities are likely to be spaces co-inhabited by our children. As the mother of teenagers, I inhabit online spaces not to talk *about* my children, but to talk (and interact playfully in other ways) *with* them.

Poster's characterization of the Internet as a social space rather than a tool, together with Madge and Connor's emphasis on the performativity of maternal identity in online communities, intersects with cultural theorist Allucquére Rosanne Stone's (2001) emphasis on relationships with technology that are characterized by playfulness. Like Poster, Stone rejects a conception of computers as tools extending the human will, arguing that this framework for thinking about digital technologies is rooted in "a human work ethic" that renders invisible the beliefs and practices of many playful cyber communities, including many programmers, hackers, and discussion groups (12–14). Distinguishing between those who play with technology ("Creative Outlaw Visionaries") and those who build and sell it ("Law and Order Practitioners"), Stone suggests that the paradigm of computers as tools makes sense only from the practitioner's perspective. Visionaries, however, are "thoroughly accustomed to engaging in nontrivial social interactions through the use of their computers—social interactions in which they change and are changed, in which commitments are made, kept, and broken, in which they may engage in intellectual discussion, arguments, and even sex." Thus, Visionaries "view computers not only as tools, but also as *arenas for social experience*" (Stone 2001,15). Unlike the Law and Order Practitioners who view computers as little boxes containing information, Visionaries understand that "inside the little box are *other people*" (16).

Technomoms are a maternal version of Stone's "Law and Order Practitioners." In this mode of being, mothers are characterized by a use of technology rooted in the maternal work ethic; we are not playful. In suggesting that we embrace the subjectivity of cyborg mothers, I am advocating we become Stone's "Creative Outlaw Visionaries" who use technology for play—both with our children and with our maternal identities themselves. As Lugones (2003) suggests, the "metaphysical attitude" characterizing playful "world"-traveling does not expect the worlds we enter (including cyberworlds) "to be neatly packaged, ruly" (95). As "world"-travelers, in cyberspace as well as in other spaces, "we are not self-important, we are not fixed in particular constructions of ourselves, which is part of saying that we are *open to self-construction. . . .* We are not wedded to a particular way of doing things. While playful, we have not abandoned ourselves to, nor are we stuck in any particular "world." *We are there creatively.* We are not passive (96).

To recognize communication technologies as opening new social spaces is to recognize computers and other electronic and digital devices as offering us new opportunities for traveling to the worlds of others and trying out new versions of ourselves as inhabitants of those worlds.[4] "World"-traveling in the electronic age, however, requires us, as Stone (2001) argues, to "rethink some assumptions about presence."

> Presence currently is a word that means many different things to many different people. One meaning is the sense that we are direct witnesses to something or that we ourselves are being directly apprehended. . . . Another meaning is related to agency, to the proximity of intentionality. The changes that the concept of presence is currently undergoing are embedded in much larger shifts in cultural beliefs and practices. These include repeated transgressions of the traditional concept of the body's physical envelope and of the locus of human agency. (16)

Intimacy, as sociologist Gill Valentine (2006) notes, has been typically assumed to require physical proximity: "The word 'close' is a synonym for intimate, and literal closeness is often assumed to be essential for familiarity and commitment" (367). Yet, as the number of families "living apart together" indicates, physical distance need not bring an end to intimacy (367–68).[5] For Valentine, as for Poster and Stone and other theorists of technology, viewing technology as an arena for social experience enabling familial and other forms of intimacy is closely linked to the advent of the Internet: "[t]he Internet expands the opportunities for daily meaningful contact between family members locked in different time–space routines at work, school, traveling, and so on. In this sense, online exchanges and daily Internet use are adding a new dimension, rearticulating practices of everyday life and lived spaces" (371–72).

Although it is true that the Internet adds new dimensions to our relationships, I am less inclined than most cultural theorists to insist on an essential difference between new digital, communication technologies and earlier "tools of networking" such as the telephone or old-fashioned paper correspondence. As Gray (2002) notes, such a distinction functions to separate the technological "haves" (the "digerati") from the technological "have-nots" (the "technopeasants"). This class distinction is important to consider in addressing the social inequities involved in the distribution of and differential access to communication (and other) technologies (133–34). In thinking about transformations in the way intimacy is lived, however, what is important is Stone's point about presence in shared social spaces. The telephone, as well as the Internet, snail mail, as well as email, allow for intentional social interaction between agents—including intimate and transformative engagement between family members—that is not grounded "in the physical facticity of human bodies" (Stone 2001, 17). It is in order to capture the array of technologies that may be understood as "arenas for social experience" for at least some users that I speak here simply of technologies of co-presence.

What all technologies of co-presence have in common is that they restructure—to a greater or lesser degree—our experiences of ourselves as agents in space and time. As Poster notes, "the vectors of space and time are drastically reconfigured" by the computer. Bodies move almost instantaneously through space and time with/in the technological vehicle; "the simultaneity of email and chat modes on the Internet completely erases spatial factors and implodes time" (Poster 2001, 26). It would be inaccurate to indicate that the telephone "erases space" or "implodes time" in the same ways as the Internet; nonetheless, as the Bell Telephone slogan "reach out and touch somebody" indicated (and as a thriving phone sex industry still indicates), the phone does allow us to move through space and time with/in it. This experience of moving through space and time becomes intensified with cellular phone technologies that allow us to reach out (and be reached) wherever we may be. The cell phone may thus be envisioned as "an entry-level cyborg technology" (Clark 2004, 27). Today, cell phones and the Internet are frequently combined (for those who can afford it) into one technological instrument.

For some, like cultural theorist Paul Virilio (1986, 1995), technologies that permit us to transgress time and space give rise to dystopian anxieties. In *La Vitesse de Liberation*, Virilio (1995) worries that online chat groups and other social spaces may promote forms of eroticism that threaten to destroy loving relationships and undermine fundamental social institutions such as the family:

> The end of the supremacy of physical proximity in the megalopolis of the postindustrial era will not simply encourage the spread of the single-parent family. It provokes a further more radical rupture between man and woman, threatening directly the future of sexual reproduction . . . the Parmenidean rupture between masculine and feminine principles broadens to allow remote acts of love. (130)

Virilio's dystopian vision highlights the heteronormative anxieties that may underlie concerns about social spaces ungrounded by relations of physical proximity. It is not the family—much less love itself—that is endangered by relationships without physical presence. What is threatened is a particular historic arrangement, namely, the heterosexual, nuclear family (Poster 2001, 115). At the same time as technologies of co-presence destabilize the boundaries of the nuclear family formation, however, they enable, promote, and respond to new forms of love and families. In queering time and space, technologies of co-presence make room for queer love and queer families (as well as queer sex). As Halberstam (2005) argues, the models of temporality and place-making practices that emerge within postmodernism allow for creative, non-normative organizations of community, identity, embodiment and agency (6). What I am arguing is that these creative non-normative organizations or "assemblages" that emerge within postmodernism include new forms of kinship, new relationships between parents and children and, most important for my purposes, new forms of maternal identity, maternal embodiment, and maternal agency.

Response-abilities: Choosing Love, Choosing Motherhood

```
LAX practice cancelled. Riding bus home. Can
   you get me at 3? [02:31:35 PM]
I'm at work. [02: 35: 21 PM]
No. Rain. Aww poo. [02:40:26 PM]
I'll love you even if you are wet :) [02:42:02
   PM]
Love you too, mommy [02:43:10 PM]
```

—Text message between Dakota
(fifteen years old) and me, March 23, 2009

In contrast to Virilio's claim that technologies of co-presence threaten the reproductive family and thus humanity's future, Haraway (1991) argues that coming to terms with our cyborg identities includes rejecting the dichotomy between us (as vulnerable subjects) and machines (as threatening objects). Identifying as cyborgs thus allows us to accept our pleasure—including maternal pleasure—in machine skills and technological communications not as a sin (or some sort of false consciousness) but simply as an aspect of embodiment: "[t]he machine is not an *it* to be animated, worshipped, and dominated. The machine is us, our processes, an aspect of our embodiment. We can be responsible for machines; *they* do not dominate or threaten us. We are responsible for boundaries; we are they (Haraway 1991, 180).

What does it mean for a cyborg mother to be responsible for boundaries? Haraway's reminder that *we* are responsible for our technological embodiments provides a response to feminist concerns about the threats posed by the blurring of boundaries between work and home. Although communication technologies *may* "extend work [including mother work] and one's availability into all periods of time and into all places," this is not an *inevitable* consequence of cyborg identity (Rakow and Javarro 1993, 148; see also Edley 2001; Gurstein 2001). In particular, although technologies of co-presence enable "presence at a distance," they do not require—from mothers or others—that we respond *without thinking* to all calls on our time and attention.

Indeed, they may enable the critical distance necessary for love that is reflective and transformative. Cyborg mothering (as opposed to techno-mothering), in giving *us* responsibility for boundaries, is a practice that provides the opportunity to resist self-sacrificing ideals of motherhood. Such practices are especially important in the context of the "new momism" that insists on standards of perfection for mothering that are both unrealistic and debilitating for women (Douglas and Michaels 2004; see also J. Warner 2005).

When my daughters would call or text me to collect them or missing items they desired (a rather frequent occurrence before they were old enough to drive), I would need to determine on a case-by-case basis the reasonableness and urgency of their requests. Did their immediate needs really necessitate dropping the activities in which I was currently engaged? Making such determinations often was easier to do via technological means than it was in a face-to-face context. Distance permitted time to think before instinctively rushing to their aid. I could take the necessary moments for a considered response before returning their texts or phone calls.[6]

To see the importance of distance to the feminist transformation of maternal identity and practice, it is useful to consider the reasons mothers leave their children—for work, for sexual freedom, or for other autonomous pursuits. Examining the story of Lilith, a woman who chose to leave her husband and children, sociologist Petra Büskens (2004) asks "what happens to motherhood when it occurs outside the conventional nuclear or single-parent family?" (106). Her answer is that mothering, as a practice, is re-invented. The act of leaving, Büskens suggests, "can be understood as one way of resisting the totalising institution of self-sacrificing/desexualizing mothering" (109). By leaving her familial home, a mother "opens up the space to be something other than a mother," creating a room—and perhaps even a home—of her own. Once she has established her own autonomy, Lillith re-establishes a connection with her children, ultimately inviting her teenage daughter and sons to share this space with her but as contributing members of a shared household manifesting mutual care and responsibility. By "altering the terms and spaces from which she mothers," according to Büskens, she "repositions the whore within the madonna, or the woman within the mother," thus deconstructing notions of selfless, asexual, instinctual mothering (109). In view of Lillith's return to mothering, Büsken contends, Lillith is best understood not as leaving her *children* but rather as leaving "the hegemonic *institution of mothering*" (116, emphasis mine). Leaving, for Lillith and others like her, may be most accurately viewed as *"a strategic withdrawal on the mother's behalf geared to disrupt and reorganise the terms on which parenting is conventionally organized"* (117).[7]

Cyborg mothering likewise may be seen as a strategy for reorganizing (deterritorializing) the terms of mothering. Communication technologies make it possible for mothers to be present to their children; they also make it possible to live autonomous lives outside the confines of the nuclear family on an intermittent or a more permanent basis. Achieving such autonomy need not require "leaving" one's children but it does require intentionally and consciously reorganizing the terms on which, and spaces and times in which, mother and child are present to one another. This is crucial if we are to avoid becoming martyrs resentful of our children's calls upon our time.

As bell hooks (2000) notes, love is a choice. Love is not, however, always experienced that way. Love often may feel involuntary and beyond our control as captured by the phrase, "falling into love." Or it may feel obligatory, as though we have no option but to love another, as a mother may feel obliged to love her children. For cyborgs, however, love is more clearly a choice. The would-be cyborg lover does not just fall, against her will, into her lover's arms. She makes conscious decisions, for example, to say this rather than that in her electronic correspondence and to send or not send her flirtatious messages. Similarly, the cyborg mother does not just instinctively respond to her child's cry. She makes conscious decisions to turn the baby monitor, cell phone, online indicator, or other communication device on or off. And each time a communications device beckons her, she must make a conscious decision to answer or not answer the call. Cyborg love is thus more likely to be experienced as a practice of freedom. Through various circuits and send and delete buttons and on and off switches, we can, in Oliver's words, "choose to close ourselves off to others or we can choose to open ourselves toward others" (220).

In addition to choosing whether to open ourselves to others, we choose *how* to open ourselves to others. And we leave records of our choices—their traces are on voice mail, message machines, email archives, and social networking "bulletins" and "walls." These traces do not guarantee but they do make it more likely that we will be vigilant about our choices on each occasion that we make them. The secret lover hesitates to leave a message on her lover's answering machine for fear it will be overheard and in that hesitation has the opportunity to reflect on what she is doing. The cyborg mother chooses her tone of voice and words to her child to more carefully reflect loving concern when she reprimands or cautions her child via electronic communication than she might in the exasperation of the in-person moment. Moreover, where vigilance is not practiced at the moment of decision making, the historical record left enables learning through post-encounter analysis and interpretation. As Oliver (2001), following hooks, also suggests, it is "only through vigilant reinterpretation and elaboration of our own performance" of opening ourselves toward others that we can maintain a loving attitude: "love is not something we choose once and for all. Rather, it is a decision that must be constantly reaffirmed through the vigilance of self-reflection" (220–21).

This is, then, the liberating aspect of loving from afar. As Oliver notes, space is not empty and thus distance need not be experienced as "unbridgeable, empty, or alienating" (213). It is "the gaps or spaces between" the lover and the beloved, the mother and child, that open up possibilities for "communication and communion" that may exist but are not as readily discernable when we are in close proximity or enmeshed in relationships that seem "natural" rather than voluntarily constructed (221). Insofar as cyborg identities enable this form of subjectivity, we would do well to embrace rather than resist them. Technologies of co-presence are not artificial and inadequate bridges between subjects. Instead, they make possible extensions and transformations of ourselves that engage in the critical self-reflection necessary to loving one another consciously and intentionally across emotional and cognitive as well as geographical and temporal boundaries.

Cyborg identities are not, however, the only way of cultivating subjectivities that are response-able to others. Nor do technologies of co-presence (whether virtual or material) guarantee the development of selves that engage in critically self-reflective love—as anyone knows who has visited a chat room, engaged in e-mail correspondence, or even passed notes in a classroom. Crossing the boundaries that divide self and other is never easy and we too frequently cannibalize or abject the other instead of truly meeting them. The difficulties of meeting the other (rather than colonizing or merely tolerating them) are frequently pronounced in relationships between mothers and their teenage children. In light of this, the notions of choice, freedom, and love raised in this chapter require closer examination.

6

Control Freaks and Queer Adolescents

There's No Place Like Home

Our family is weird, Mom . . . and I wouldn't have it any other
way.

—Dakota (eleven years old), December 25, 2004

On Christmas Day, the first winter holiday following the separation of
her parents, my younger daughter proclaimed her family strange and
gave us her blessing. Present at the moment of my daughter's procla-
mation and blessing—in addition to myself—was my new partner, my
not-yet-ex-husband, his new partner, our older daughter, Tomeka, and
my seventy-year-old father (who had traveled from Canada to join our
newly configured family in Florida for the holidays). We had all spent
the previous evening (Christmas Eve) together celebrating a slightly
belated Chanukah and winter solstice with my daughters' Jewish godmother (or "grandmother") and her children and grandchildren (known
to my daughters as their aunts, uncles, and cousins). My dad, the girls,
and I would be departing in a few days' time to spend part of our
holidays with Tomeka's extended (Guyanese and Jamaican-American)
birth family. At the moment, we were all playing a slightly risqué and
somewhat silly game of charades and having a good time.

My father would later report back to my sisters that it was "just
like *Little House on the Prairie*," evoking a cultural reference for the

extended, happy family that speaks strongly to his generational and rural roots. This way of describing my extended family of choice, although clearly intended as a compliment, illustrates the ways in which "ordinary perception . . . straightens up anything queer or oblique" (Ahmed 2006, 92). I am delighted that my father felt "at home" in the shifting landscape of my family and its complicated domestic space. Yet, his analogy between my family and the rather traditional, albeit extended, family of an earlier era highlights our perceived goodness by rereading the multifaceted and complicated connections conjoining various members of my chosen family through a narrative that aligns us with the familiar. My family, of course, departs significantly from the (homogenous, white, Christian, heterosexual) family to which Laura Ingalls belonged in her little house on the prairie.

Our family is, in my daughter's words, "weird" and, as her mother, I am gratified that she is able to recognize and willing to accept our difference from "normal" families. We are a transracial, multiethnic, multireligious, multigenerational family extended across cities, states, and countries and we embody differences in sexual identities and politics, and the lifestyles, values and temporalities connected to differences in social class and rural versus urban living. Moreover, our kinship is largely constructed and voluntary, not biologically given or legally protected. This is true of the parent–children relationships as well as extended kinship networks of aunts, uncles, and grandparents. Neither my older daughter's birth mother, nor my daughters' other mothers (parental partners) have any legal parental status although they choose to be in our daughters' lives and my daughters choose—at least some of the time—to be in theirs. During the several years we were separated but not divorced, even the custodial rights of my husband and I were largely dependent on mutual good will.

In their teens, my daughters reacted quite differently to the notion of family by choice on which they have been raised. Although both of my daughters have felt entitled to define their own family boundaries— including who they will and will not accept as mothers—my younger daughter has largely embraced (sometimes with resignation, but often with pride) what she deems the "weirdness" of her family. In contrast, at fifteen, Tomeka declared to us that her friends were her family and the rest of us—birth, adopted, and step kin alike—were simply "random strangers." For the following two years, she asked on numerous occasions to be "emancipated" from us as her family.

What does it mean to choose one's family? Who gets to choose? And how might the notion of "chosen family" replicate, as well as resist, normative ideologies of the familiar? In this chapter, I explore the liberal ideologies of individualism, rationalism, and privacy underlying the notion of "chosen family." Although I am not the first to notice paradoxes associated with the notion of choice, I explore the tensions in the rhetoric of chosen family by means of examining the struggles engendered with mothering alienated teens. Individualistic conceptions of the subject as the locus of choice, I suggest here, give rise to a self–other divide that manifests itself in (among other ways) the emergence of power struggles between parents and adolescent children within the family, wherein teenagers desire liberation from adult prohibitions perceived as threatening to their subjectivity. Conceptions of the choosing self as an idealized rational agent simultaneously render the adolescent's subjectivity culturally unintelligible and thus in need of containment by her parents. Drawing on the work of queer theorists such as Judith Butler (1993) and José Muñoz (1999), as well as the work of French feminist Julia Kristeva (1982), I argue that these familial battles between adolescents and their parents (most notably their mothers) are irresoluble insofar as they are premised on a politics of abjection that define the self in terms of the Other that one is seeking to escape or control. Practices of the self based on abjection, moreover, give rise to strategies of power that replicate the politics of colonialism and tolerance.

To recognize the ways in which the politics of colonialism and tolerance take place within (and not merely outside of) familial homes is to recognize a central limitation of liberalism's distinction between the private and public spheres and the risks of unwittingly importing this distinction into feminist, postcolonial, and queer theoretical thinking about either politics or families. Using Bonnie Honig's (2001) analysis of our yearnings for home and interrogating Bernice Johnson Reagon's (1983) distinction between political coalitions (as sites of unsettling difference and danger) and the home (as a safe retreat from political struggle), I suggest in the last part of this chapter that if home is not to become a site of colonization, then it needs to become a site of coalitional politics.

Chosen Families, Choosing Subjects

The notion of "chosen family" emerging from the gay liberation movement of the 1980s distinguished kinship organized around principles of love (including non-normative forms of love) from kinship premised on biological or "blood" ties, enabling lesbians and gay men who were estranged from (or exiled from) the straight families into which they had been born to reclaim and reconfigure kinship for themselves. According to anthropologist Kath Weston (1991), the focus on love "deemphasized distinctions between erotic and nonerotic relations while bringing friends, lovers, and children together under a single concept . . . well suited to carry the nuances of identity and unity so central to kinship in the United States" (107). Thus, "love makes a family" became the rallying cry of gay politics by the late 1980s, when struggles for domestic partner benefits and the right to parent emerged as important political struggles.

In response to the inability of traditional kinship narratives to capture changing configurations of family in the western world, the rhetoric of "chosen families" as used in the 1980s by lesbians and gay men has subsequently been adopted—some might say appropriated— by heterosexuals to describe family configurations that depart from traditional norms. Despite the criticisms of this enlarged definition of family by some (see, e.g., Lasch 1987), theorizing family as determined by choice has the clear advantage of recognizing gay and lesbian families, families created through reproductive technologies, openly adoptive kinship networks, blended families, and other polymaternal and "weird" families *as families*. At the same time, the rhetoric of chosen families, *as chosen*, poses certain difficulties.

One potential difficulty is the lack of reciprocal recognition that may characterize such families. As Carol Levine (1990) notes in her analysis of how AIDS requires responsiveness to changing conceptions of family, the answer to "who counts as family?" will reflect, in large part, the beliefs and interests of the person answering the question (35). "In the language of significant others," as Weston observes, "significance rest[s] in the eye of the beholder" (109).

Noting that the gays and lesbians she interviewed "tended to depict their chosen families as thoroughly individualistic affairs, insofar as each and every ego was left to be the chooser" (109) and that few rituals marked the formation of gay families, Weston (1991) remarks that "emergent gay families sometimes raised problems of definition and mutuality: I may count you as a member of my family, but do you number me in yours?" (113). This problem of definition is in keeping with those experienced in many polymaternal families. Once kinship is detached from its biological and legal moorings, it is always possible for an asymmetry to exist in our relational connections. Lack of recognition by those whom we love often is painful. I have experienced this pain when my older daughter cast me as "stranger" rather than mother and when her birth mother has refused to return my calls. I have created this pain when I could no longer reciprocate my husband's sense that we were best friends who would be together forever. I have witnessed this pain on occasions when my children have refused to accept my partner as a mother, and during the periods when my daughter's birth mother has disappeared from her life. However, in analyzing *real* kinship as opposed to idealized kinship, acknowledging the possibility of such pain and disappointment within families is important. Here, the asymmetrical nature of choosing kin might be viewed as a strength, rather than a limitation, of the notion of "chosen families." More troubling, from a theoretical vantage point, is the portrayal of unfettered subjectivity contained in an individualistic conception of "chosen families." The notion of family as a creation built upon personal choice risks replicating dualisms such as nature/culture, necessity/choice, self/other, reason/unreason, and private/public. In so doing, it threatens to obscure the complex dynamics of families and important facets of mothering within families.

In speaking of families of choice, we need to take care not to oppose such families to our families of origin in ways that instantiate dichotomous thinking about nature and culture. As noted earlier in considering adoptive families, chosen families cannot be mapped onto a template of the biological family (despite a long history of attempting to do so). At the same time, families created through formal or informal adoption may violate an adoptive child's complex identity if they deny the role of biological origins and physical embodiment to a child's sense of self. Moreover, adoptive families deny a birth mother's status as a mother when they insist that social mothering is the only form of mothering that matters. Similar considerations apply to families created through reproductive technologies such as egg donation and surrogacy, to lesbian families, to stepfamilies, and to a wide variety of other polymaternal families wherein the mother or mothers who participate in childrearing may be distinct from the mother who gestates and gives birth to a child (who may herself be distinct from the mother to whom the child is genetically related). If we wish to respect mothering in *all* of its dimensions, as well as the complex subjectivities of children, we will need to refrain both from reducing kinship to biological connections and from privileging nurture (choice) over nature (biology) in family formation.

We should also avoid the assumption that families of choice are *always preferable* to families of (biological or other) origin. It is clear why lesbians, gay men, and others who have been subjected to criticism, exclusion, or even violence by their childhood families might view the homes they create as adults as preferable to the homes in which they were raised. Resistance to heteronormative ideals of the family as a procreative unit by those who are sexually queer is also readily understandable. Nonetheless, in opposing families of choice (as a good) to procreative families or other families of origin (as less than good), an ideology of chosen families risks replicating the Hobbesian distinction between the (nasty and brutish) state of nature and the (rational and relatively safer) civil society that allegedly succeeds it. This would be a mistake. There is nothing *intrinsically* dangerous about nature (including biological procreation), nor anything *essentially* safe about social formations (including families of choice). In some cases, the social institutions we create, including the families we choose, may be less than friendly, safe, or hospitable environments. Not all of our choices are good choices, as evidenced by the number of women (and sometimes men) who tolerate abuse by their chosen partners. Moreover, even good choices may involve risk and challenge. Intimacy with others includes a willingness to be open and thus vulnerable. Related to this, intimacy with others may and frequently does include challenges to our most cherished beliefs and practices, including beliefs about and practices of the self. Finally, in at least some and perhaps many cases, the families into which we are "naturally" born (or otherwise placed without our consent as children) may be among the family relationships we *choose* to retain as valuable once we are adults. This may be because of a shared history, because we enjoy relations of mutual respect, trust or comfort with our parents, grandparents, siblings, cousins, aunts, or uncles, or it may be a choice to retain these familial connections despite—or even because of—the challenges with which they present us. I willingly retain a close connection to my family of biological origin, despite the physical distance that separates us, for all of these reasons: history, respect, trust, comfort, *and* challenge.

In other circumstances, we may choose to retain our connections with our biological families (as well as kin created through law) because we remain physically, economically, legally, or psychologically dependent on them—or because they remain dependent on us. My husband and I remained married for several years after our separation, in part, because he relied on my health insurance benefits. My older daughter and I retained a connection—however tenuous—throughout her adolescence because she was economically and legally dependent on me. As this suggests, "choice" is probably misconceived if opposed to "necessity." As liberal theorists have argued since the seventeenth century, rational choices are often choices aimed at enabling our survival and well-being. According to Thomas Hobbes (1651), we choose, if we are rational, to submit to a sovereign agent (the Commonwealth), willingly "chaining" ourselves to civil laws in order to secure for ourselves a peaceful existence and defense of our property. According to John Locke (1693), relationships within the procreative family are likewise the outcome of rational calculation and choice. Locke denies it is a natural relationship that binds the son to the father, arguing that filial loyalty is a product of reason: knowing that his father can choose whether or not to leave him an inheritance, the son chooses to follow his father's wishes. Similarly, Locke contends, a man and woman choose to marry because reason dictates that this is the best way to satisfy their desire and raise their children (secs. 72–73). The specific examples of rationality emanating from liberal theory require critical interrogation and I return to a discussion of reason and unreason later. For present purposes, however, I wish simply to highlight that, as Locke's description of the family suggests, "choices about family relationships are not free of material considerations, even if a language of freedom justifies these material decisions" (Lehr 1999, 24).

As Frye (1983) argues, choices are always made "within a matrix of options" that expand insofar as one holds gender, race, class and other forms of privilege and contract under circumstances of sexual, racial, economic and other forms of oppression (113). Katie Cannon (1988) notes in *Black Womanist Ethics* that "the cherished assumptions of dominant ethical systems predicated upon both the existence of freedom and a wide range of choices have proven to be false in the real-lived texture of Black life," as well as other situations of oppression (75). White feminists and queer activists have critiqued the procreative family as decreasing rather than increasing the freedom of women and gay men and there is, undoubtedly, some truth in this critique. Nonetheless, the assumption that we are *always* liberated by separating ourselves from such families clearly reflects biases of race, class, age, and ability. For people of color whose families have been torn asunder by slavery, indentured servitude, war, child trafficking, and other forms of economic and political violence, separation from one's biological kin is not likely to be configured as a personal choice that increases one's freedom. For those of all races who lack material privilege or physical independence, a relatively stable home including a reliable breadwinner and/or caregiver may appear an attractive choice should it be among the options available. The fluidity and ambiguity of family boundaries prized by those who celebrate families of choice may appear risky to those (including children) who do not enjoy economic independence or physical or psychological autonomy. At the same time, such fluid and ambiguous families may be a *necessary* choice for those with meager resources. Indeed, the fluidity and ambiguity of family boundaries denoted by the notion of "chosen family" have been long-standing characteristics of families of color and white working-class families for whom colonialism and poverty have necessitated the creation of (emotional, political, and material) support networks indistinguishable from kinship (Caulfield 1984; Dill 1988; LeBlanc 2003). To describe these created families as the result of free choices made by completely unfettered subjects occludes the matrix of constraints within which such choices are made.

As Weston herself notes, "choice" is an individualistic (and bourgeois) notion that highlights "the subjective power of an 'I' to formulate relationships to people and things, untrammeled by worldly constraints" (110). This depiction of the abstract choosing agent, unmoored to any particular context, presumes that one's choices are not limited by constraints of time, place, or opportunity. Moreover, this notion of the autonomously choosing self as a free and rational agent isolates the self from its relationships to others. In so doing, it presumes that the subject has an authentic reality that precedes the relationships in which one chooses to engage. This conception of the self—like essentialist understandings of sexual identity as having a fixed authenticity preceding sexual performance and erotic engagement—is implausible. Moreover, it erects a self/other divide that becomes impossible to escape.

There is a distinct irony in the depiction of an autonomous subject freely choosing family connections for him or herself as though his or her present subjectivity was not formed within an already existing history, including a familial history. Among the dialogic contexts within which our subjectivity is built, maintained, and developed (as well as challenged, damaged, or even destroyed) is the context of our family of origin—especially, some would argue, the context of a mother–child relationship (see, e.g., Grosz 1990; Kristeva 1987; Oliver 1997). Indeed, our widespread cultural practices of maternal profiling—practices that hold mothers responsible for their children's choices and emphasize maternal fitness as crucial to a child's well-being—presume that a child's subjectivity and agency emerge within the familial context into which it is born (or fostered or adopted). These cultural practices and the standards of maternal fitness they embody are problematic, as I earlier argued. Resistance to practices of maternal profiling, however, need not deny the fact that childhood experiences within a given family (or families) do, indeed, play a role in the formation of our subjectivity. This context is among the *given* relations from which our present *choices*—including our chosen families—make sense. Our relationships with our mothers (and others) do not determine our subjectivity; neither, however, are they irrelevant to it.

The difficulty that gives rise to maternal profiling is not the recognition of the central role of mothering in the formation of a child's subjectivity within contemporary Western cultures. Mother–child relationships *are* a formative (albeit not determinative) influence on subjectivities as they emerge within a culture premised on the patriarchal, heterosexual, nuclear family as a primary site of child development. The problem of maternal profiling (and its close relative, mother-blaming) arises when we mistake this contingent historical development of the family for an essential and necessary one and the normative subjectivity that is supposed to emerge from it as both possible and desirable. In the heteropatriarchal nuclear family, the dialogic context of mother–child becomes the central symbiotic dyad from which an autonomous self is supposed to emerge, but cannot. Conservative theorists have suggested that a child's autonomy from his or her mother is to be nurtured by ensuring that the marital coalition between husband and wife is the central dyad in a family and is not supplanted by an intergenerational mother–child alliance (see, e.g., Mann et al. 1990). In contrast, I have been suggesting that enabling a child's formation of self requires undoing the dyadic relations of self and other (whether inter- or intragenerational) that undermines a truly interactive and thus dialogical model of reality. When, for example, we replace the mother–child relation with a mothers (and others)–child(ren) relation, we enable a child's subjectivity (as well as a mother's subjectivity) to be reconfigured as constituted by a complex and interrelated set of relationships, "past and present, realized and sought" (Whitbeck 1989, 62). Such a subject is not isolated from its family relationships; neither, however, is it subsumed by any one of them.

A core advantage of childrearing within extended "chosen" families (whether configured by open adoption, separation and repartnerings, the inclusion of lovers, other mothers, friends and neighbors, or in some other way) is that they enable the emergence of a multifaceted subjectivity built *in relation to* rather than *in opposition to* others. The mere inclusion of diverse persons within one's chosen family will not, however, on its own, undo the self/other opposition that underlies much of Western liberalism and which emerges vividly in struggles between Western mothers and their adolescent children. Undoing this also requires that our dialogic practices refrain from straightening that which is queer—including what I have come to consider the potentially queer subjectivities of many teenage children in the contemporary Western world.

Mothering the Other

Spring 2007: Mothering her is impossible—or at least it feels that way. Yesterday, she phones me to bring her lunch at school because she can't possibly eat what is being served. She is fifteen and perfectly capable of making a lunch to take with her if she doesn't like the school lunches. But (on this occasion) I avoid the lecture and matter of factly explain that I am at work and cannot bring her lunch. She hangs up. Last week she didn't conform to dress code and I needed to bring her the appropriate pants. This took an hour out of my work-day—an hour and a half actually, if I count the time spent looking through the piles in her room for something identifiable as a pair of black pants. Two weeks prior to that, her school (a charter school for at-risk teens) called to inform me that she was refusing to remove her lip and nose piercings and that a parent would need to pick her up if she would not conform to code.

Today, Tomeka calls from school to inform me that her permission slip for the end-of-year field trip to a theme park was due a week ago. This is apparently my fault, although I've never seen the permission slip nor heard about the field trip before now. Can I come to the school to sign the relevant forms—now? I do, but don't successfully avoid lecturing her on being more responsible. As I am driving her home, I inquire about her summer plans as her father, other mothers, and I (and our family therapist) have agreed that she needs to do something besides hang out unsupervised with an equally at-risk peer group. She says she is going to get a job at the driving range, picking up balls. As we drive by the range on the way home, I pull in so she can get an application form. She swears at me, accuses me of

treating her like "a three-year-old," and refuses to get out of the car.
Once home, she pitches a fit about the fact that "there is no food in
the house" (the cupboards and fridge are full). Apparently, I am "poi-
soning her" by purchasing soy milk and brown eggs and too many
vegetables (much of which is a concession to her recently stated, but
short-lived, desire to be vegan) and demands that I buy her "some
fucking groceries in this lifetime" so that she doesn't "starve to death."

I accuse her of being utterly unreasonable. She accuses me of
being "a control freak." We are at an impasse that feels all too familiar.

I am, according to my daughters, more "strict" than their father. It
is true that I am more likely than their father to request (occasionally)
that they clean their bedrooms, to insist that they attend school, to ask
where they are going and when they will be home when they go out,
and to set curfews. I also remind them that I would like to see some
basic civility practiced in our home. I have "grounded" my daughters
either materially (by confining them to the house) or virtually (by taking
away their computer or phone privileges) when they fail to comply with
my rules. Moreover, I am the one who has been responsible (much to
my daughters' chagrin) for establishing counseling sessions for various
members and permutations of our family as we have dealt with issues
ranging from learning disabilities and truancy to depression, anxiety,
and antisocial behaviors. I was also the one who decided—after consulta-
tion with Tomeka's father and other mothers and a family therapist—to
enroll Tomeka in a school for at-risk students after numerous truancies,
detentions, suspensions, and expulsions during eighth grade at the local
public school. And, yet, I wouldn't identify myself as "controlling." (Of
course, no one ever does.) My standards on room cleanliness are pretty
low (namely that they refrain from growing biohazards in their rooms);
I have never insisted that my daughters earn "As" in school, merely
that they do their best; and I give my daughters considerable latitude
in choosing their friends and social activities (even when these choices
are different than those I wish they would make).

If I were to be cast in *Little House on the Prairie*, I would, I fear,
be typecast as Mrs. Oleson, mother of Laura's bratty classmate, Nellie
Oleson. Mrs. Oleson had no idea how to control her daughter and was
implicitly blamed for her daughter's narcissism, self-indulgence, and
general lack of manners—character vices presumed to be the result
of having been "spoiled rotten." Both of my daughters are capable
of bratty, narcissistic, and disrespectful behavior that my own mother

would not have tolerated (and many contemporary mothers still do not). I often wonder if I have been too lax with my daughters. Indeed, both my older daughter's birth mother and my partner frequently suggest that I am too easy with Tomeka (and also, perhaps, with Dakota) and that I should discipline her more firmly. Perhaps they are correct. By 2008, at sixteen years of age, Tomeka has dropped out of school (despite my cajolings, insistings, and groundings) and has had numerous (fortunately, minor) run-ins with the police. At home (when she is home and not off god-knows-where with god-knows-who), Tomeka is consistently angry and belligerent with me and any other family member who crosses her path. Dakota claims that she "cannot live with her [sister]" anymore and the "cannot" here betrays a desperation that goes beyond mere sibling rivalry. Living with anger as a constant toxic presence in our house is taking its toll on all of us. Tomeka, of course, returns her sister's antipathy, re-emphasizing that she does not want to live with any of us. And, yet, live together we must. (A quick glance at the expense of residential schools and counseling centers for Tomeka rules out this option and dividing my daughters into separate household residences seems not to be an option either: My ex-husband—now unemployed—cannot afford to take on either child full time; neither my partner nor my husband's partner is willing to become a primary caretaker for Tomeka and both of them live outside of Dakota's school district; although Tomeka's birth mother offers to take up guardianship of Tomeka at one point, this offer is later rescinded due to her own struggles as a single mother in the midst of a severe economic recession.)

At some point during her sixteenth year, I tell Tomeka that she needs to decide whether she (a) wants to be a part of our family—in which case she needs to abide by certain familial norms or (b) wants to simply treat our house as a hotel—in which case she may come and go as she pleases, but should not request anything of me (or others) besides basic shelter and food. She selects the second option. Although I subsequently spend much of my time feeling guilty about allowing her to be a street urchin, Tomeka still feels I am trying to control her life. She paints "FUCK YOU" in two-foot letters across the wall of her room, reiterating her now familiar demand to be "emancipated" from our family. I explain to her that no court is going to award her emancipated minor status given her total lack of income and bring her a bucket of paint and a brush to repaint her wall. The truth is, however, that I would like to be emancipated from these daily familial confrontations as well. We both begin silently counting down the months until she turns eighteen.

According to Shannon Winnubst (2006), liberalism configures freedom as an escape from limitations that is enabled in two ways: by the transgression of the boundaries that contain us as subjects and by the liberation from prohibitions that seek to regulate our behavior (18, 119). Boundaries are allegedly neutral limitations that serve to differentiate subjects from one another—separating and connecting us by the physical boundaries of our skin, the walls of our homes, our national borders, and so forth (as well as by the virtual boundaries created by our use of technologies). Prohibitions are acknowledged to be less than neutral as limitations that seek to shape our behavior and desires in particular ways (120). From a post-structuralist perspective, however, the two types of limits (and thus also our transgressions of them) are intimately intertwined. Foucault (1967, 1978, 1979), for example, explains how particular forms of subjectivity and particular types of bodies emerge from (and thus are not repressed by) particular forms of prohibition and discipline: The confinement of social outcasts in seventeenth-century Europe produced the subject characterized by madness or mental illness (with its increasingly fine-tuned psychiatric distinctions); the development of the prison and its related economy of punishment during the nineteenth century produced the juvenile delinquent (as well as a diversity of other criminal "types"); and the elaboration of Victorian taboos into a richly scientific discourse of sexuality produced the homosexual (as well as a host of other deviant sexual identities). It is through these and other definitions of non-normativity, Foucault contends, that the boundaries of the normative subject are established.

As Butler (1993) argues, the deviant subjectivities (identities) that circumscribe the boundaries of "bodies that matter" are themselves disavowed as subjects (as autonomous selves with the full rights of citizenship) through a process of their expulsion:

> This exclusionary matrix by which subjects are formed . . .
> requires the simultaneous production of a domain of abject
> beings, those who are not yet "subjects," but who form the
> constitutive outside to the domain of the subject. The abject
> designates here precisely those "unlivable" and "uninhabit-
> able" zones of social life which are nonetheless densely popu-
> lated by those who do not enjoy the status of the subject, but

whose living under the sign of the "unlivable" is required to circumscribe the domain of the subject. This zone of unin-habitability will constitute the defining limit of the subject's domain; it will constitute that site of dreaded identification against which—and by virtue of which—the domain of the subject will circumscribe its own claim to autonomy and to life. In this sense then, the subject is constituted through the force of exclusion and abjection, one which produces a constitutive outside to the subject, an abjected outside, which is, after all, "inside" the subject as its founding repu-diation. (3)

As Tomeka approaches the age of majority, I worry incessantly that she will find herself living in the "uninhabitable zones" that Butler describes, as one of those multitudes who "do not enjoy the status of the subject." It is not merely Tomeka's transgressions of prohibitions—both others and mine—that give rise to this worry. It is the *ways* in which she transgresses limits that is of concern. Whether one becomes the "right kind of subject"—or, indeed, whether one becomes a subject at all—depends not merely on whether one obeys or transgresses pro-hibitions but on whether one transgresses them in *appropriate* ways (Winnubst 121). There is, for example, a multitude of "appropriate" ways of missing school. Excusable absences may include attending a family member's funeral; participating in an academic, artistic, or ath-letic competition; or being sick. It is not the act of missing school itself, nor even the repetition of such acts that produce a deviant sub-jectivity. (My younger daughter sometimes misses classes for other scheduled academic or extracurricular activities and student-athletes do this repeatedly without being marked as deviant.) It is the *inap-propriateness* of one's transgressions from which a deviant subjectivity emerges. If one violates the prohibition on school absences (as Tomeka has) because one would rather sleep or party or simply because one is "sick of school," one becomes marked as a truant and expelled (tem-porarily or permanently) from the student body.

As queer theorist José Muñoz (1999) explains, drawing on the work of linguist Michel Pêcheux (1982), there are three modes in which a subject may be constructed by ideological practices: identi-fication with discursive and ideological forms (the "Good Subject"); counteridentification or rebellion against the identificatory sites offered by dominant norms (the "Bad Subject"); and disindentification with dominant ideologies (wherein one neither opts to assimilate within dominant structures nor does one strictly oppose them) (11). I concur with Muñoz that "working on and against" normative ideologies by trying to transform cultural logics from within (disidentification) is a political strategy preferable both to "buckling under the pressures of dominant ideology" (identification) and to "attempting to break free of its inescapable sphere" (counteridentification) (11–12).[1] Thus, it is much to my dismay that, during their adolescence, my daughters appear to have positioned themselves respectively as the "good child" (Dakota) and the "bad child" (Tomeka).

Dakota's claim to be "good" emphasizes the fact that she succeeds academically and gives me (relatively) little trouble, typically conforming—or at least pretending to conform—to the rules set by me, her other mothers (including her friends' mothers), her father, her teachers, or others. In situating herself as the "bad child," Tomeka resists every norm that I or any other adult might (attempt to) impose. The difficulty with Dakota's "good girl" strategy is her uncritical identification with structures of power and domination. The difficulty with Tomeka's "bad girl" strategy is that she does not (yet) recognize that counteridentification simply "validates the dominant ideology" through marking its boundaries by deviance (Muñoz 11). Part of me, I confess, sometimes admires my elder daughter's chutzpah. As someone who (like my younger daughter) felt frequently compelled to live up to the image of the good girl during my youth, I sometimes silently applaud Tomeka's willingness to resist social norms and authorities. At the same time, I am appalled and ashamed to be cast in the role of the bad mother—both by the social authorities my daughter defies and by my daughter herself (no doubt, a remnant of my desire to be a good girl). And I agonize about what will become of Tomeka in a society that punishes, marginalizes, or ignores those who do not conform to its regulatory norms. I hope that she will learn (before she ends up in a permanently uninhabitable zone such as addiction, homelessness, or prison—which are the stuff of my maternal nightmares) that strategies of counteridentification unwittingly replicate the very systems that one hopes to counter.

For now, however, resolute in her conviction that no one else has the right to "be the boss of [her]," Tomeka alternates between scoffing at and swearing at each authority who dares to curtail her freedom. When her psychiatrist chides her for not taking her medications as prescribed, Tomeka accuses her of being "fucking stupid." When her teacher insists she actually write something on the examination paper that has been circulated, Tomeka crushes the paper into a ball and throws it at her teacher. When the police bring her home for breaking curfew, Tomeka laughs at their "stupid laws." On one evening, an officer leaves my home with the parting words, "I pity you, ma'am." His pity mirrors that which I have received from Tomeka's schoolteachers and guidance counselors at myriad parent–teacher conferences scheduled to address her truancy and other misbehaviors. Such pity is preferable to blame, but it comes at a cost—sympathy for me is usually correlated with the judgment that my daughter is no good (which is, of course, precisely how she has chosen to situate her identity). My failures to control her or to be able to reason with her are interpreted as caused by traits intrinsic to Tomeka's character; she is uncontrollable, ungovernable, and incorrigible.

All mothers have been taught to blame ourselves for our children's perceived deficits. Mothers are typically held responsible for their children's behavior; thus, if a child is bad, the mother is presumed to be bad also. This correlation of child and maternal profiling plays itself out most obviously in cultural depictions of mothers and children of color and in cultural stereotypes of low-income mothers and their children (depictions and stereotypes that frequently intersect). As Patricia Hill Collins (1990) notes, the failures of black children to succeed at school as well as their disproportionate representation among the incarcerated frequently has been blamed on the perceived inadequacies of the black matriarch (76). Similarly, welfare and other low-income mothers have been blamed for passing on a culture of poverty to their children, including the vices of laziness and overbreeding (Douglas and Michaels 2004).

I am thus surprised, amid this culture of mother-blaming, to discover that others do not (always) blame me for my child's behavior. In fact, I am often awarded the benefit of the doubt by the authorities that my daughter defies because of my race, class, and professional status combined with my dutiful participation in school activities and polite engagement with authorities (many of whom are, no doubt, unaware that I am both divorced and queer).[2] Because I appear to fit the profile of a "good mother," they do not immediately assume that I am the cause of my daughter's defiant behavior. The difficulty is that authorities seem to presume that if mothering (nurture) isn't the root of my daughter's bad behavior, then it must be attributable to my daughter's own nature (an inference that blocks from vision a whole host of other factors that could be implicated in a child's rebellious behavior).

Much to my chagrin, the likelihood of this profiling of my child as a "bad seed" increases when authorities discover that she is an adopted child (presumed to have inherited bad genes and/or to have been permanently scarred by her separation from her biological mother). Scientific research on adoption and crime indicating a genetic basis for criminal behavior supports the "bad seed" theory of my daughter's behavior (see, e.g., Brennan et al. 1996). So too do depictions of adopted children in popular culture. Consider, for example, the outright evil embodied by adopted children in films such as *The Omen* or more recently *Orphan*. Even in the television series, *Little House on the Prairie*, it was the adopted child, Albert, who—although far from evil—was the most likely of all of the Ingalls' children to get into trouble. These days, however, my daughter's adoptive status is largely overshadowed by the fact of her developmental status. I am frequently the object of pity (rather than blame) simply because my child is a teenager.

For more than a century, those studying adolescence have interpreted it as a stressful and crisis-ridden time characterized by symptoms such as violence, rebellion and other forms of antisocial behavior, egoism, narcissism, self-indulgence, contradiction, primitive anxiety, depression, sexual and bodily disturbance, perversity, and promiscuity.[3] Some have even likened adolescence to schizophrenia, neurosis, or borderline personality disorder (see, e.g., Kernberg 1984; Sullivan 1953). The list of "symptoms" used to pathologize adolescence closely mirror stereotypes of sexual queers. For example, the notion that adolescents suffer from "sexual and bodily disturbance" has a close parallel in psychiatric diagnoses of gender-identity disorder as applied to transgender, transsexual, and even gay and lesbian individuals. The notion that adolescence is characterized by "perversity and promiscuity" parallels criticisms of those adults who refuse to contain their sexual pleasure to the confines of heterosexual, monogamous couplings. And the notion that adolescents are narcissistic and immature closely mirrors criticisms of sexual queers as people who refuse to "grow up" and "settle down." Unlike queerness, however, which is frequently viewed by dominant ideologies as a (bad) choice, adolescence functions as a biological explanation (an explanation in terms of "natural" developmental, neurological, and/or hormonal causes) that allows white, middle-class children who are rebellious, like the white, middle-class mothers who kill their children, to be seen as "mad" rather than "bad."

Like infanticide, youth crime and deviance is a constant source of fascination for the media[4] and a similar dynamic operates in explaining it.

Because heteropatriarchal constructions of motherhood cannot countenance the notion that a good mother would produce a bad child, children from "good families" (i.e., white, middle-class households) who come into contact with the juvenile justice system are likely to be excused as mentally unstable (and thus referred to counseling rather than detention centers). Adolescence provides just such an excuse. While childhood is viewed as a time of innocence and dependence, a time when children are in need of protection and training, adolescence is "*expected* to be an age of deviance, disruption, and wickedness" (Brown 1998, 3). Raging hormones, anger, depression, and a variety of symptoms that have caused psychologists to liken adolescence to borderline personality disorder, schizophrenia, and other disorders are viewed as a sort of temporary madness over which neither mothers, nor the children themselves, have much control.[5] As Winnicott (1963) suggests, there is only "one real cure for adolescence" and that is "the passage of time" (79).

The pity that I receive from various authorities and the empathy I receive from other mothers of teenagers help me to maintain my own sanity during my children's adolescence (as do the little blue pills that my doctor prescribes for me). Yet, the core problems that pervade my home and family remain unresolved. At sixteen years old, with an eighth-grade education and no employment prospects, Tomeka drops out of school. She also drops out of counseling, art lessons, music lessons, and our family. She refuses to take medications for attention deficit disorder or for depression and increasingly self-isolates. When at home, she sleeps most of the day, exiting her bedroom only to forage for food or to complain that we have none. We correspond by notes left on the kitchen table (when she is home) or by text message (when she is not). We rarely have an in-person conversation anymore and when we do, they are rarely pleasant interchanges.

We are each other's Other and neither one of us likes the vision of ourselves that we see through the other's eyes. I am a teacher and a scholar. I love books, theatre, and public radio. I am self-disciplined, hard working, punctual, and conscientious. I am quiet and (usually—or at least I used to be) gentle and patient. Against these standards that I set for myself, Tomeka can, I suspect, only see herself as a failure. She hates school and does not have the attention span for books or plays or news commentaries. She lacks discipline, avoids work, is oblivious to deadlines, and rarely shows up anywhere on time. She is loud and uncensored and (often, although not always) angry and impatient. Put in more positive terms, however, Tomeka is a free spirit (and a quite "normal" teenager). She loves talking on the phone, social networking, hanging out with her friends, and listening to loud music. She is an artist who likes to paint on the walls of her room and create her own drama; she does not believe in coloring inside the lines or following someone else's script. She is a stand-up comic with a caustic wit. She is spontaneous. She is self-expressive. She prefers feeling to thinking. Against *these* standards, I suspect I would be viewed as (and that Tomeka does view me as) a failure. I am introverted, stoic, and more comfortable reasoning than emoting. I live a life governed by deadlines and responsibilities with less room than I might like for spontaneity. I have little patience for drama that is not performed on a stage; I cannot draw, and although I read music competently, I lack the ability to create or improvise a song.

How, then, do we meet each other as mother and daughter?

The Mother as Other

According to Julia Kristeva (1982), the child must abject the maternal, the object that has created him or her, in order to become a subject. Drawing on Lacan's (1977) model of psychosexual development, but providing a more central place for the maternal in her explanation of the subject's psychosexual development, Kristeva suggests that the prelinguistic infant becomes a linguistic subject through the process of abjection. In its earliest stage of development (what Kristeva calls "the chora"), the infant does not distinguish itself from its mother or even the world around it, ingesting everything around it without acknowledgment of boundaries. (This is the stage, according to Lacan, that one is closest to "the Real" or the pure materiality of existence.) During the next stage of an infant's development, the infant begins to establish boundaries between itself and the maternal, thereby creating boundaries between self and other that must, according to Kristeva, be established as a precondition for language. She says:

> The abject confronts us . . . within our personal archeology, with our earliest attempts to release the hold of *maternal* entity even before ex-isting outside of her, thanks to the autonomy of language. It is a violent, clumsy breaking away, with the constant risk of falling back under the sway of a power as securing as it is stifling. (13)

Kristeva views this stage of abjection as *"a precondition of narcissism"* (13) or the subsequent mirror stage of development. During the mirror stage, the young child identifies with its own image (Lacan's "Ideal-I" or "ideal ego"). This simplified, bounded (idealized) version of the self establishes the grounds for what becomes the creation of phantasies in the fully developed subject by establishing the "imaginary order" (Lacan 1977) that allows the subject to enter the symbolic order. As the child acquires language, he or she is yet further separated from the Real (both the material world outside oneself and one's own internal chaos). The mirror stage, as well as our entry into the symbolic order, is, however, troubled by the subject's relation to the abject, which is its necessary founding condition:

> The more or less beautiful image in which I behold or recognize myself rests upon an abjection that sunders it as soon as repression, the constant watchman, is relaxed. . . . Abjection is therefore a kind of *narcissistic crisis.*" (13–14)

Because abjection is the repudiating condition that grounds both subjective identity and the symbolic order, and because it never ceases to challenge both, the boundary that separates the subject from its abject is "permanently brittle" and subject to periodic disintegration (13). The brittleness of the boundaries of subjectivity presents a challenge to those who—like children striving to become adults—wish to become real. (As the skin-horse advises the velveteen rabbit, becoming real does not happen for "people who break easily.") Arguably, adolescence is a period in which the brittleness and instability of subjective identity is pronounced. As Denis Flynn (2004) suggests, "[a] normal transition through adolescence involves some measure of disturbance . . . [and] alternating periods of integration and disintegration" (175).

The struggles with both subjective identity and the symbolic order experienced during adolescence suggest, although Kristeva herself does not, a connection between adolescence and abjection.[6] As literary theorist Carol Coats (2004) notes, the concepts of adolescence and abjection are both structurally and logically compatible (142–47). In psychoanalytic terms, adolescence requires "a conscious reinscription of the body" or a redrawing of the boundaries of the self. This reimagining of oneself as a sexual body requires a movement from disgust to eroticism as the bodily crevices and orifices that emit and accept fluids are no longer disowned as abject but accepted as part of one's erotic self. Adolescence also requires a resetting of the boundaries between self and other. In attempting to re-establish or rediscover an "Ideal 'I,'" the adolescent faces questions of alienation (who he or she is not) and identification (who he or she is or will be). These renegotiations of the boundaries of the self, moreover, take place within a context characterized by the reintensification of conflicts between law (prohibitions) and desire. Parental controls are loosening and yet the adolescent is apt to feel pressured by "diffuse and conflicting demands and prohibitions from everywhere all the time" (Coats 145). Insofar as the narcissistic crisis that Kristeva identifies with abjection is caused by "two seemingly contradictory causes," namely, *too much strictness on the part of the Other*" combined with the *"lapse of the other"* (1982, 14), one could expect that crisis to be resurrected during adolescence.

On the social level, adolescence, like abjection, "breaches and challenges boundaries" (Coats 142). As Coats indicates, adolescence is an "in-between time" where what the subject believes about children is challenged, as is what he or she hopes for and values in maturity. Coats aptly describes the challenge of adolescence as "trying to become an adult without becoming adulterated" (142). Although meeting this challenge cries out for strategies of disidentification, the adolescent frequently forges his or her identity through strategies of identification and counteridentification. Striving for social recognition from her peers but not wishing to stand out, the adolescent (as constructed in the developmental chronology of the contemporary western world) "seek[s] the terms of individuation within affiliative groupings," while "reaffirming her distance from the socially abject" (143). As Coats suggests:

> Under the logic of abjection, my identity depends on gathering to me those who bolster my illusion of totality (that is, those who are like me), and pushing away those people who remind me of my difference, my lack. . . . As long as I can [counteridentify] with the not-me, I can maintain a benevolent distance. But when I begin to realize it could be or is me, I have to readjust my distance and benevolence because of the intrusion of the Real. (155)[7]

When my daughter says that her friends are her family, she announces subjective boundaries based on an affiliative identification with those who are like her (those who enjoy the same music and share her sense of fashion and her flair for the dramatic). When she says (screams, writes, paints) "fuck you" at home, she is not only (re)establishing clear boundaries between herself and the maternal but is also (emphatically) refusing to assimilate herself to the social norms I value by rejecting any and all prohibitions and limitations I might seek to impose. She is thus simultaneously abjecting me (as that which haunts and disrupts the borders of her subjectivity) *and* indicating her own willingness to persist as an abject Other (who haunts and disrupts the borders of my subjectivity). As a subject emerging from abjection, she views me as a "control freak." The language of "control" captures the fact that I am (whether my prohibitions are strict or not) attempting to interpellate her into a subject position of subjugation ("as long as you are living under my roof, you WILL clean your room"), a subject position that Tomeka consistently resists.[8] The language of "freak" is equally important, however, as this characterization of me speaks not to limits in the sense of prohibitions that I impose on her, but instead to the boundaries of her subjectivity itself. The freak or freakish is that which is "not-me," that which repulses and must be expelled from the self. In casting me as a freak, she counteridentifies with me as her abject Other.[9]

Because, for my part, I do not see myself as a "control freak" (my response to this is to say that this is "not me"), I find my daughter's words, actions, and emotions unintelligible. She is, I conjecture, "unreasonable." I do not know how to engage such unreason. It makes me anxious; it makes me angry; it paralyzes me. I want to eject this otherness from my home, from my life, but I cannot. She is a minor; I am responsible for her. More than this, however, I am her mother (regardless of her age) and thus defined in relation to her at the same time as I find myself in opposition to her. She does, indeed, haunt the borders of my subjectivity. Phenomenologically, Kristeva's description of what it feels like to be "beset by abjection," is an apt description of my predicament:

> [W]hat is abject, the jettisoned object, . . . draws me toward the place where meaning collapses. . . . It lies outside, beyond the set, and does not seem to agree to the [superego's] rules of the game. And, yet, from its place of banishment, the abject does not cease challenging its master. . . . it is a brutish suffering that "I" puts up with, sublime and devastated, . . . I endure it. . . . A massive, opaque and for-

gotten life, now harries me as radically separate, loathsome. Not me. Not that. But not nothing, either. . . . A weight of meaninglessness, about which there is nothing insignificant, and which crushes me. (1–2)

This meaninglessness has political as well as phenomenological implications, as Kristeva's language of tolerance ("I endure it") indicates. As Winnubst notes, those of us living in late modernity "habitually live in the space of assumed reason," granting privilege to that which is meaningful and criticizing (epistemologically, morally and politically) that which is meaningless (139). Too often, our disavowals of meaninglessness (viewed as a lack of reason) take the form of projecting our anxieties "onto raced and sexed Others," Winnubst cautions (139). This, of course, precisely parallels what I do when—rather than engaging the space of my home as "a space in which meanings are endlessly contested" (139)—I project my anxieties onto my daughter, contending that *she* is unreasonable. Although I do not attach her unreason to her race or her sex, I do seek to resolve my anxieties through abjection. In order for me to retain my belief (hope?) that I am a good mother (and thus am the "right kind of subject"), I infer that *she* must be the problem. I take her to psychologists and psychiatrists and counseling, hoping that through talk therapy or medications or behavior-modification techniques or in some other way, she can be "managed." This is the colonizing impulse, the desire to render the other less threatening by bringing her in line with one's own sensibilities through strategies of containment and prohibition. When containment and prohibition strategies do not work, I fall back on the strategy that Flynn (2004) notes is commonly used by the parents of teenagers, namely, enduring my situation while wishing adolescence would "just go away" (176). This is the position of tolerance, a begrudging acceptance of the other's difference mixed with the hope that one will not have to "put up with" that difference any longer than necessary.

It is tempting to make excuses for myself here. My intentions have been good. I have been attempting to act in the "best interests of my child." I have been trying to protect her, to provide her with opportunities, to prevent her from becoming a socially abject Other. All of this is true. But it is also true that I am among those who have abjected her. In recognizing the parallels between my engagement with my daughter and what Winnubst calls "the twin politics of colonialism and tolerance" (122), I re-learn a lesson I already knew (or thought I knew): the personal *is* political. Far from the idyllic notion of home yearned for by social conservatives and critiqued by many feminist, queer, and other critical theorists, family may be the place wherein we are *most* directly challenged to remain open to the Other.

Home and/as Coalition

There's no place like home

—Dorothy, in *The Wizard of Oz*

In *Democracy and the Foreigner*, political scientist Bonnie Honig (2001) observes that we are frequently ambivalent about the notion of home, torn between "home-yearning" on the one hand (desiring a place where "people know me and I can just be me") and, on the other hand, "escape" from home (desiring a place where I can never "just be"; where my sense of self is continually challenged and expanded) (xiv). This ambivalence is, she suggests, aptly illustrated in *The Wizard of Oz*. Dorothy leaves home because (like many adolescents) she feels her family doesn't understand her and has mistreated her. Her aunt and uncle have allowed Ms. Gulch (a personification of unjust prohibitions) to take away her beloved dog, Toto, and then—exacerbating the injury—they have ignored her anger and sorrow, sending her away ("not now, Dorothy") in order to concentrate on their preparations for an impending twister. Dorothy also leaves home, however, because farm life in Kansas is dull (as emphasized by the lack of color in the start of the film); Dorothy seeks adventure and the challenge of the new. In searching for a new home, Dorothy does encounter the challenges of the new; Oz is certainly more colorful than Kansas and full of unexpected creatures and dangers. However, Dorothy also discovers that Oz is neither safer nor more just than her childhood home. Indeed, Ms. Gulch is simply re-embodied in Oz as the wicked witch against whom the bureaucratic wizard is ineffectual and the munchkins are powerless (Honig 2001, xiii). After correcting Oz's injustices herself, Dorothy thus seeks to return to Kansas.

Honig suggests that this narrative illustrates the inadequacies of both nostalgia for home as a place of origin (the protective procreative family, community, or homeland of our birth) *and* of the desire for home as destination (a family, community, or nation of "choice" where we imagine we will find unconditional acceptance, "just as we are"). The ambivalence of our longing for a home of origin while yearning for a new home is captured, Honig observes, by Dorothy's claim in *The Wizard of Oz* that "there's no place like home" (see also Rushdie 2008). On the one hand, this can be read as a yearning for home ("there's no place like *home*," followed by a wistful sigh). On this common reading, home is positioned as a "unique, wonderful and irreplaceable" place to which nothing else can compare. Alternatively, however, Dorothy's words can be read with a different intonation and meaning ("there's *no place* like home"), indicating that there *is nowhere* that lives up to our mythological dream of home—including home itself (xiii). It is this latter reading that Honig recommends, suggesting that *both* nostalgic yearnings for an earlier form of home and family that was unitary in its needs and concerns *and* the desire for a future form of home and family that will be unified and unconditionally accepting of us are premised on a version of home, self, and family more imaginary than real.

Bernice Johnson Reagon (1983), in her well-known article, "Coalition Politics," likewise advocates that we abandon the yearning for home as a place of unity, harmony, and unconditional acceptance. Contrasting the space of coalition politics to that of a home, Reagon notes that the space of coalition is not a safe or nurturing space where unsettling differences can be locked out. Distinguishing nurturing work from the important but risky work of coalition building, Reagon suggests "[c]oalition work is not work done in your home. Coalition work has to be done in the streets. And it is some of the most dangerous work you can do" (359).[10] This distinction between political coalitions (as sites of unsettling difference and danger) and the home (as a safe retreat from political struggle) is reiterated in many subsequent feminist and queer critiques of identity politics. Martin and Mohanty (1986), for example, suggest the home is a place of containment and entrapment that suppresses difference. Similarly, Teresa De Lauretis (1990a) advocates "leaving or giving up a place that is safe, that is 'home'—physically, emotionally, linguistically, epistemologically—for another place that is unknown and risky," depicting family, self, and home as "held together by the exclusions and repression that enable any ideology of the same" (22). Likewise, Jenny Bourne (1987) and Ien Ang (1995) argue against political "homelands" that stifle genuine political engagement by seeking commonality and absorbing difference.

These critiques of "home" reflect conservative ideals of the home as the place where we can "batten the windows and block out the noise" (Mahanay 2009), as a "refuge and sanctuary from the troubled world we live in" (Call 1997). They also reflect the nostalgic musings of male philosophers on the home as an uncontested space, safe from the risks and dangers of the outside world. Male theorists frequently have spoken of houses, homes, and dwellings as places of shelter, security, belonging, and pleasure. Likening human inhabitance of homes to birds in nests and other animals in their shelters, Gaston Bachelard (1994), for example, speaks of the sense of "well-being" and "contentment" that creatures feel when huddled in their "refuge" where they are "concealed" from potential dangers outside their home (91–95). For Heidegger (1927), anxiety (where the world feels alien and other) is incompatible with feeling at home; that which is strange or "uncanny" is viewed as the opposite of home—a place characterized by that which is customary, familiar and secure (176).

As social geographer Linda McDowell (1999) suggests, such theorists "seem to be harking back to a pre-industrial idyll" (72)—a Victorian vision of home such as that advanced by John Rushkin (1867) who speaks of the "true nature of home," as follows:

> [I]t is the place of peace—the shelter not only from all injury, but from all terror, doubt and division. Insofar as it is not this, it is not home; in so far as the anxieties of the outer life penetrate into it, and the inconsistently minded, unknown, unloved, or hostile society of the outer world is allowed by either husband or wife to cross the threshold, it ceases to become home. (82)

As Rushkin's description illustrates, during the industrial era the home became an idealized place viewed as the primary locus of love, empathy, and care. Such conceptions of home as a place of respite from the outside world deny the labor and struggle that "[go] into constructing and maintaining a dwelling, turning a house into a home," thus erasing the gendered (and also frequently classed and raced) politics of homemaking (McDowell 1999, 72). In thinking about the familiar and the familial (if they do so at all), male philosophers are able to romanticize the home by virtue of keeping it at a safe distance, close enough to see but not close enough to disrupt. Ahmed (2006) notes that Husserl, for example, speaks of the domestic world that takes place around him as he writes—the veranda, the garden, and the children in the summerhouse—as "yonder." His peace and well-being as he sits at his desk depends, it seems, on being surrounded by—yet *undistracted* by—the noise and work of the familiar, that is, home (28–31). Clearly, Husserl's writing was not interrupted by angry teenagers storming into the house complaining that he was starving them. Nor, it seems, were Bachelard's, Heidegger's or Rushkin's contemplations ever marred by incessant fretting about the whereabouts and well-being of their adolescent daughters.

Unlike their male counterparts, feminists contemplating the home have recognized the labor involved in housework and child care. From Charlotte Perkins Gilman's (1898) criticisms of the domestic slavery of women to Judy Syfers' (1971) classic essay "Why I want a Wife" and beyond, feminists have highlighted the gendered division of labor that goes into making a house a home. Critical race theorists and socialist feminists have further noted the ways in which the division of labor that supports homemaking is frequently raced and classed (see, e.g., Collins 1990; Rio 2008). Feminist emphasis on "the personal as political" further emphasized the physical, emotional and sexual abuse that women and girls have suffered in families (see, e.g., Dworkin 1989). Lesbians, gays, and queers, like feminists, have frequently viewed the home as a site of gender and sexual oppression—a place frequently characterized by the toxicity of the closet, the threat (or actuality) of exile, a place one needed to escape in order to be free. As these feminist and queer critiques of the family were becoming commonplace, postcolonial theorists were offering incisive analyses of "homelands," including scathing critiques of nationalistic identities as forged by the abjection of foreign Others. Before 9-11, the domestic policies as well as the foreign policies of overdeveloped nations were already being theorized as procuring the "safety and security" (and comfort and privilege) of white, Anglophone subjects by the exploitation and exclusion of racialized Others (depicted as dangerous intruders against whom "our home" needed to be defended) (see, e.g., Ang 1995; McClintock et al. 1997). Given the feminist emphasis on women's confinement, exploitation, and abuse in the home and the queer emphasis on gay's and lesbian's invisibility and oppression within families based on conceptions of normative sameness, combined with postcolonial critiques of the exclusion, subjugation, exploitation, and oppression of racial and ethnic minorities by normative conceptions of citizenship, it is not surprising that by the late twentieth century, many scholars and activists began critiquing the desire for home as a dangerous fantasy built on the repression and exclusion of difference. When Reagon cautions us not to "get comfortable" in our "little barred room" (where we have locked out difference) because we "cannot survive there," she draws on feminist understandings of home as a carceral institution in which women have been imprisoned (358). When, using a different metaphor to characterize the home, Reagon suggests that we cannot (and should not attempt to) retreat to the "womb" or look for "a bottle with some milk in it and a nipple," she evokes the sense that the desire for home is childish and immature. Thus, for Reagon, the desire for home stands directly opposed to the "old-age perspective" needed to build successful political coalitions across differences of gender, sexuality, and race (348).[11]

Reagon's essay (based on a presentation to the 1981 West Coast Women's Music Festival) addresses the false unity and violence of exclusions enforced by particular normative (in this case, white and lesbian) definitions of "woman" held by feminist organizers and many attendees. In this context, she is speaking specifically about how such normative definitions of "woman" make her (a straight, black woman) uncomfortable—or less than "at home" in this space—and, moreover, how her presence (as well as the presence of others who differ from radical feminist norms) unsettle normative understandings of "woman," thus making the "women-only" gathering at which she speaks feel less safe and less nurturing than it had been prior to the admission of those who were different. Critics of nationalism explore a similar dynamic within the politics of the multicultural nation. "Foreigners" and immigrants frequently feel less than completely "at home" within a nation that defines citizenship in terms that normatively exclude them—and the nation they have joined, in turn, feels less safe than previously with these "different" citizens present (a point that is particularly pertinent in the United States post 9-11). I do not disagree with these analyses. Nor do I disagree with the claim that in order to overcome these violations and exclusions, we will need to be willing to stretch beyond our comfort zones and take risks. I am troubled, however, by the implications of such arguments that "home" represents a refuge or retreat from difficult political work. In particular, I am troubled by the claim—made explicit by Reagon, but implicit in many critiques of identity politics overlapping with her own— that "it is very important not to confuse . . . home and coalition" (360).

I find the distinction between home and coalition troubling for several reasons. First, the distinction raises difficulties for our understanding of political coalitions. For example, I find it unlikely that political coalitions can be maintained for any duration unless *some* degree of safety and trust is present—which means that successful political coalitions require some of the central attributes of our ideal of home. We need to think about ways to engage difference in the public sphere by creating (relatively) safe spaces in which it is possible to take risks. Second, and more crucial to the present discussion, the distinction between home and coalition raises difficulties for our understanding of homes. I agree with Iris Young (1997) that there may be aspects of the ideal of home that are worth reclaiming (and reconstructing). Certainly, children need places that are (relatively) safe and where they can feel loved. But it is not children alone who need this. We all do, if we are to continue to grow and develop and reach Reagon's "age-old perspective" (where we are not merely "little meager human-body-mouth-talking all the time") (Reagon 352). Yet, there is a parallel between the ways in which particular normative definitions of "woman" or "straight" or "citizen" impose a false unity accompanied by the violence of exclusion and the ways in which normative definitions of "home" as a "womb-like" refuge impose a false unity accompanied by the violence of exclusion. By uncritically replicating the conservative ideal of the home in feminist, queer, antiracist, and postcolonial politics, we reify the very distinction between private and public domains we wish to counter. We also erase (as do conservatives) the wide variety of ways in which people create, inhabit, and think about homes.

I certainly do not experience my home as a refuge from the outside world characterized by homogeneity and comfort. My home is spread out over cities, counties, and countries. Moreover, the persons who inhabit my home shift and change—both in the sense that there are not the same persons here, wherever "here" is, at all times *and* in the sense that each individual member of my family changes over time (sometimes, in the case of menopausal mothers and moody teenagers, within the space of a few minutes). Difference thus marks my home not merely in the sense of diversities of group identity (e.g., age, gender, ethnicity, or class), but also in terms of the complexity of each individual's subjective identity—including mine—as it fluctuates and changes in the material (and virtual) presence of others. Because my home is a site of ongoing movement, difference and negotiation (both materially and socially/psychologically), I do not equate being at home with feeling complacent or settled. Indeed, I frequently experience "home" as more akin to a site of political struggle than to a womb.

I suspect that most homes—and not just my own—are sites of political negotiations requiring adjustments, flexibility, and compromise among diversely situated subjectivities. Clearly this is the case in the postmodern Western family, characterized as it is by commuter relationships, divorce, remarriage, and a variety of fragmented and reconstituted families. Such homes will inevitably involve some degree of conflict and difference and thus the ability of a home's inhabitants to shift their perspectives (and quite often their material bodies and possessions as well) to meet one other. The idea of home as an uncomplicated refuge from political struggle makes even less sense when applied to postcolonial families who have been geographically dispersed or displaced by enslavement, war, or poverty. Many of these families, including those that have migrated to the West, struggle with internal tensions linked to the opposing values of cultural tradition and westernization or modernization (L. Ahmed 1999). Home is certainly complicated by the politics of class (and frequently race) for women of any nationality employed as domestic workers, especially if they reside in the same place they work (Stasiulus and Bakan 1997). Indeed, the lists of political struggles that may complicate home are practically endless. Even within the traditional, nuclear Western family home defended by conservatives one would expect differences to arise among its inhabitants. As Honig (1996) conjectures:

> [A]s anyone with siblings must know and as spouses in all domestic situations can surely attest, the practice of teaming up with someone who could possibly kill you is not the opposite of home; it perfectly captures one of the defining features of family life itself. What children and/or spouses do not establish temporary alliances with and against each other? (268)

Honig thus suggests that we need to "resignify home as a coalitional arrangement," thereby "accepting the impossibility of the conventional home's promised safety from conflict, dilemmas and difference" (270). I agree wholeheartedly that home is best thought of as related to, rather than opposed to, coalition building. At the same time, I want to avoid claiming that all homes are, by virtue of internal conflicts and differences, thereby coalitional. I do think that all homes are invested with political struggle (they are not places of unity providing respite from such struggles), but these struggles can take different forms. Sometimes the home is invested with the politics of colonization (the attempt to suppress, repress, or exclude difference), sometimes with the liberal politics of tolerance (the begrudging acceptance of difference), and only sometimes with the politics of coalition (the commitment to engage difference as a positive force of challenge and growth). Nonetheless, Honig certainly points us in the right direction by highlighting the difficulties with imaginary versions of home premised on unity. The home should not be remembered or imagined as free from the "power relations that entangle every home" (Sabra 2008, 90).

To see, rather than ignore, familial power relations is to recognize that our home (and indeed every home) is "unhomely" (Bhabha 1992). When we uncover the hidden or repressed political histories (of, e.g., sexism, racism, heterosexism, and colonialism) that characterize our homelands and domestic spaces, the public (world) and private (home), as Bhaba suggests, "collapse into each other," giving rise to the uncanny sense that our home is not really a home. He describes this moment of recognition as follows:

> To be unhomed is not to be homeless, nor can the "unhomely" be easily accommodated in that familiar division of social life into private and public spheres. . . . [T]he home does not remain the domain of domestic life, nor does the world simply become its social and historical counterpart. The unhomely is the shock of recognition of the world-in-the-home, the home-in-the-world. (141)

This is the shock of recognition that Minnie Bruce Pratt (1984) encounters when she comes to understand "the limits that [she] lived within" as a white child raised in the racially segregated southern United States and "how much [her] memory and [her] experience of a safe space to be was based on places secured by omission, exclusion, or violence, and [her] submitting to the limits of that place" (26). It is also the shock of recognition I feel when I see (really see) for the first time that the political strategies of colonialism and tolerance are not merely "out there" in the world but are being replicated *inside* my own home *by me*. I have been "domesticating difference" by trying to control and manage it (Honig 1996, 257). But, as Honig suggests, to take difference seriously is to see conflict as "inescapable" and "ungovernable":

[U]ngovernability is precisely what difference threatens us with. To take difference . . . seriously . . . is to affirm the inescapability of conflict and the ineradicability of resistance to the political and moral projects of ordering subjects, institutions, and values. Moreover, it requires that we recast the task of democratic theory, and move it beyond that of simply orchestrating multiple and conflicting group needs and towards a new responsiveness to that first task's tendency to involve democratic cultures and institutions in violent and resentful dynamics of identity/difference. It is to give up on the dream of a place called home, a place free of power, conflict and struggle, a place—an identity, a form of life, a group vision—unmarked or unriven by difference and untouched by the power brought to bear on it by the identities that strive to ground themselves in its place (258)

Although Honig is speaking here of communities and nations, her remarks become applicable to rethinking familial homes when we recognize the collapse of the public and the private into each other. In familial homes, as in nations, ungovernability is precisely "what difference threatens us with." My daughter is ungovernable. But this is not a fact about her; it is a fact about difference itself. In families, as in the polis, conflict is "inescapable" and resistance is "ineradicable." This means that we need to recast the task of mothering—like the task of democratic governance—as something more than "orchestrating" the needs of diverse and conflicting subjects (or groups of subjects) and respond instead to the ways in which such attempts to orchestrate and govern replicate "violent and resentful dynamics of identity/difference." What might maternal thinking and practice look like if we "give up on the dream of a place called home, a place free of power, conflict and struggle"?

7

Queering Familial Solidarity

Polymaternalism and Polygamy

May 2010: It is Mother's Day. I am having lunch with my partner and visiting friends from Switzerland. My own daughters are not with me (I will be driving to their father's house after lunch to meet them for a movie date). Our lunch companions have a preschool-aged child with them, however, and our conversation turns toward parenting. When they inquire what life with teenagers is like, my partner responds, "like boot camp." Although this is a view I've been known to espouse before, in hindsight I regret this view of life with my daughters and suggest that I have begun to think about it as more closely aligned to the difficult work of coalition building.

What does it mean to think of a family as a site of coalition? In speaking of coalitional families, I attribute to them three primary characteristics. First, such familial assemblages are characterized by multiplicity (or what Honig calls "ineradicable difference"). This is an *ontological* characteristic of coalitional families—a fact about the nature of their *reality*. The reality of multiplicity is most pronounced in complicated families that require the ongoing coordination of multiple households and diverse groups of people. However, as I also have suggested, multiplicity may be a characteristic—manifested to a greater or lesser degree—of all families. Yet, in some families—and perhaps in most families at least some of the time—this ontological fact of real difference is ignored or overshadowed by an emphasis on commonalities (which may, in reality, also exist; difference and commonality are not mutually exclusive).

Thus, the second characteristic of coalitional families pertains to their *epistemology*: Coalitional families *understand* that their family is characterized by multiple and ineradicable differences. As I have suggested at various junctures throughout this book, non-normative families such as those created through open adoption, divorce and repartnerings and practices of queer kinship are more likely to understand (or come, over time, to understand) multiplicity as a deep and abiding characteristic of family composition. Although non-normativity in family formations is not a guarantee of such understanding (some adoptive, blended, same-sex, and other polymaternal families may try to mimic "as-if" biological, procreative families), the perspective of non-normativity may offer an epistemic advantage. It is for this reason, among others, that non-normative family configurations may be a useful starting place for (re)theorizing mothering. Acknowledging such differences is not, however, sufficient for familial coalition.

Crucial to coalition in familial as well as other contexts is a *normative* (or ethico-political) dimension: coalitional families do not merely acknowledge difference; they also *value* engagement with difference. As such, coalitional families do not seek to eradicate difference through tactics of colonization, nor do they merely tolerate difference. Instead, families characterized by coalitional sensibilities place value on the different contributions made to a family by members with different talents, capacities, and dispositions as well as different needs and vulnerabilities. Familial contributions to the group must be understood here as going beyond caring for and about other family members and domestic spaces. In the case of very young, very old, very ill, or cognitively or physically disabled members of a family, for example, contributions may include demonstrations of human vulnerability and interdependency, as well as resistance to and critiques of forms of caretaking that diminish, devalue, or misunderstand the needs of the one cared for. In transracially adoptive families or other families of mixed race or mixed ethnicity, the contributions of some members may include exposing and disrupting assumptions of white privilege. Teenagers' contributions, including the contributions of queer youth, may include efforts such as troubling or unsettling familial norms (including norms of sexual propriety). Moreover, because the subjectivities of family members emerge from different positionings within the family (e.g., as mother or daughter or son; as birth mother, adoptive mother or stepmother; as father or grandfather or uncle; as oldest child, youngest child, or middle child; etc.), each will contribute different perspectives in constructing or reconstructing family histories, stories, and memories and thus, to familial self-definition. And because the subjectivities of family members are also forged by the inhabitation of different extrafamilial contexts (prefamilial histories, work, school, hobbies, friendships, etc.), contributions to one's family also will include bringing home what one has learned during one's travels to worlds outside the home. In a coalitional family, one engages these and other differences as a site of potential growth and transformation.

Coalitional families, then, are characterized by their long-term commitment to noticing, valuing, and engaging difference within the context of a network of intersecting and overlapping intimate relationships. The commitment to engaging difference is important here. A coalitional family is not one in which families adopt an "anything goes" relativism about difference.[1] Coalitional homes are sites wherein questioning, discussion, critique, and struggle take place. However these engagements occur in ways that are responsive to others and responsible to our relationships. In coalitional families, disagreement is not a reason to abandon a kinship relation. Nor is kinship a reason for abandoning disagreement. What binds a coalitional family together as an assemblage is a shared commitment to engaging differences, learning from them, and risking the subjective and intersubjective transformations that may emerge from the engagement of those differences.

One reason it may seem odd to think about families as coalitional entities is that when we think about political coalitions, we frequently think of them in terms of what Jodi Dean (1996) calls "conventional solidarity." Conventional coalitions are groups that form not on the basis of love but on the basis of "shared adherence to common beliefs, values, or goals" (18). Sometimes the shared goals of such groups include liberation (from, e.g., exploitative working conditions, racial subordination, or gender oppression). In such political coalitions, it is not necessary that we like each other; what is important is that we are able to put aside our differences in order to achieve a shared ideal. Conventional solidarity is not, however, the only form of coalition. Following the typology forwarded by Dean in her *Solidarity with Strangers*, we may contrast conventional solidary with "affectional solidarity" (a solidarity that grows out of intimacy) and "reflective solidarity" (a solidarity characterized by a commitment to working through and across differences). Dean suggests that conventional solidarity is best suited to temporary strategic alliances aimed at specific short-term goals, whereas affectional solidarity captures the connections of intimacy that sustain friendships and kinship, arguing for the importance of reflective solidarity to sustaining coalitions forged among members of a heterogeneous public.

The distinctions Dean highlights between short- and long-term alliances (or between temporary and more lasting assemblages of multiplicity) are crucial, as is her claim that continued coalition among heterogeneous groupings requires us to work through, rather than around, differences. If families are, however, sites of ineradicable difference, then reflective solidarity will be as necessary to the survival of affectional coalitions of kinship as it is to the survival of political coalitions in the public sphere. Put another way, insofar as the familial coalitional assemblage breaches the boundary between the private and the public spheres, it is necessary to view affectional and reflective solidarity as necessarily intertwined. To (very) loosely paraphrase Kant, reflection without affection is empty, affection without reflection is blind. Only through their unison can love arise (Kant 1855, A 51, B 75). This is the message of several texts about polygamy released in the past decade. In this chapter, I critically examine three of these cultural texts—*Big Love, Sister Wives,* and *Love Times Three*—with a focus on how coalitional mothering may emerge as both an ideal and a practice in the polygamous family.

It is commonly assumed that polygamous families are inevitably heteropatriarchal and thus could not be queer. However, this assumption—like the assumption that mothering is an inevitably heterosexist practice—has prevented strategic coalitions among those interested in creating non-normative kinship relations, as well as between those practicing queer kinship and those practicing queer sex. I place polygamous families on the spectrum of polymaternal families alongside adoptive families, stepfamilies and same-sex families precisely in order to avoid the distinction between "good" queers and "bad" queers that undermines what could be a truly queer political movement. On one reading—the homonormative reading—of "good" queers and "bad" queers, monogamous couples (but not polyamorous or open sexual relationships) should be awarded traditional marriage and parental rights. On another reading—the antinormativity reading—all forms of intimacy and kinship (especially if state sanctioned) are suspect as inadequately queer. On this latter reading, a "bad" queer is anyone—regardless of sexual orientation—who seeks familial belonging. *Big Love, Sister Wives,* and *Love Times Three*—as their titles suggest, provoke us to think beyond the boundaries of normative forms of intimacy. Thus, they challenge us to enlarge our conceptions of familial solidarity—and in particular, our conceptions of solidarity between mothers—beyond both the domestinormative and the antidomestic.

Big Love: The Coalitional Assemblage
of the Polygamous Family

The present historical moment is one characterized by a plethora of polygamist "coming-out" narratives. U.S. television series such as *Big Love* (which aired on HBO from 2006 to 2011) and *Sister Wives* (which began airing on the Discovery network's learning channel, TLC, in 2010) have captured the public's attention with their respective portrayals of fictional and real-life suburbanites who have careers, drive their children to school in minivans, and attend block parties, while practicing the principle of plural marriage. *Oprah, Dr. Phil, The Rosie Show, The Ellen DeGeneres Show, Anderson,* and a host of other television and radio talk shows have devoted multiple episodes to interviewing polygamists and every major U.S. and Canadian news station has covered topical issues relating to polygamy. Television, radio, print, and tabloid news have reported on the raids of polygamous compounds and the arrest and trial of Warren Jeffs, the president of the Fundamentalist Church of Jesus Christ of the Latter Day Saints (FLDS Church) and of Winston Blackmore, a religious leader in the polygamous community of Bountiful, British Columbia. Even FOX (the extreme right–leaning U.S. television station that nonetheless features the gay-friendly series *Glee*) piloted a series about a man on the verge of entering multiple marriages (*Lone Star*) in 2010 (the series was canceled after only two episodes). The past half-dozen years have also witnessed the production of several novels, memoirs, films, made-for-TV movies, and documentaries about polygamy (e.g., *The 19th Wife, The Lonely Polygamist, Sister Wives, Love Times Three, Favorite Wife, Daughters of Zion, Escape, Stolen Innocence, In God's Country, Banking on Heaven*).

What should we make of the American fascination with polygamy at this moment in time? Many have suggested that curiosity about polygamy may be explained by its titillation factor (see, e.g., Kanazawa 2008). And to be sure, in series about and interviews with polygamous families of choice, the media has frequently milked this interest, highlighting questions about sexual schedules and sleeping arrangements

as well as questions about male sexual stamina and female sexual jealousies. In news coverage of criminal prosecutions of polygamous compound patriarchs and interviews with women who have escaped from
polygamous compounds, stories of child brides, rape, and sexual sub-
servience have been the most prominent headlines. Our fascination—
and disgust—with violations of sexual taboos, however, will not explain
why the close attention to polygamy arises at this particular historical
moment, a moment marked by culture wars over the changing face
of American kinship and, most specifically, marked by a heated debate
between those who passionately advocate and those who vehemently
oppose the legalization of gay marriage and gay adoption.

The *Big Love* series, which marks the first sympathetic U.S. media
portrayal of a polygamous family, was created and written by gay life
partners Will Scheffer and Mark Olsen. *Big Love* follows the Henrickson family, a Mormon family composed of Bill Henrickson, his three
wives, Barb, Nicki, and Margene, and their nine children. Together,
they live in the suburbs of Salt Lake City practicing "The Principle"
of plural marriage and navigating the complexities of a secret kinship.
Throughout the first four seasons, it is the toxicity of living a closeted
life that, in large part, drives the family drama: the possibility that their
polygamous practice could become public knowledge threatens Bill's
livelihood, as well as the careers, friendships, extended family relationships, and social standing of the wives and their children.

Because of the ongoing threat of being "outed," combined with
the desire for social recognition and tolerance for their form of life,
the Henricksons come out as polygamists at the end of the fourth and
penultimate season. By framing the polygamy narrative in terms of the
toxicities created by living a closeted life and the risks and social appro-
bation faced in coming out of that closet, *Big Love* draws intentional
parallels between polygamous relationships and same-sex relationships.
Indeed, during a 2007 radio interview with Terri Gross of National
Public Radio's "Fresh Air," Scheffer and Olsen credited the Republi-
can passage of DOMA (legislating that marriage must be between one
man and one woman) as pivotal to their idea for the series. Indicating
that they conceived the series about a polygamous family "shortly after
the second Bush inauguration," Scheffer and Olsen claimed it was a
response to "the excesses of . . . the dialogue [concerning] what is and
what isn't a family, what is a marriage, what isn't a marriage" and "what
society chooses to value in both those arenas" (Gross 2007).

The reality TV series, *Sister Wives*, which began airing during
Big Love's final season, likewise raises questions about the legitimacy

of social and legal norms governing marriage and family in the United States. In large font, the promotional materials for the show instruct the viewer to "rethink love," "rethink marriage," and "rethink family reality." Featuring Kody Brown, his four wives, Meri, Janelle, Christine, and Robyn and their fourteen children, *Sister Wives* provides curious viewers a glimpse into the "real" workings of a polygamous family and the discrimination they face. Like the fictional Henrickson family featured on *Big Love*, the Brown family worries about finances, struggles to balance the needs and schedules of various family members, and must deal at first with the difficulty of living secret lives and subsequently with the turmoil—including loss of jobs and criminal investigation—that ensues when their story goes public.

Closely paralleling both of these television series is the recent memoir of the Darger family, *Love Times Three*, co-written by Joe Darger, his three sister wives, Vicki, Valerie, and Alina, and three of their now adult children. Indeed, the Darger family posits they were an inspiration for *Big Love* creators Olsen and Scheffer, noting that the creators drew on a 2003 cover issue of *Mormon Focus* featuring the Darger wives and their suburban family. The series, they contend, details episodes from their own lives (such as family meetings, the triple "honey-do" lists, the outing of a polygamist wife after her child successfully nominates her for a "mother of the year" award, and the inclusion in their family of a wife who has experience with and connections to compound life) (Darger et al., 3–4). Like *Sister Wives*, however, the Dargers' memoir is less interested in allying itself with struggles for same-sex marriage than it is in silencing public concerns about polygamy.

Whether drawing parallels between same-sex and polygamous families, as Olsen and Scheffer do, or carefully distancing themselves from the "salacious" activities of gays and lesbians, as the Browns and Dargers do, all three contribute to a queering of our public discourse on kinship. Notably, each of these sympathetic portrayals of polygamy highlight homosocial bonds between strong women who actively resist both monogamy and monomaternalism. This new face of public polygamy, as exemplified in the lives of middle-class suburbanites, contrasts itself sharply to the heteropatriarchal form of polygamy that governs our social imagination. Indeed, despite the Browns' and Dargers' claims to be "normal" families, polygamous families of choice resemble queer polyamorous relationships as much as they resemble "normal" families.

Although American participants may characterize polygamous relationships as plural marriage, only the first marriage is recognized

by the state. The result is that other wives are legally free to leave if
and when they wish—along with any children borne to them. This
freedom for women inhabiting plural marriage is highlighted in *Big
Love*'s first season when two of the wives of a polygamous union do
leave their family and run off together, leaving their husband and first
wife unhappily monogamous. Like other kinship assemblages unsancti-
fied by the state, including polyamorous relationships or those formed
through open adoption or separations and repartnerings, the polygamous family of choice blurs any sharp distinction between queer and
straight practices of kinship. Many (although I do not think all) women
in polygamous families are heterosexual and yet they "do family" in
non-normative—and many would say "perverse"—ways. Moreover, as I
suggest here, women in polygamous marriages are largely homosocial.
What should we make of women who have sex (and babies) with men,
yet orient their private lives around other women?

Here, I suggest that in thinking about polygamous families—as
in thinking about other queer forms of kinship—we need to shift our
attention away from the politics of sexual identity and toward the politics of solidarity.[2] What distinguishes queer practices of kinship, in part,
from more normative practices of kinship, as I argue more specifically
below, is an admixture of affectional and reflective solidarity that may
eclipse the desire for unity enmeshed in conventional solidarity. This
is not a matter of sexual identity although it may well be a matter of
learning, in Ahmed's (2004, 2006) terms, to *re-orientate* our affections
and attentions in ways that involve critical reflection on our alignments. It also involves "practices of the self," in Foucault's (2010, 2011)
terms, that are free, courageous, truthful, and transformative. I do not
argue that all polygamous families embody such critically reflective re-
orientations and transformative practices of the self. Nor am I arguing
that any particular polygamous family does so consistently and without
exception. Like the other kinship practices I have considered here,
polygamous families *both* resist *and* replicate normative practices of
family making. Because the polygamous family is so frequently vilified
by conservatives and progressives alike as a site of heteropatriarchal
excess, however, this part of the argument hardly needs rehearsing.
Thus, my primary focus here is on the ways in which polygamy constructs an alternative to heteronormativity through queer practices of
solidarity—practices that challenge us, perhaps, to critically reflect on
our own political alignments and practices of abjection.

Queer solidarity may, at first pass, seem an oxymoron. This is
because we so frequently think of solidarity as requiring allegiance to

shared conventions. In groups based on conventional solidarity, as Dean (1996) suggests, the expectation that one will "adhere to the norms of the group" is the "primary attribute of membership"; thus group norms become "boundaries beyond which one *as a member* cannot go" (18). As such, conventional solidarity lends itself to the politics of colonization. The politics of colonization is clearly embodied in the character of Warren Jeffs, who stands as an exemplar of our worst fears about polygamous life and was added to the FBI's "Ten Most Wanted" list in May 2006. "President and Prophet, Seer and Revelator" of the FLDS Church, Jeffs is reported to have controlled all of the property where the Church's members lived and claimed the sole authority to perform marriages and to assign wives to male members of the Church. Demanding complete obedience of his followers, Jeffs instructed women to be subservient to their husbands and rewarded loyalty of male constituents by awarding them more wives. Those perceived to be disobedient were punished by reassignment of their wives, children, and homes to other men (Goodwyn et al. 2005). Exerting substantial control over the children borne into his congregation as well, Jeffs became notorious for arranging marriages between teenage girls and older men, and for exiling young men from the Church to reduce the competition for a limited supply of women (Hylton 2007). In 2011, Jeffs was convicted of the sexual assault of a twelve-year-old girl and a fifteen-year-old girl whom he claimed as his "spiritual wives" and sentenced to life imprisonment.

As the exposure of spiritual and familial life under Warren Jeffs' rule makes clear, conventional solidarity as the requirement to adhere to shared practices, values and goals may transform a community or a family into what ex-FLDS member, Carolyn Jessop, terms "a prison camp" (Jessop and Palmer 2008, 2). That conventional solidarity is ill-suited to the long-term project of negotiating and understanding difference *among* group members also is illustrated, however, in less egregious cases of conventional solidarity within families. The affectional solidarity between the members of the fictional Henrickson family, for example, as portrayed in *Big Love*, is frequently threatened by the politics of conventional solidarity. Throughout much of the series, Bill Henrickson puts "faith first" and his family second, the wives squabble about who can and cannot be trusted to uphold The Principle, and the teenage children struggle with what it means to live within a family that demands strict allegiance to the articles of faith that bind the family. Although family votes are a common process whereby important decisions affecting the family are made, Bill frequently attempts (albeit unsuccessfully) to control the actions and orientations of other family members. Although the reality TV polygamist, Kody Brown (frequently described by commentators as a laid back "surfer dude"), is much less authoritarian than the fictional Bill Henrickson, *Sister Wives* also provides a glimpse into the "father knows best" tendencies of an independent polygamous family. In season 2, when the family faces criminal investigation and worries they may be torn apart by the state, Kody makes the decision they will move from Salt Lake City to Las Vegas, despite the objections of some of his wives and his older children, asserting that *he* is the family "leader" and, regrettably, is thus responsible for making this difficult decision on behalf of the larger "we."

Importantly, attempts to enforce obedience to family conventions are not unique to polygamous families. *Any* family that demands shared adherence to particular practices, values and goals may transform into a boot camp or even a site of exile (as many gay and lesbian youth are aware). Like political coalitions that are premised on identity politics,[3] a family that practices the politics of containment and/or exclusion by setting rigid boundaries on membership (a "party line," as it were, from which one cannot veer too far without risking abjection) demands the suppression of difference in the name of a core unity. Nonetheless, most families (including my own) enact practices of conventional solidarity at least sometimes, as do most mothers (as well as fathers). The colonizing impulse behind demanding unity on principles and practices one holds near and dear is exceptionally hard to avoid. Like Bill Henrickson or Kody Brown, I have been guilty of practicing a form of "we" saying. For example, I may issue the edict that "we don't talk like that in our family" in response to the use of sexually or racially derogatory terms. Inevitably, my daughters' response to me on such occasions is to point out the obvious fact that they (as a part of the "we") just did. In pointing this out, they are not necessarily resisting my instruction to refrain from speaking in ways that put down or exclude others (although they may resist my principles also). What they are resisting (and rightly so) is my exclusion of them as "family" by a particular rhetorical use of "we."

Slippages into the politics of colonization (and its twin sibling, tolerance) may be countered, in part, by the affectional solidarity of group members. As "associations of emotional affirmation," families—like other social groupings based on affective connections—are not united merely by shared values and practices, but by feelings and practices of "mutual care and concern" (Dean 17). Representations of polygamous life on compounds such as those presided over by Warren Jeffs emphasize the group's unorthodox (polygamous) conventions but rarely provide us with representations of genuine affection between family members. It is the seeming absence of affectional solidarity in these sites of kinship that is, perhaps, what truly horrifies us. *Escape,* Carolyn Jessop's memoir of life in Colorado City, Arizona, for example, details a childhood with a depressed and violent mother followed by a loveless marriage featuring disillusionment with her husband and conflict with her sister wives and little affection for the family's children. Although the risks she takes to gather all of her (biological) children and take them with her as she "escapes" the compound indicates concern for their well-being, she recounts subsequently having to "learn to hug and kiss [her] children again." "In the FLDS," she observes, "women are not supposed to show affection to their children. It's conferring value on an individual, and only the prophet and the head of the family are allowed to do that" (Jessop 2008). Jessop's portrayal of polygamous compound life is mirrored in *Big Love* wherein most (albeit not all) mothers and fathers living in rural compounds appear incapable of genuine intimacy with each other or with their children.

In contrast, the narratives of "independent" polygamous families highlight love, affection, and care. In *Love Times Three,* the Darger women note that plural marriage "requires of each woman a constant, gentle empathy for her sister wives and a respect for boundaries and fairness," emphasizing that when there are multiple partners, there are multiple "perspectives and feelings [that] must be considered" (159). Their desire to live a polygamous life is framed as a desire to enlarge their conception and practice of love: "the whole point of living this way," they state, "was to see how closely we could model Christ's teachings about love, acceptance, care, and compassion" (161). A similar theme resounds in the dialogue of *Sister Wives.* In the prologue to each episode, Kody Brown states "love should be multiplied not divided." Although *Sister Wives* features religious motivations for polygamy much less prominently than *Love Times Three,* the Browns' practices embody ongoing attention to the needs of others, exemplifying an ongoing balance between "saying this is what I want and need and offering up to others what they want and need." In both the Brown and Darger families, older children (as well as adults) care for younger children; siblings (as well as adults) are attentive to and respectful of the differences among them and when one member of the family is "really struggling, the others [are] there for her" (*Sister Wives,* season

2, episode 11). As the Dargers note, there are aspects of polygamous families that may be helpful to raising children to be open to the needs of others: in a big family, "children learn to be unselfish, to be helpful, and to understand [and respect], from an early age, a wide range of personality types" (207).

Affectional solidarity, as explicated by Dean, is both primary and particular. It is primary because a child's "earliest experiences of relations of love and affection provide the basis for self-trust and for the ability to engage with and respond to the needs of the others" (17). It is particular because it "responds to and validates the other as a unique individual" with specific needs, talents preferences, capacities, dispositions, and vulnerabilities (17–18). The "we-feeling" of affectional solidarity stems from "the immediacy of our tie to another" and our awareness of the "specialness and exclusivity of a relationship attuned to complexities of individual specificity" (18). The primacy and particularity of affectional solidarity is illustrated by the bonds of trust and care among the Browns' children in *Sister Wives*. The generosity with which the existing Brown children accept their new siblings (and look out for them at their new school) after a fourth wife and her children from a previous marriage are added to the family is particularly noteworthy. Although differences must be negotiated (as the previous Brown children note, their new brother and sisters were "raised differently than [them]" and thus cry more readily over skinned knees and bruises), few of the animosities that sometimes exist between stepsiblings appear to be present. Nor do the Brown children appear resentful of their new mother, as stepchildren may be. Indeed, they appear to have internalized the notion that "love is to be multiplied, not divided."

Affectional solidarity captures an important ideal for contemporary Western families in emphasizing the intimacy, primacy and particularity of many familial relationships.[4] As *Escape* and *Big Love* illustrate, however, not all family members are capable of such solidarity. For some family members, such as Carolyn Jessop's husband and *Big Love*'s Bill Henrickson, affection may be dependent on the willingness of family members to be contained by the norms of a family's conventional coalition (the shared beliefs, values, and goals that set the boundaries of the family's self-definition). Jessop recounts her husband's technique of "breaking" an infant (preparing it for obedience) through slapping her baby and then holding it under running tap water so it choked while it screamed. The damage done when affectional solidarity is absent during childhood is evidenced by the years of "therapy and hard work" that Carolyn Jessop notes were needed to re-establish intimacy between herself and her children, enabling them to finally thrive. The damage done to children deprived of affection is also represented in *Big Love* via the fictional characters of Bill Henrickson and his second wife, Nicki. Both exiled from their (compound) families of origin who were unwilling or unable to provide them with early experiences of love and affection, Bill and Nicki, as adults, are frequently unable themselves to adequately engage with and respond to the needs of others, including their own children. Their own difficulties as parents become particularly pronounced when dealing with teenage children who resist their own teachings: Bill is dismayed when his eldest daughter rejects plural marriage in favor of a monogamous relationship; Nicki, who associates intergenerational relationships with the abuse of young women on the compound, is horrified when her teenage daughter develops a romantic relationship with a much older teacher.

Bill and Nicki's deteriorating relationships with their teen daughters highlight the ways in which affectional solidarity may miss the mark with regard to particularity, as well as primacy. Responding to and validating the other as a unique individual is considerably more difficult than it sounds, even in families where intimacy is primary. Learning not to project our own histories, needs, values, capacities, and dispositions onto the other is no easy achievement; moreover, acknowledging the differences between oneself and the other is frequently made more difficult (not less so) in the presence of a "we-feeling" that easily reduces self and other to a singular unity. This is what happens when Nicki projects her own past as an abused young woman onto her daughter's present choices. It is also what happens in my own family when I project my own desires (say, for educational success and economic independence) onto my daughters, failing to recognize that their paths may be different than my own.

This suggests that within coalitional families, just as within coalitional associations in the heterogeneous public, what Dean terms "reflective solidarity" is also necessary. Reflective solidarity is a form of solidarity founded on a respect for difference. Here the bonds that tie people together are created through "discussions and questions" and "shared expectations of recognition and response" (16), what Dean sums up as a *"mutual expectation of a responsible orientation to relationship"* (29). Reflective solidarity (like Oliver's response-ability) rests in "our awareness of and regard for those multiple interconnections in which differences emerge" together with "an openness to difference which lets our disagreements provide the basis for connection" (16–17).

Openness to difference and a commitment to working through disagreements is a primary feature of the independent polygamous families featured in *Big Love, Sister Wives,* and *Love Times Three.* In all three, family meetings, as well as more private conversations between smaller subgroupings of kin, are featured as sites of discussion wherein each party is recognized, disagreements are voiced, and responses are respectful. In *Love Times Three,* the Dargers emphasize the importance of good communication that validates the feelings of others (168, 211) and the core family values of responsibility, respect, honesty, self-control, selflessness, accountability, and repentance (248). These values are frequently—if sometimes imperfectly—exemplified in the dialogue between various family members in *Sister Wives.* In addition to allowing us to eavesdrop on (some of) their family meetings and private dialogues, each episode features a metanarrative wherein the adult members of the family (and sometimes the children) collectively reflect on the challenges they have recently faced (e.g., jealousies, hopes and fears that arise when the newest wife joins their family, financial challenges, stressors related to the criminal investigation of the family, or the difficulties of finding suitable homes for everyone when they relocate). Although this show (like all "reality" TV shows) is scripted and we cannot know more than we are shown, the meta-narrative conversations—as well as the family meetings and more private "do you have a moment?" conversations—are a striking mixture of candor, self-reflection, and acknowledgment and respect for one another's differences. The capacity for critical self-reflection and compassionate listening that pervades conversations between the Browns appears to be the result not merely of rehearsing a script (although they may do this also), but of a communicative practice and related practices of self-improvement and self-transformation in which all members are regularly and necessarily engaged. As the first wife, Meri, notes, "one of the benefits of polygamy is that . . . you are forced to examine yourself and your treatment of others," to "confront your own weakness of character and work on being the best wife, sister and mother you can be" (Brown et al. 2012, 102, 108).

Big Love likewise highlights a relationship between sister wives (and other family members) embodying a reflective solidarity that accepts and works through differences. As a fictional vehicle, *Big Love* is able to portray these differences quite starkly. Here the sister wives represent the coming together of three distinct communities: the LDS community that repudiates polygamy (Barb), an FLDS polygamist community (Nicki), and the secular world (Margene). They also embody the coming together of three distinct affective styles: Barb is reflective and spiritual, Nicki is fearful and status seeking, Margene is affectionate and sexual. Tensions and reconciliations between the three—as well as between them and their common husband and children feature prominently in the series, demonstrating the contention of the real-life Brown family that in a polygamous family, "relationships are complex and they are constantly changing" (Brown et al., 10).

In contrast to affectional solidarity (where the "we" is based on mutual feelings of concern) and in contrast to conventional solidarity (where the "we" is based on shared principles and objectives), in reflective solidarity, the "we" is based on shared responsibility for engaging difference.

> [W]e appeal to others to include and support us because our communicative engagement allows us to expect another to take responsibility for our relationship. Here we recognize the other that is neither immediate nor restrictively mediated. We recognize her in her difference, yet understand this difference as part of the very basis of what it means to be one of "us." (Dean 1996, 39)

Reflective solidarity, as Dean describes it, includes an affective element (expectation, she notes, is a feeling) and also requires an element of concrete particularity. However, reflective solidarity does not reduce to feelings (nor, I think, does love). Moreover, reflective solidarity does not require "that we completely recognize the other person as the 'person she is'"; instead, it requires that "we give the other *the space to be* the person she is" (39, my emphasis). Respect for the differences between family members (even if we do not understand those differences) is a crucial characteristic of coalitional families, as is the "messiness" and permeable boundaries of reflective solidarity (29), the recognition of interdependence and shared vulnerability in coalitions of reflective solidarity (45), and the conception of struggle as "both an aspect of community and a vehicle for changing communities without recourse to violence," including the violence of exclusion (179). As Dean notes, reflective solidarity as a shared practice of engaging difference does not predetermine membership in or contribution to the "we" that is formed by that shared practice.

In the face of external, public norms that abject them and internal differences that challenge them, the Henricksons, the Browns, and the Dargers struggle to hold together their respective complicated families by loving one another across personal and cultural differences. Ultimately, however, all three polygamy narratives are about the solidarity among sister wives. While husbands are away working, courting new wives, and battling persecution, it is the women as a coalitional sisterhood who share domestic and parenting responsibilities, pool resources, and negotiate diverse values and styles of caregiving. *Big Love*, *Sister Wives*, and *Love Times Three* all emphasize that the principle of plural marriage is one wherein women marry not only a husband, but become eternally united to each other. For this reason, as all three narratives emphasize, men cannot consider courting another wife without the permission of their present wives. That courtship is a family affair is represented in scenes of group dates in *Big Love* and by kinship between women in *Love Times Three* that precedes their respective marriages to a common husband. (Valerie and Vicki Darger are twin sisters; Alina is their cousin.) In *Sister Wives*, Meri's, Janelle's, and Christine's embrace of Robyn as the fourth wife and *their* new partner is symbolized by a Claddaugh ring (a traditional Irish ring given as a token of friendship, love, or marriage worn by each of the sister wives) which the current wives jointly select and present to their new wife on her wedding day (season 1, episodes 5 and 7).

Public interest in the relationships between sister wives is fueled by the assumption that women in polygamous marriages compete for a man's affection (see, e.g., the October 26, 2007 episode of *The Oprah Winfrey Show*). In response to this assumption, independent polygamous women are quick to note that their choice to live as polygamists stems, in large part, *from the desire for kinship with other women*. The Darger wives emphasize their status as "soulmates," noting that it is the belief in "our female connection that drives our commitment to each other and gets us through tough times. Our friendship and love have grown over the years, to the point where little jealousies are far outweighed by the knowledge that my sister wives always have my back" (Darger et al., 170). In *Sister Wives*, Robyn responds to the assumption that polygamous women must have "low self-esteem" by noting polygamy is "really about the girls . . . it's a girl party" (season 2, episode 6). All four of the Brown women emphasize their desire to have wives. Christine is particularly adamant about this, noting that she "never wanted to be married to just a man. I wanted sister wives more than a husband" (season 2, episode 3); her tag line in the prologue to each episode is "I like sister wives; I wanted a family, not just a man." The importance of homosocial relations between women is similarly emphasized in other independent polygamist narratives. In *Big Love,* for example, we frequently see the Henrickson wives holding hands and embracing; it is Barb (not Bill) with whom Nicki shares her first waltz. In this series—the only polygamist narrative to explore a woman's marriage to more than one man—it is also notable that Margene's decision to defy the marital convention of "one man, many women" stems not from loving another man but from her deep affection for an ex-sister wife; Margene marries her ex-wife's (Ana's) Serbian lover in order to stop his deportation and thus Ana's own planned departure from the country.

The reduction of polygamy to a heteropatriarchal form of kinship underserving of the label "queer" fails to note the explicit resistance to both monogamy and monomaternalism voiced by women who choose polygamy. In an NPR interview, Julie Halcomb, author of the blog, "A normal polygamist family," emphasizes the "loneliness" of monogamous marriage, as well as the burdens; "everything always fell on me as far as the housework, the raising of the children" (Polygamists share their life, 2011). It was Julie, not her husband, who sought to explore polygamous options. In *Love Times Three,* the Darger wives emphasize the advantages of mothering as a collective. Noting that their children refer to them collectively as "the moms," Vicki describes their co-mothering relationship as follows:

> We each have our own parenting personality, which together makes us a good team. Alina is protective, but also fun and really good at relating to teenagers. Val is easy-going and a mentor, but less strict because she doesn't like conflict. I'm strict, but also like to let the children experiment. It's nice to have another mom to lean on for help when I need to give special attention to a child, or when I'm not sure which approach to take to a difficult situation. (211)

The Brown sister wives emphasize the freedom that comes from sharing domestic tasks and a husband. Janelle, who prefers working outside the home to doing housework, resounds a theme from Judy

Syfers' early feminist essay, "Why I Want a Wife," noting that, in having sister wives, she gets *both* a "tremendous home life" *and* "get[s] to do what [she] wants to do" (episode 1). Meri, who enjoys time to herself, "can't imagine" being solely responsible for her husband, noting that "when we go to family reunions and I see family members who are monogamous, I often wonder, 'How can you have your husband around all the time? When do you have time for yourself?'" (Brown et al., 111, see also season 2, episode 5). Reflecting on such candid self-revelations in her review of *Sister Wives* for *The L.A. Times*, Mary McNamara wonders if the future of feminism might lie in polygamy, likening the Brown clan to a "matriarchy" in which "one man is quite enough" because "what a gal really needs around the house is more women" (McNamara 2010).

That a man need not mediate sisterhood between polygamous wives is the parting message of *Big Love*. When Bill Henrickson dies during the series finale, the flash forward depicts the sister wives and their children continuing as a familial assemblage that gives each member the space to be and become who and what they desire: Barb continues her feminist journey toward priesthood, giving a blessing to their first grandchild; Margene is supported in her desire to pursue humanitarian work by the other mothers who care for her (their) children as she goes overseas; and Nicki continues to search for her place in the world, but finally seems assured of her place in their family. Although a fictional happy ending, the *Big Love* finale embodies an important, but overlooked truth about polygamous families. Women may—and frequently do—continue as close friends and allies with sister wives from previous marriages; they also may continue to live together after a husband has died and children have left home (Darger et al., 162).

Good Queers, Bad Queers

In exploring the fluidity of and freedom for women within a plural marriage, *Big Love, Sister Wives,* and *Love Times Three* explicitly counter a common criticism of polygamy, namely, that it is "harmful to women's equality and thus is contrary to a liberal egalitarian democracy" (Calhoun 2005). This criticism of polygamy has been advanced by critics of same-sex marriage who argue that abandoning marriage norms of "one man, one woman" will open the doors to harmful polygamous practices. Much as the U.S. colonization of Afghanistan has been justified by arguments about the patriarchal oppression suffered by women living under Taliban rule, those who seek to uphold "traditional" definitions of marriage justify legislating normative forms of intimacy by invoking fears about the well-being of women under alternative regimes. Indeed, this is the explicit analogy that governs the anti-polygamy stance of documentaries such as *Banking on Heaven*. In this film, footage of women in long-sleeved, high-collar, ankle-length dresses roaming the prairies are interlaced with footage of ex-FLDS members who provide stories of women being beaten, forced to have sex and become child brides and statements from concerned legislators who state that polygamist compounds are sites of "massive corruption and violations of human rights" with "many striking similarities to the Taliban." Arguing that the politicians who "brag about liberating the women of Afghanistan and Iraq" need to "liberate the women and children of Colorado City," the filmmakers descry the ways in which the FLDS religion treats women as "chattel" and "breeding machines."

Homonormative advocates of same-sex marriage (like homonormative gay patriots) support this fear mongering by likewise pathologizing polygamy and carefully differentiating it from their own (monogamous) practices of intimacy. As the coming out narratives of polygamous families of choice indicate, however, we cannot simply assume that polygamous marriages are *always* more gender inegalitarian than monogamous ones. To generalize all polygamist husbands as "abusive" and all polygamist wives as "uneducated" or "oppressed" is, as the Dargers contend, tantamount to "characterizing all monogamists based on the abusive behavior of actor Charlie Sheen or the infidelity of golfer Tiger Woods" and the submissive nature of women who tolerate such behavior (vii–viiii).

If the assumption that all polygamous marriages involve heteropatriarchal oppression is unwarranted, the proper response to opponents of same-sex marriage who challenge, "And why not also polygamy?" may be "indeed, why not polygamy?" (Calhoun 2005).[5] The question, "why not polygamy?" is precisely the question raised in an early episode of *Big Love* by Roman Grant, self-proclaimed Prophet and patriarch of a polygamous compound (Juniper Creek), who pronounces at a press conference that polygamists are "just like . . . homosexuals" and deserve the same "rights to live in peace" as were granted to homosexuals by the Supreme Court's affirmation of privacy rights (episode 3). It is also the question raised by the Browns' lawsuit demanding the decriminalization of polygamy—a lawsuit drawing on the *Lawrence v.*

Texas precedent which struck down state sodomy laws as unconstitutional intrusions on the "intimate conduct" of consenting adults.[6] The argument in favor of decriminalizing polygamy is only persuasive, however, in light of the depiction of *Big Love's* and *Sister Wives'* portrayals of gender egalitarian marriages—marriages contrasted explicitly to the patriarchal marriages existing on polygamous compounds. Thus, underlying the (positive) contention that polygamous marriage is analogous to same-sex marriage is a troubling distinction between "good" polygamists and "bad" polygamists that closely parallels the distinction between "good" (mature, nonthreatening) gays and lesbians who seek monogamous marriage rights and other queers who have not yet abandoned their repugnant sexual practices.

The background to the Henrickson's private lives in *Big Love* is an entangled past with the Juniper Creek compound on which Bill and Nicki were raised. Unlike Carolyn Jessop, however, Bill and Nicki have been unable to fully "escape" their past. Because those at Juniper Creek (most notably the Prophet Roman Grant, who is also Nicki's father) threaten to reveal the Henrickson's family's secret, Bill is drawn into battling the compound in a series of ploys that endanger his family. By the fourth season of *Big Love*, critics began to complain about the overcomplicated plot lines, bemoaning the fact that the series had become a convoluted "crime drama" that had lost its focus on the internal dynamics of the Henrickson family. In the words of one critic, "the shenanigans with the caricatured weirdos at Juniper Creek feel like distractions . . . that overwhelm the family's story" (Sepinwall 2010). The convoluted battles between the Henricksons and the "weirdos" inhabiting the Juniper Creek compound, however, as well as the murderous rivalry between Juniper Creek and a rival polygamous compound, play an important role in the series.

The Juniper Creek storyline reminds us that the Henricksons' happy suburban polygamous experiment exists against a background of patriarchal excess, corruption, and control. This is highlighted in Bill Henrickson's speech as a newly elected Utah senator during *Big Love's* fifth and final season. Having outed himself as a polygamist, Bill assures his constituency that although he "believes in plural marriage," he will "correct extremism, fundamentalism, and abuses" (episode 43). Bill is thus situated as the (relatively) benign patriarch who allows his wives a significant amount of freedom and power. In contrast, Roman Grant (a character loosely based on Warren Jeffs) is the corrupt, absolute master of Juniper Creek, a place where constituents (especially women and girls) are intentionally kept poor and powerless and incest and pedophilia run rampant. Reminding us just how far such corruption can go, Hollis Green, the leader of a rival polygamous sect, is the ultimate terrorist—the man in the wilderness with a cache of automatic weapons who brands people who won't do business with him and sends his transgendered wife, Selma, out to assassinate his enemies. As one commentator suggests, the Greens embody the nightmare that occurs "when all law is abdicated except the law of the Father and the cross-dressing Mother" (The moth chase, 2010). By setting the Henricksons' polygamous practices against the backdrop of such sexualized excess (incest, pedophilia, transgenderism, and sadism), the suburban, middle-class family is rendered "normal."

A similar dynamic pervades the positioning of "real-life" suburban polygamist families as "normal" and unthreatening. Both the Browns and the Dargers explicitly distance themselves from FLDS beliefs and practices, arguing that, as *independent* fundamentalist Mormons, their culture and family life is "vastly different" than that practiced by members of the FLDS—emphasizing the consensual nature of their own marriages and their respect for the autonomy of women and children and denouncing "underage marriage and abuse of any kind" (Darger et al., 11, see also Brown et al., 3–8). When asked by a friend if she had to marry her uncle and if her dad molested her, Madison, one of the Browns' daughters, doesn't interrogate this stereotype of polygamy; instead, she emphasizes the difference between her family and FLDS families, responding, "That's not us. That's sick and wrong to me" ("Former FLDS teens" 2011). The Browns also emphasize their difference from FLDS members in terms of dress and lifestyle, noting that—unlike other Mormon fundamentalists—they and their children "dress . . . modernly, . . . watch TV, go to the movies, play computer games, go to parties, and listen to popular music" (3).

The new public face of polygamy emerging from representations of polygamous families of choice contrasts sharply with the image of polygamy as an institution that stifles difference and dissent. Both the Brown and the Darger families feature independent, strong-willed women who work outside the home and who voluntarily choose to live "a polygamous lifestyle." Neither family demands that the children follow their parents' path, and they educate them through a mixture of home schooling and public schooling that exposes children to religious principles and kinship practices different from their own. In short, these exemplars of suburban polygamous families seem "to operate with cooperation and even democracy: never does it seems like [the husband] lays down the law for everyone else" (Barney 2011).

Insofar as the narrative of the suburban polygamous family resists portrayals of polygamy as heteropatriarchal and abusive, such families become easier to embrace as both "feminist" and potentially "queer." Yet, insofar as the narrative supporting a positive portrayal of polygamous families uncritically adopts a form of metronormative neoliberalism, its potentially radical discourse about the changing face of American kinship is recuperated by a homonormative discourse that we might term *polynormativity*. The modernity and progressiveness of independent polygamous families contrasts to the primitive, barbaric, backward nature of compound life in a narrative that equates being "progressive" with neoliberal accumulation. This dynamic is clearly illustrated by Oprah Winfrey's ongoing coverage of polygamy stories.

In 2007, Oprah aired an episode, "Polygamy in America," that explicitly contrasted the lives of suburban polygamists with polygamy as lived on rural compounds. The episode opens with an interview with Valerie Darger of *Love Times Three* fame discussing the complications of polygamous life including, notably, the middle-class difficulties of scheduling sports events and music lessons for all of their twenty-three children. The viewer is then shown rows of "palatial homes" in Centennial Park, Arizona (one of the nation's largest suburban polygamist communities) and introduced to Richard, a successful businessman with three wives who owns one of these homes and provides his wives with "everything they need to be happy." A wife notes her freedom, contending that if a wife was unhappy, "[she] would leave, simple as that." From here, the coverage shifts to Colorado City, where Carolyn Jessop, ex-FLDS member and author of *Escape*, serves as a guide. The viewer is informed (by Jessop, as no one on the compound she has discredited will meet with them) that in Colorado City, constituents are "isolated" with "no television, internet, radios or newspapers" and an enforced dress code and hairstyles for women. The poverty and isolation of Colorado City is contrasted with the affluence of Centennial Park where "Richard has five flat screens in his house"; Centennial Park residents, we are assured, are "a much more liberal people."

The neoliberal values and capital accumulation of polygamists in Centennial Park is also the focus of two 2011 episodes of *Our America with Lisa Ling*, a series hosted by the Oprah Winfrey Network self-described as reporting on "some of the most challenging, thought-provoking issues in society today. . . . with stories ranging from polygamy and amateur porn, to sex trafficking and veterans with PTSD." Tellingly entitled, "Modern Polygamy: Spotlight on a Young Polygamist Family" (October 23, 2011) and "The Story Continues: Modern Polygamy" (December 4, 2011), these episodes highlight the happy life of twenty-eight-year-old Isaiah and his wives (aged twenty and twenty-eight) and their young children. When we first meet the young family, they are making sushi in the kitchen of a modest trailer park home; by the time of the follow-up coverage five months later, they have "moved up" into a more spacious Centennial Park home with multiple bedrooms and baths. Ling posits that they are "the poster family for polygamy," contending that this family and the others she has met in Centennial Park "defy the stereotypes of polygamy."

The stereotypes of polygamy are highlighted, however, in the *Oprah Winfrey's Show*'s 2009 "exclusive" report, "Oprah Goes Inside the Yearning for Zion Polygamist Ranch" (March 30, 2009). The Yearning for Zion ranch in rural El Dorado, Texas (population: 1,951)—like the polygamist compound in Colorado City (population: 4,668)—was once presided over by the notorious Warren Jeffs. The guide on this occasion, however, is Carolyn Jessop's ex-brother-in-law and the new Prophet, Willie Jessop, who attempts to position life on the ranch as normal small town life. Explaining that members of the FLDS resist the word "compound" as a word connoting restriction, Willie Jessop insists that the ranch is "like any other town." At the same time, he notes—prior to introducing Oprah to the residents—that they have "no TV" and thus people "aren't going to know who you are." Although members of the ranch, including various constituencies of women and children, maintain Jeffs' innocence and contend they are both happy and free ("we don't get forced into anything"), Oprah is clearly skeptical. Such skepticism may be warranted—it is certainly possible that residents are self-censoring out of fear of compound leaders; it is also possible that (like suburban polygamists) they simply wish to make a good impression and dispel stereotypes about a life to which they are, themselves, committed. What is noteworthy here, however, are the ways in which Oprah's disbelief centers primarily on the idea that one could be happy leading a life absent of most modern amenities, fashion, and culture.

Oprah begins her interviews of ranch residents with a group of second graders. Trying to make casual conversation, she asks what toys they like to play with and what stories they like to read. This seems an odd question to the children who do not have toys and storybooks; they contend they "don't want to play"; they like to "work" and likewise read "with purpose." Similarly, when Oprah asks a group of teenage girls what they do for "fun," they suggest they "go to school for fun." Although Oprah does ask the teens about whether young girls are forced to marry against their will (which they deny), the bulk of her time with them is spent exploring the lifestyle differences between them and other contemporary teenagers. Attempting to display themselves as technologically modern, the girls show Oprah they have cell phones, while admitting they don't play video games or have computers. Attempting to present themselves as culturally knowledgeable, they assert they have, in fact, watched television and movies; but the films they list—*Chicken Little, Winnie the Pooh*—instead demonstrate the vast gulf between themselves and their urban and suburban counterparts. Their discussion about fashion produces further disbelief from Oprah. When the girls attempt to highlight the differences in their long "peasant" dresses—with one stating, quite plausibly, that although their dresses may "look the same" to outsiders, they say to each other, "where'd you get that dress?!"—Oprah laughs uncontrollably. A similar rhetorical strategy, verging on ridicule, pervades Oprah's discussion with older women about their allegedly identical hairstyles; "I have to ask," Oprah says, "what's up with that 'poof'?" When the women point to differences among their hairstyles, Oprah cannot see the differences. When they claim a common desire to backcomb and braid, the viewer is clearly intended to share Oprah's suspicion that anyone would voluntarily choose to adopt such a coiffure.

As Scott Herring (2010) notes in *Another Country: Queer Anti-urbanism*, the metropolitan is typically codified as "the terminus of queer world making" and the dismissal of the rural is both "commonplace" and "chronic" (4–5). Herring identifies six "analytic axes" of "metronormativity" (15–16), each of which is embodied in the narratives distinguishing suburban and rural polygamists. The "narratological" axis of metronormativity, which depicts flight from the country to the city as a "one-way trip to sexual freedom," is prominently featured in Jessop's memoir (and other narratives) of "escape" from FLDS "compounds" wherein women's and girls' sexuality is held hostage. What Herring terms the "racial logistics of metronormativity" are featured in the "normative ideals of whiteness" that characterize depictions of "good" polygamists much as they characterize depictions of "good" queers. (Notably none of the suburban polygamists featured on television series or interviews are Muslim, African immigrants, or other people of color). The third, "socioeconomic" axis of metronormativity is readily evident in stories about suburban polygamist communities characterized by consumerism, class mobility, and prosperity—characteristics sharply contrasted to the poverty of rural polygamist life. The notion that city queers are "more progressive" than rural queers—Herring's "temporal" axis of metronormativity—is clearly paralleled in representations of suburban polygamists as "more liberal" than the "backwards" polygamists who reside in the desolate rural areas of Colorado City, Arizona and El Dorado, Texas. Closely intersecting with both the socioeconomic and temporal depictions of city and country lives is the "epistemological" axis of metronormativity, namely, the notion that those who live closer to the city are more "in-the-know." Because of their isolation from city life and their lack of most modern communication devices such as television and the Internet in addition to their exclusive home schooling, rural polygamist children and adults are largely depicted as ignorant and uneducated. Among the things of which rural polygamists are ignorant, as highlighted in Oprah's depictions of people on the Yearning for Zion ranch, are the norms of fashion. Thus, on the sixth, "aesthetic" axis of metronormativity, suburban polygamists are featured as more "sophisticated, fashionable, and cosmopolitan," whereas rural polygamists are marked as "aesthetically intolerable" (16, 22). In general, the "affectations, manners, foodways, dress, comportments, and other displays" which mark some queers as better than others also mark those polygamists who have escaped rural life and moved to the suburbs as "naturally superior," thus giving us (and them) license to "morally despise" their rural counterparts (20–21).

Of course, we do not always despise those whom we see as inferior; often we pity them. In *Relocations: Queer Suburban Imaginaries*, Karen Tongston (2011) notes that queer subjects are "thought to be in emotional, aesthetic, and physical peril in nonurban environments" because they lack choices (5). Indeed, "the very question of queer choice portends the emergence of an enlightened liberal subject from out of the darkness" (152). This is, indeed, the leading motif of sympathetic portrayals of the modern, suburban polygamous family—a motif that renders rural women's assertions that they too practice polygamy *by choice* largely inaudible to the citified listener. What should we make of the claim of the Zion ranch sister wife who claims (echoing the assertions of suburban sister wives) that living with other women is a chosen path to spiritual enlightenment that enables her to better know and improve herself? How should we assess the claim of Carolyn Jessop's daughter that she is "not brainwashed" and has returned of her own free will from the city to the Zion ranch because she "loves it" and misses her "old life, family and religion?" Can we hear the pain expressed by the Zion ranch mothers who had children removed from their custody during a raid on the compound that turned their lives "upside down?" These counter-urban narratives—also documented during Oprah's "exclusive" visit to the Yearning for Zion ranch—are largely occluded by a metronormative framework that characterizes the speakers from which such counter-narratives emanate as too unsophisticated to be taken seriously as free agents.

Intersecting with our metronormative assumptions and further impeding our ability to hear these women in "peasant" attire who proclaim to choose their lives on the ranch (and to be harmed by our interventions in that life) is a liberal discourse of freedom and autonomy that has become "naturalized" in feminist (and perhaps also queer) scholarship (Mahmood 2004, 13). According to the liberal feminist "topography of freedom," a woman (or other individual) cannot be considered free unless her actions result from her "own will" rather than from "custom, tradition or social coercion" (11). As Mahmood argues in *The Politics of Piety*, this leaves us unable to understand the Muslim woman's piety as anything other than an act of false consciousness. Similarly, I argue, we are hampered in understanding the Mormon fundamentalist woman's words and actions as anything other than a "deplorable passivity and docility," because we fail to understand her words and actions from within her own discourse—a discourse that is not formulated within the (feminist) parameters of coercion and consent, nor within the (queer) parameters of resistance and recuperation (15, see also 9–14). That a woman might willingly conform to religious edicts and prophesies (as well as to aesthetically intolerable-to-us modes of fashion) becomes unintelligible within a "teleology of progressive politics" guided by "the narrative of subversion and reinscription of norms" (9).

The result—for feminists such as Oprah and also, I am suggesting, for queers like us—is an entrenched dichotomy between "good" (independent and autonomous) polygamists and "bad" (coercive and submissive) polygamists—and between "good" mothers (who help their children escape compound life) and "bad" mothers (who defend FLDS practices). The seductiveness of these dichotomies disrupts the opportunity for reflective solidarity between us and the monstrous—or pitiable—(m)other, thereby undermining our ability to engage responsibly (and response-ably) across difference. Like "first-world" framings of transnational adoption, metronormative, politically "progressive" framings of polygamy lead us to rush in to "save the children" (and, in this case, perhaps also the women) for "their own good," too easily forgetting that in so doing, it is we—and not some monstrous other—who are practicing a politics of colonization.

The Politics of Love

A politics of love is necessary in the sense that how one loves matters; it has effects on the texture of everyday life and on the intimate "withness" of social relations

—Sarah Ahmed (2004)

Big Love, Sister Wives, and *Love Times Three* (and perhaps also the narratives of other polygamous women, if we could learn to hear them) help us to differentiate love as a feeling from a politics of love that requires critical reflection on the relations between self and others. Independent polygamous families appear, like other forms of queer kinship, to be assemblages of multiplicity based on respect for difference. Refusing to be fashioned out of the pair and untethered by legal (or uniform genetic) ties, these families illustrate the multivalent and tenuous threads that hold complicated families together. Because of our tendency to project homogeneity onto rural, community-based polygamous families, we are less likely to view them as a model for queer kinship. Nonetheless, they too refuse to be fashioned out of dyadic (monogamous) couplings and proprietary definitions of either erotic or maternal love. Moreover, the tenuous nature of their kinship is illustrated by the raids on their communities that continually threaten to tear them apart. In order to respect the tenuous threads that connect the members of polygamous (and other queer) families internally—as well as to strengthen the potential affiliations and alliances *among* queer families, it is important to attend to the practical, epistemological and phenomenological—as well as affective—dimensions of love. Together, these dimensions point the way to a politics of love that may produce solidarity between mothers and their children and among mothers themselves.

The *practical* dimension of love is summed up in hooks' (2000) reminder that "love is as love does" (13). Viewing love as an action (rather than a feeling) reminds us that how we love (or fail to love) has consequences for which we bear ethical responsibility (13–14). This dimension of love is exemplified by a mother's commitment to preserve her child(ren)'s well-being, protect them from danger and facilitate (without controlling) their physical, intellectual and emotional growth and development (Ruddick 1995, 68–69, 123). Maternal love, understood as a form of *doing*, must be distinguished from a mother's interior feelings or thoughts. As feminist scholars have often noted, children frequently cause their mothers the "exquisite suffering" of ambivalence: "the murderous alternation between bitter resentment and raw-edged nerves, and blissful gratification and tenderness" (Rich 1986, 21). Mother love is "intermixed with hate, sorrow, impatience, resentment and despair" (Ruddick 1995, 68). These mixed feelings and ambivalent attitudes characterize motherhood from its inception (the new mother who fantasizes about shaking her child until it ceases screaming) through the caregiving years (the mother of the adolescent who may also wish to murder her child) and beyond (the mother of the adult child who continues to struggle with her child's opposition to a mother's own principles). Fantasizing about killing one's child is a quite different matter from committing filicide, however. As Ruddick correctly suggests, the mother who "pictures herself" flinging a screaming infant at a window but acts to protect that child from her own angry impulses, loves her child (67). From the "practicalist" perspective that Ruddick develops, maternal love resides in and is tested by what a mother *actually does*.

Emphasis on the practical dimension of love is an important antidote to the self-flagellation many mothers undertake when they discover that loving feelings toward their children do not arise instinctively or consistently. It is also critical to undoing racist and classist conceptions of "good" mothering. The mother work of women of color and poor women who struggle to ensure the survival of their children and of the (ethnic, rural, or other) communities those children inhabit exemplifies love as a form of doing. Maternal love is embodied, for example, by mothers who work long weeks to put food on the table, tell oral histories to their children, teach their children survival skills and comb (or backcomb) their hair, as well as in the collective community-building work of women in neighborhoods, churches, schools, reservations (Collins 1990, 1994) and also, we might conjecture, on polygamous compounds. As Collins suggests, reflecting on such things as "relationships among family members" may be a symptom of racial

and economic privilege (1994, 48). As her term "motherwork" suggests, the commitment of mothers to children is manifested in their
individual and collective labor.

Closely related to the practical dimension of love is an *epistemological* dimension of love. As hooks (2000) reminds us, "understanding knowledge as an essential element of love is vital" because our
knowledge—of each other, of ourselves, and of love itself—informs the
work that we do (94–95). For Ruddick, the maternal thinking associated with the tasks of keeping a child safe and fostering her growth is
"knit together" by "attentive love." As earlier discussed, Ruddick's attentive maternal love (love that sees "the *child's* reality" without "seizing
or using him") is closely related to the notion of "loving perception"
as developed by Frye and Lugones. As such, it stands opposed to the
"arrogant perception" that characterizes the colonial love practiced by
some transracially adoptive mothers and critiqued by Moffat, Borshay
Liem, and others. Attentive love, as an element of the politics of love,
likewise stands opposed to practices of removing children from homes
simply because their families are unconventional.

If we think about attentive love as the combination of "a cognitive capacity—attention—and a virtue—love" (Ruddick 1995, 119), we
recognize its close affinity with feminist philosophical notions of virtue
epistemology and of epistemic responsibility. Response-able mothers
and lovers, like Lorraine Code's (1992) responsible knower, will exhibit
virtues such as honesty, openness, humility, and a concern for normative realism (how things "really" are). In practicing these epistemic
virtues, mothers will avoid both "epistemic indolence" ("a reluctance
to enquire further lest one face the necessity of having to reconsider
a wide range of treasured beliefs") and "epistemic imperialism" ("the
belief that a stereotyped person or situation is summed up" and can be
claimed as part of one's "stock of cognitive possessions") (Code 191–92).
The response-able mother is one who brings the virtues of reflection
and self-reflection to the task of communicative engagement required
by Dean's reflective solidarity. She will bring these virtues to bear both
within her own practice of mothering and in her relationships with
other mothers.

Both the practical and the epistemic dimensions of love are
important to what we might term a *maternal ethics of love*, an ethical practice that is akin to a practice of solidarity. The practice of
solidarity that I hope to evoke in speaking of an ethics of maternal
love extends beyond a mother's solidarity with her child(ren) toward a

solidarity between and among mothers. In her work on the role love plays in the development of subjectivity, Theresa Brennan (1992, 2004) argues that "living attention" (or love) from those who care for us is foundational to the development of our identity and our sense of agency and empowerment in the world. Brennan's notion of "living attention" informs Oliver's notion of "response-ability" (the ability to respond to and to address others) as the founding possibility of subjectivity. If subjects are produced in dialogic contexts, as I have suggested, then "the ego *is* insofar as it bears witness of itself to the other. . . . It is . . . the relationship of telling oneself to the other, that solidifies the ego" (Oliver 2001, 206). We can only come into being then (as mothers and as others), if somebody else gives us and our words "living attention." According to Brennan (1992), this task typically falls to women who are socialized—as mothers, wives, and helpmates—to provide living attention to others. While women's attention enables the self-image of men and children "to cohere," and thus "clears a space" in which men and children may "act upon the world," men (like Warren Jeffs, but also like many less vilified husbands) are taught to appropriate women's living attention and redirect it elsewhere (e.g., toward their own work or social status) (218–19). The result is that women may be "immobilized" by men who demand "a surplus of living attention" (234).[7] Under these circumstances, we (as mothers) need an ethics of maternal love that accommodates our need to receive (as well as give) love. We too need living attention in order to do our work. A practice of solidarity with each other, then—as lovers, co-mothers, sister wives, friends, or allies—is critical not only to facilitating our children's well-being, but also to facilitating our own coherence and agency as ethical subjects.

Both the practical and the epistemological dimensions of love are related to its *phenomenology*. Ahmed (2006) suggests that love is what literally "gives us a certain direction" (19). Yet, within our dwelling spaces, some loves (or objects of love) may be "out of reach," which is to say that they "may not even get near enough to 'come into view' as possible objects to be directed towards" (90–91). There are consequences to the different orientations love gives us, including consequences for our thinking about love itself. Mothers (and theories of motherhood) that focus on transmitting middle-class (white, neoliberal) values and privileges to children within the contexts of nuclear, heterosexual, monogamous families are more likely to conceptualize mother–child love as a dyadic (and perhaps also possessive) relationship between a (one) mother and child, whereas mothers (and theories of motherhood) that focus on mothering within non-normative circumstances are more likely to think about the love between mothers and children as loving attention that is circulated among mothers, communities, and the community's children.

Although love is not simply a feeling, "emotions shape the very surfaces of bodies, which take shape through the repetition of actions over time, as well as through orientations towards and away from others." Thus, attending to emotions can show us how our "actions are reactions, in the sense that what we do [and what we know] is shaped by the contact we have with others" (Ahmed 2004, 4). This, no doubt, reveals itself in my own work as well as in the work of most scholars of motherhood. My project (as a mother and as a theorist of mothering) begins with the love of two children, one an adopted child of color, the other a white child borne to me. These diverse points of contact lead me to desire sisterhood (loving solidarity) between my children, as well as between myself and my adopted daughter's birthmother. The love that "pulls me" towards particular, concrete others (affectional solidarity) can, as Ahmed notes, be "transferred towards a collective, expressed as an ideal or object" (political solidarity) (124). Indeed, it is my love for my daughters and the particular concrete others—a proliferating diversity of other racial-ethnic and white, queer and straight, working- and middle-class mothers—who sustain them (and thereby also me) that leads me to the ideal of polymaternalism espoused throughout this book, as well as to the ideal of home as a place of coalition and the ideal of love as a practice of solidarity.

Noting that emotions (from the Latin term *emovere*, "to move, to move out") are also about "attachments or about what connects us to this or that," Ahmed observes that "what moves us, what makes us feel, is also that which holds us in place, or gives us a dwelling place" (11). This being "held in place" may be interpreted as being "stuck" (being bound, chained, immobilized, obligated) or it may be interpreted as being "held together" (being coherent, connected, intelligible, response-able). Queer ambivalence about love, like feminist ambivalence about home, reflects opposing constructions of intimacy as simultaneously disempowering and empowering.[8] Discarding or leaving behind habitual ways of seeing, knowing, and understanding others (getting unstuck) is frequently a prerequisite to knowing them better, more intimately. As Oliver (2001) notes, "[a]s soon as I am sure that I know you, that I know what you will do next, I have stopped having a relationship with you and instead have a relationship with myself, with my own projection onto you. When I think that I know you, our relationship is over" (210). For this reason, Oliver contends, recognition must be reconceptualized as "a form of love that requires bearing witness to what cannot be seen," namely that which differentiates or stands between us (210).

As I have earlier suggested, it may be the "gaps and spaces between" the lover and the beloved, the mother(s) and child(ren) that make "communication and communion" possible (221). That which stands between us can also be that which brings us together, like a kitchen table or a conference table. This is Hannah Arendt's (1958) metaphor for relationship: "To live together in the world means essentially that a world of things is between those who have it in common, as a table is located between those who sit around it; the world, like every in-between, relates and separates [us] at the same time" (52). On Arendt's metaphorical understanding, the material world that stands between us is what gives rise to our difference and keeps us from collapsing into each other, losing both our individuation and, along with it, our relation to one another. If the table were to suddenly vanish from our midst, the "persons sitting opposite each other" would be "no longer separated but also would be entirely unrelated to each other by anything tangible" (53).

Using a less neutral and more sensory metaphor (evoking the image of a diaper table, perhaps, rather than a kitchen table or conference table), Gloria Anzaldúa (1998) suggests that what stands between us is *la mierda* or "a mountain of *caca* that keeps us from seeing each other" (528, see also Anzaldúa 1990, 146). Anzaldúa's metaphor reminds us of the differences we need to work through in order to see (really see) one another, as well as the repulsion we may experience in doing that work. From some positions (typically those of lesser privilege), it may be easier to see the *caca* heaped on the middle of our conference table (in the midst of our public spaces) or on the middle of our kitchen table (in the midst of our domestic spaces). But seeing it and working through it (rather than around it) is crucial if we, as mothers and as scholars of motherhood, are to work together, play together, or dine together at this table.[9]

Maternal love, as a love that bears witness to that which stands "between" mothers and children, mothers and others, and between mothers themselves and between children themselves, is a practice of solidarity—a commitment to continue coming back to *la mierda* long after a child has outgrown its diapers. In coming back to the table—

as many times as necessary—and working through whatever mountain is heaped atop it, maternal love embodies the faith and hope that
through practicing communicative engagement across difference, we
might create spaces "safe enough" for our children—and ourselves—to
risk the vulnerability of intimacy and develop a "responsible orientation to relationship" (Dean 1996, 29). Maternal love as a practice of
solidarity attempts to move beyond the dichotomy of home/not home
and safety/risk, to work toward an "ideal of home as a site of the risk
of connection, of sustaining relationship through conflict . . . an ideal
of home as a space of mutuality *and* conflict, of love *and* its risks and
struggles, of caring *and* conflictual connections to others" (Wier 2008a,
8, emphasis mine).

Maternal love as a practice of solidarity is also what makes us,
as mothers, real. Through shifting landscapes of home, through shifting relationships with our children and other mothers (and others),
through ongoing processes of shared meaning making, and through
ongoing struggles for change, we are held together. To accept love as
a practice of solidarity is to value the "we" over the "I" not as a practice of self-sacrifice but as a practice of ongoing self-transformation.
To value the "we" (both others and the relationships we share with
them), we must be willing to "expose ourselves to uncomfortable truths
[such as our own implication in relations of power] and to engage in
self-critique and transformation" (Weir 2008b, 128). In my own case,
recognizing my daughters, their other mothers and others as analogous
beings through something other than the power of colonial love (that
seeks to transform *them* into my image) has required "re-cognizing"
myself (126). My capacity to identify with and love others (as a part of
a "we" that includes them) has involved, as Kristeva (1991) suggests,
developing a capacity to identify with my own strangeness, a capacity
to accept, respect, care for and love the parts of myself that have been
repressed, excluded, abjected, or alienated. This is a project that has
only begun in these pages.

Epilogue

November 2010: Tomeka has locked herself in the bathroom again. This time, we are at my partner's house. I have called my ex-husband and his partner here as well—to stage an intervention. Tomeka is now eighteen, but still without a high school diploma or a job and she is pregnant. I am not ready for this. Nor, we are trying to convince her, is she. She is angry with me, with all of us, and determined to keep this baby. Although I do finally convince her to see a doctor and get a sonogram to determine how far along she is (and thus her time frame for decision making), she has already made up her mind. My teenage daughter is going to become a mother.

Around the same time I discover Tomeka is pregnant, my father is falling ill. I fly home to Canada for the winter break, during which time I visit with my bedridden, pain-wracked father, provide what assistance I can to my sister, Brenda, who has become Dad's primary caregiver, and proofread myriad due-tomorrow college application essays for Dakota, who has accompanied me on the trip. In summer 2011, in quick succession, I become an orphan (as my father dies a painful death from rectal cancer), a grandmother (as Sophie Elizabeth Park-Ozee emerges into the world), and an empty nester (as my younger daughter leaves for college).

In giving the eulogy for my father in May, my sisters and I each reflect on his capacity for unconditional love and his support for each of us despite our significant differences. (I am philosopher with a tendency—or so my family tells me—to have my head in the clouds; Brenda is a homemaker and the family nurturer and caregiver; Susan is an accountant with her feet firmly on the ground.) At my father's wake, we hold hands; we cry together; we laugh together. My youngest niece notes that although we can each be individually "grouchy" as moms, we are "cool" when we are together. It is true. In fact, I have harbored silent fantasies in the past of what it might be like for us to live and raise our children together—somewhat like the Henrickson or Brown or Darger family, as "sister wives" but without any husband.

I return home to Orlando literally just in time for Dakota's high school graduation. (My flight from Calgary to Orlando is delayed indefinitely and in a tone of voice resembling, I imagine, someone desperate who might be armed and dangerous, I explain to various airline agents that I must return home *now*; that arriving tomorrow is simply *not an option*. Luckily, I do not *look* armed and dangerous, but instead present as a harried and hysterical white mother; my story evokes sympathy from a ticket agent who gets me rerouted immediately.) After the high school graduation ceremony, my partner and I (and my ex-husband) share a celebratory lunch with our daughters, Dakota's high school friends, and their parents (two of whom, Karen and Cathy, have been Dakota's other mothers for the past seven years). The following day, Dakota, her friends, her other mothers (with two fathers in tow), and I travel to Maryland where we are jointly chaperoning their attendance at the World Odyssey of the Mind competition. Despite our differences (in sexual orientation, political beliefs, and caregiving styles), Karen, Cathy, and I, like my sisters and I, are a good team.

The following month, I drive to west Florida where Tomeka is now living with her birth mother, Trish. I know—through Tomeka and by virtue of the fact that Trish will not return my phone calls—that Trish is angry with me. I am unsure why (since she will not speak to me about it), but speculate it is either because she blames me for Tomeka's predicament or for not taking Tomeka and the baby-to-be into my own home or, perhaps, because of the alleged homophobia of Trish's fiancé or some combination of these things. Nonetheless, when I meet Tomeka and Trish at the hospital where Tomeka is being induced, Trish is friendly and gives me an embrace. As Tomeka finally goes into labor, Trish holds her right leg and I hold her left leg as the midwife coaches all of us through the delivery. Although Tomeka's boyfriend is also present, I barely know him and doubt that he will be a lasting presence in our lives. Thus I am focused on the perfect (and in this case quite literal) triangle of mothers and daughter in the delivery room. Although I remain apprehensive about what is to come in the next several weeks, months, and years, this shared moment is perfectly as it should be. When a (male) physician arrives to observe the proceedings, he asks who Trish and I are. I explain that we are Tomeka's mothers.

He gives me half a wink and says, "Oh, I understand." He doesn't, of course, but I don't explain further. An hour or so later, without the physician's assistance, Sophie Elizabeth pokes her head and then the rest of her body into our world—a world in which, thus far, she only has one mother, but nine grandmothers and great-grandmothers who, unbeknownst to her, will work in tandem to mentor and guide her (and, no doubt, occasionally annoy her).

In August, my partner, Claudia, and I drive to Tuscaloosa with Dakota who will be starting university there the following week. Here too, I reflect that the triangulation of professor-mothers and academic-daughter is as it should be. Despite struggles along the way and my previously felt need to negotiate differences between my partner and daughter, they have now forged a relationship for themselves no longer requiring my presence in the middle; I can now relax into my third point in the triangle. As Dakota, like Tomeka, enters a new stage in her life, she will be supported by multiple mothers who—via phone calls, emails, text messages, Facebook posts, video conferencing, and in-person visits—will encourage, support, console (and occasionally nag) her. As I enter a new phase in my own life, I am immensely grateful to all of the other mothers who have been, are now, or will be in the future, present in my life and the life of my daughters.

In her well-known and much contested essay, "Compulsory Heterosexuality and Lesbian Existence," Adrienne Rich (1980) asks why women's intimate connections to one another have been hidden, disguised, marginalized, and excluded in a wide range of writings, including feminist scholarship (632). Arguing that it is "not enough" for feminism to acknowledge lesbian existence as a matter of sexual preference, Rich argues for recognition of a "lesbian continuum" that recognizes diverse forms of "primary intensity between and among women," including "the sharing of a rich inner life" and the "giving and receiving of practical and political support" in addition to explicitly sexual contact with another (658–49).

In part, this book has attempted to respond to the exclusion and marginalization of women's intimate relations with one another within feminist scholarship on motherhood. As others before me have noted, much feminist theorizing about motherhood has implied that mothering takes place within the contexts of nuclear, heteronormative families. More recently, studies of lesbian motherhood have found their place within our feminist canon; yet, as Rich contends, it is "not enough" for feminist theories, including feminist theories of motherhood, to acknowledge lesbianism as the sole location of resistance to hetero-patriarchal or heteronormative institutions. The "not enoughness" of the move toward inclusion of lesbians in our theories of mothering is further indicated by contemporary queer critiques of same-sex marriage and parenting as a homonormative practice. Lesbian mothering illuminates the possibility of mothering as a cooperative practice between women, a practice that highlights intimacy between women while challenging the ideology of monomaternalism and the heteronormative Oedipal picture of child development. As I have been arguing here, however, the affective triangulation of maternal desire that resists the heteronormative principle of "one and only one mother per child" (monomaternalism) exists on a continuum that may include, for example, families formed through open adoption, through divorce and recouplings, and through polygamous kinship. In these and many other contexts of communal childrearing, mothering may reveal itself as a queer form of breeding (a practice that breeds queerness), rather than as the compulsory activity of reproducing heteropatriarchal, heteronormative, and domestinormative forms of life. If mothering is not a solo activity and home is not a fixed and static place wherein such activity takes place, then we are challenged to rethink motherhood as an identity, mothering as a practice, and the scholarship of motherhood as a field of study that can be pursued in isolation from queer theory.

Just as Rich's notion of the lesbian continuum was widely criticized for diluting the meaning of the term "lesbian," my own insistence on a continuum of polymaternal families might be criticized for diluting the meaning of the term "queer." Can heterosexual breeders be portrayed as queer without marginalizing those with non-normative sexual identities? Might my inclusion of (heterosexual) divorce-extended, adoptive, and polygamous families under the umbrella of "queer" families further the divide between those sexual minorities who argue that "they are just like everyone else" and those who claim difference because of their sexual practices? My response to these concerns, as contained in the preceding pages, is twofold. First, queer theory and activism has already blurred the boundaries of identity politics. The move from lesbian and gay studies to queer theory (and from lesbian and gay politics to queer activism) was a move that decentralized the importance of sexual identity, emphasizing instead notions of performance and performativity. In keeping with this, the emphasis throughout this book has been on what it means to mother queerly rather than on what it means to be a queer mother. My interest is in a range of practices of mothering that (intentionally or unintentionally) begin to queer the meaning of motherhood by (consciously or unconsciously) resisting the reproduction of heteronormativity. We may wish that all queer performances and practices were conscious and intentional, but a queer reading of performances enacted by those who identify as straight, like a queer reading of literary texts written by straight authors, is not undermined by attributions of authorial intent. What people *do* and how their performances may be interpreted is a separate matter from their self-perceptions and understandings. Just as those who identify as queer may act in (homo)normative ways, those who identify as straight may perform queer acts.

Second, the queer critique of breeders has been centered on the ways in which biological reproduction in normative familial spaces has reproduced straight (heteronormative, reprosexual, repronarrative, domestinormative) forms of life. If, as I have argued here, mothering often exceeds and resists biocentric narratives, if familial intimacy frequently resists our attempts at domestication, and if home exists in queer times and spaces, then there is no reason for queer theorists to exclude mothering as a practice or as a topic of study allegedly opposed to the development of non-normative forms of life. My hope is that just as the engagements of feminist theory with postcolonial theory and of queer theory with postcolonial theory have challenged and enriched both feminist and queer understandings of gender, work at the intersections of feminist theory and queer theory (as these intersect with postcolonial theory) may challenge and enrich our current understandings and practices of motherhood. Perhaps such enriched understandings of motherhood will even breed some rather queer (theoretical and physical) offspring.

Notes

Introduction

1. Race and class privilege are not, of course, the only variables that shape our conceptions of good mothering; sexual orientation, marital status, ability, weight, age, and a host of other factors also shape our ideals of what it means to be a "real" (i.e., good) mother.

2. See, for example, Johnson (2005), Johnson and Henderson (2005), Moraga (1993, 2011), Muñoz (1999), J. M. Rodriguez (2003), and R. T. Rodriguez (2009).

3. Thanks to an anonymous reviewer for posing these questions.

Chapter 1

1. Consider, for example, Judith Jarvis Thomson's (1971) classic defense of abortion wherein she likens the inconveniences of pregnancy to being kidnapped and involuntarily hooked up to a violinist who needs use of one's kidneys to live, and—in another analogy—likens the fetus to a burglar who has invaded one's home. In both cases, the fetus is simply a stranger that usurps and depletes a woman's resources. Frye (1983) is explicit about this, contending that the rejection of motherhood may depend on a woman being free to see the fetus as a parasite. Although it is true that the fetus depends on the life blood of its maternal host, reducing the pregnant woman's experience to the experience of parasitism ignores the emotional and relational complexity that frequently attends decisions to abort, transfer or continue a relationship with the growing life inside oneself.

2. Yates was originally convicted of capital murder and sentenced to life imprisonment. However, on appeal she was found to be not guilty by reason of insanity—with a history of psychosis and postpartum depression—and committed to a high-security mental health institution. Provoked by the Yates and Schlosser cases, Texas State Rep. Jessica Farrar introduced a bill to the Texas legislature in March 2009 that would establish infanticide as a crime distinguishable from murder (Appel 2009). Such legislation, if passed, would

259

be unique in the United States, but would make Texas law compatible with the laws of many other industrialized democracies, including Australia, Canada, Great Britain, France, Greece, Italy, Japan, Norway, and Sweden, as well as Brazil, Colombia, India, the Philippines, and Turkey.

3. Lavergne et al. (2008), Rivaux et al. (2008), and MacGruder and Shaw (2008).

Chapter 2

1. See also Fanon (1967), Anzaldúa (1987, 1990), and Lugones (2003) on the phenomenon of double-consciousness arising from inhabiting a peripheral body. By drawing on this notion here, I do not intend to obscure the significant differences between postcolonial bodies and adoptive bodies. Insofar as adoptive maternal bodies frequently embody class and race privileges used to appropriate the labor of postcolonial bodies, the differences between the two have important political consequences as I discuss in detail in the following chapter. Here I merely wish to emphasize a particular methodological parallel between postcolonial and adoptive epistemologies.

2. Some feminist legal scholars have sought to address the unjust outcomes of surrogacy and other custody cases by highlighting the unique nature of mothers' gestational experiences—arguing that the donation of sperm does not make one a parent (see, e.g., Pateman 1988; Shanley 1993; Woliver 1995). Unfortunately, a focus on women's gestational capacities as *the* differentiating factor between male and female parents implies that gender is irrelevant to adoptive parenting.

3. In light of this, it is not surprising that persons of color who know how to perform the script for whiteness and lesbians and gays who know how to perform the script for heterosexuality are among those marginalized folk most likely to be approved for adoption.

4. For discussions of the surveillance and regulation of black, Latina, indigenous, lesbian, teen, and poor mothers, as well as those who have neglected or abused their children, see Fineman and Karpin (1995).

5. Here I emphasize the importance of agency and choice to highlight how non-normative forms of motherhood, such as adoption, may function as a site of political resistance. However, the notions of agency and choice require critical interrogation, as I discuss briefly here and more extensively in Chapter 6.

6. Miller (1995) comments on the Boston Women's Health Collective's now classic text *Our Bodies, Our Selves*, but the point holds for the circulation of adoption narratives as well.

7. One notable exception was the 1992 case, *In the Matter of Evan*, where a lesbian was permitted to adopt the biological child of her partner without discontinuation of the birth mother's rights. This was the first second-parent adoption by a lesbian co-parent approved in the United States.

8. Prior to 2000, only four states (Massachusetts, Missouri, Wisconsin, and New Mexico) allowed nonbiological parents legal standing to seek visitation or perhaps custody. In 2007, several other states (Minnesota, Rhode Island, Colorado, California, Indiana, Pennsylvania, New Jersey, Washington, and Maine) granted such standing, although in a majority of these states legal standing pertains only to seeking visitation (not custody). At the most conservative end of the political spectrum is my home state of Florida. Although a State Appellate Court ruling in 2010 declared Florida's three-decade-old ban on adoption by lesbian and gay individuals and couples to be unconstitutional, in 2011 newly elected Gov. Rick Scott urged a return to "promoting adoption by marital families" that provide children with both a father and a mother.

Chapter 3

1. See Barry (2006) on the treatment of incarcerated mothers, Lindsey (1994) on the interpretation of poverty as neglect, and Fetzer (1999) on the interpretation of kinship care among Native Americans as parental neglect.

2. The kidnapping and transnational sale of babies for profit has been well documented. See Fieweger (1991), Jackson (1994), Miko (2000), Freundlich (2000), Stoler (2002), Nelson (2006), McDermott (2006), and Hübinette (2006).

3. In the wake of NABSW's critique of transracial adoption, the adoption of black children by whites decreased from 2,574 in 1971 to 1,400 in 1987 (Simon and Alstein 2000).

4. In 1992, U.S. citizens adopted 6,472 children from abroad; in 2004, the number of foreign children adopted into U.S. families was 22,991, more than tripling in an eight-year period (U.S. Dept. of State 2006, 2011).

5. Precedents cited in these legal arguments included *Brown v Board of Education* (1954), *City of Richmond v Croson* (1989), *Loving v Virginia* (1967), *Palmore v Sidoti* (1984), and *Shaw v Reno* (1993).

6. Children covered by the Indian Child Welfare Act (ICWA) were exempted from IEPA policy. However, mixed race indigenous children were not covered by the ICWA, thus limiting the Act's protection of tribal sovereignty in matters of child placement.

7. TANF was reauthorized in the Deficit Reduction Act of 2005.

8. See Posner 1987.

9. See, for example, the much-touted Minnesota study on transracial adoption conducted by Scarr and Weinberg (1976) and revisited by Weinberg, Scarr, and Waldman (1992).

10. Direct confrontations with the ghosts of one's past is a common theme among Korean (and other) children adopted into Western families. For other narratives of adult Korean adoptees returning to Korea to seek their identity and make a "home" for themselves, see Lee (2008), Trenka (2009), and Kim (2010).

11. Kim (2010) likewise suggests the importance of a "collective identity" for Korean adoptees.

Chapter 4

1. This is not to say that a child is *always* best served by having multiple, diverse parents. It is, however, to say that this option should not be "arbitrarily foreclosed" (Narayan 1999, 85).

2. See J. Warner (2005) for a provocative account of the impossible ideals of good mothering governing women in the United States.

3. There are no exceptions to standard adoption law for stepmothers—namely they cannot petition to adopt their spouse's child unless the birth mother agrees to completely revoke her parental rights (U.S. Dept. for HHS, 2012). Thus, even if a child is living with his or her stepmother the majority of the time, the stepmother rarely has the legal right to enroll children in school, provide the child with health insurance, or undertake other state-regulated acts of maternal care. Nor will she have any rights of visitation to the child for whom she has cared should her marriage dissolve. At time of writing, only sixteen states allowed second-parent adoptions by same-sex parents, leaving most lesbian co-parents in the same situation (Human Rights Campaign 2012).

4. See Edelman (2004) for an insightful critique of our fetishism of the Child as a site of innocence and vulnerability.

5. See Stanworth (1987) on nonadoptive custody disputes.

6. See, for example, Freudburg and Geiss (1986), Grimm and Grimm (1978, 1996), Keller (1991), Koehler (1990), Munsch (1982), and Turner (1990)

7. See also Kristeva (1987), Taylor (1989), Honneth (1996), Oliver (2001), and Butler (1997, 2005).

8. As Penelope Deutscher (2002) claims, in a different context, the question is not whether to "eat" others (as this is inevitable). What we must ask ourselves is how to eat "ethically," that is, in ways that respect the others' difference (130–36). This is a topic I take up from a different angle in examining abjection as circumscribing the boundaries of the self in Chapter 6.

9. As Lugones notes, her concept of "world"-traveling is "not assimilable to the middle-class leisurely journey nor the colonial or imperialist journeys." The traveling between worlds that Lugones recommends includes "risking one's ground" and "being open to surprise." "World"-traveling, she contends, thus takes us in the direction of building "deep coalitions" (98). I turn to an examination of families as coalitional entities and mothers as coalition builders in Chapter 7.

10. See, for example, Allen (1984), Anderson (1994), and Frye (1983). Many other feminists (following Rich 1986) also reject motherhood as an institution but not necessarily mothering as a practice.

11. To present barriers to children's epistemic and moral development and then, having examined children under such nonoptimal conditions, conclude

that they are incapable of such development is to undermine children's agency formation in ways similar to the ways in which women's epistemic and moral agency has been historically undermined (cf. Frye 1983, 46–47). As Hughes (1996) notes and we would do well here to remember, philosophers have often denied autonomy to women on the same grounds it has been denied to children: lack of rationality, capriciousness, and vulnerability (16).

Chapter 5

1. See, for example, Brown (1922), Gibson (1969), Wilkinson (1974), Amato and Keith (1991), Fagan and Rector (2000), Wallerstein et al. (2000), and Amato (2001).

2. See Morgan (1999, 2002) and Butler (2004) on the notion of "doing" family.

3. See also Butler (2005) for analogous considerations about the relationship between subjectivity and ethical responsibility. Butler's emphasis is on "giving an account of oneself," however, and as such requires a fairly mature form of narration that may be beyond a child's ability.

4. The metaphor of "world"-traveling seems especially apt given the proliferation of virtual spaces explicitly named as "worlds" within cyberspace: for example, "Fish world," "Zoo world," "Café world," "Mall world," "Hero world," "Mafia world," or "Farmville," among others.

5. Valentine borrows the notion of "living apart together" from Levin (2004). Levin used the term to describe U.K. families who are separated by geographical distance because of a parent's work commitments. Valentine extends the usage to embrace divorced families, diasporic families, and others. See also Holmes (2004).

6. Much of the emphasis in cybercultural studies has been on how digital technologies "speed up" time; of equal importance is how such technologies allow us to "slow down" lived time.

7. See also R. Jackson (1994) for a series of real and fictional accounts of mothers who leave their children. Although Jackson balks at turning the mother who leaves into a feminist heroine, she argues, like Büskens, that maternal departures from their children's lives are misunderstood outside of "a framework that links the personal to the social and political" (33).

Chapter 6

1. See also S. Ahmed (2004) who argues, in a similar vein, that queer discomfort is "not about assimilation or resistance, but about inhabiting norms *differently*" (155, original emphasis).

2. Like my light-skinned biracial daughter who is frequently presumed to be white because she lives with white parents, as a "femme" who lives with children, I am frequently presumed to be straight.

3. See, for example, Hall (1904), A. Freud (1936), Sullivan (1940, 1953), Kernberg (1984), and Laufer and Laufer (1984).

4. In 2008, U.S. law enforcement agencies made an estimated 2.11 million arrests of persons younger than age eighteen. Juveniles represented 16 percent of all arrests for violent crime and 26 percent of all arrests for property crimes in 2008. Nonetheless, the Office of Juvenile Justice notes that this represents a decline in juvenile arrests, thus soothing fears that had emerged in 2005 and 2006 that we might be "on the brink of another juvenile crime wave" (U.S. Dept. of Justice 2009, "Juvenile Arrests," 1).

5. Such psychological and psychiatric assessments of adolescence are now supported also by cognitive science. Caulum (2007) for example, contends that brain imaging research demonstrates that the areas of the brain responsible for impulse control and decision making are not well developed until well into a person's twenties.

6. Kristeva does not address adolescence per se in her 1982 analysis of abjection. In her 1997 work, which does address adolescence, Kristeva's description of adolescence as an "open psychic structure" wherein the adolescent questions her identity along with her capacity for language seems quite compatible with an account of abjection; yet Kristeva appears to reject such an account (136).

7. Coats talks of "disidentifying" with the not-me; however, her use of this term parallels Muñoz's discussion of counter-identification (as distinct from disidentification).

8. As explained by Althusser (2001), interpellation is the process of "hailing" through which individuals are turned into subjects. Althusser's famous example is the hail from a police officer that simultaneously recognizes and subjugates the subject who acknowledges this hailing (118). As Butler (1993) notes, for this subjugation by the law to work, we must recognize and accept this subject position.

9. See Wilson (2001) for an interesting analysis of the ways in which abjection produces the freakish and how, in freakish families, the nonfreakish may be abjected.

10. Lugones' (2003) discussion of "streetwalker theorizing" resonates with Reagon's claim that "coalition work has to be done in the streets." Lugones, however, refuses theorizing that is "held captive by the private/public split" (221).

11. Reagon's rhetorical strategy here of telling her audience to "grow up" obviously predates queer critiques of futurity and the advocacy of queer temporalities. It is nonetheless interesting to consider their juxtaposition. Being "all grow'd up" has a resonance for black women that is quite different than being a "grown up" has for white queers.

Chapter 7

1. See Dean (1996) on the difference between reflective solidarity and liberalism (178).

2. As Halberstam (2011) notes, our tendency to see heterosexuality everywhere may "blot out a far more compelling story about cooperation, collectivity, and nonheterosexual, non-reproductive behaviors" (38). Although she makes this remark in the context of critiquing the heteronormative lens through which nature was viewed in *The March of the Penguins,* I think something similar occurs in the way we view polygamy. We—and here the "we" includes many feminists and queers, as well as others—are so focused on the heterosexual and reproductive relationships between polygamist wives and their husbands that we fail to see the deep and interesting relationships between the wives themselves who engage as a homosocial collective.

3. I am using "identity politics" here in the sense critiqued by Reagon (1983) and others. This critique of identity as an inflexible categorization does not apply to recent reconceptualizations of identity such as the "transformative identity politics" advocated by Weir (2008b).

4. As noted earlier, the notion of family as a locus of affection (love and care) is a relatively recent historical notion and remains ill suited to describing kinship in many non-Western cultures wherein bonds of loyalty, for example, may supersede bonds based on demonstrations of affection.

5. A serious discussion of this question continues in Canada. The federal government commissioned a study into polygamy weeks before it introduced same-sex legislation in June 2005. The study was intended to alleviate fears that legalizing same-sex marriage might lead to constitutional challenges from polygamists. However, the study recommended that Canada repeal its anti-polygamy law, indicating that the law was discriminatory to both native-born citizens and immigrants and, moreover, harmed women in polygamous marriages who were unable to claim spousal support and inheritance rights (Campbell et al. 2005). Shortly, thereafter, Winston Blackmore, who had been arrested for polygamy, lodged a legal challenge to the constitutionality of anti-polygamy laws. In November 2011, the Supreme Court of British Columbia upheld the constitutionality of its anti-polygamy laws, acknowledging that they did, indeed, violate the Canadian Charter of Rights and Freedoms, but arguing that state intrusion was nonetheless warranted because of the harm to women and children presented by polygamy (see Reference re: Section 293 of the Criminal Code of Canada). In light of the fact that Blackmore had not been charged with incurring any specific harm (simply with practicing polygamy), the Canadian public remains divided on the issue with polyamorists, Muslims, and immigration advocates paying particularly close attention to the details of the ruling.

6. At time of writing, the lawsuit is in limbo. Lawyers for the Browns had filed an eighty-page brief challenging the constitutionality of the anti-bigamy

law under which the Browns were being investigated. Rather than filing a summary judgment motion arguing the merits of constitutionality of the state law, however, the prosecutors promised not to prosecute the Brown family for polygamy and to end the investigation, asking the District Court Judge to dismiss the case. Lead counsel for the Browns pledges he will continue to challenge the constitutionality of the law, but the Browns may lose their legal standing in light of the dropped charges against them (see Turley 2012).

7. For a similar argument based in radical feminism, rather than psychoanalytic feminism, see Frye (1983) 167–72.

8. Kipnis also captures our ambivalence about love, noting at the end of her polemic *Against Love*, that to be "against" love can mean *both* to be opposed to it (resistant and defiant) *and* to be next to it (beside it or near it).

9. As hooks (2000) also notes, love demands work—some of it distasteful. The practice of love invites us to enter a place of connection and community, which is "at the same time a place of critical awakening and pain"; faced with this many of us "turn our backs on love" (114).

References

Ahmed, Leila. 1999. *A border passage: From Cairo to America—A woman's journey.* New York: Penguin.

Ahmed, Sara. 2000. *Strange encounters: Embodied others in post-coloniality.* New York: Routledge.

———. 2004. *The cultural politics of emotion.* New York: Routledge.

———. 2006. *Queer phenomenology: Orientations, objects, others.* Durham, NC: Duke University Press.

Allen, Jeffner. 1984. Motherhood: The annihilation of women. In *Feminist frameworks: Alternative theoretical accounts of the relations between women and men,* 3rd ed., ed. Alison M. Jaggar and Paula S. Rothenberg, 380–85. New York: McGraw Hill.

Altbach, Edith. 2007. *From feminism to liberation.* New Brunswick, NJ: Transaction.

Althusser, Louis. 2001. *Lenin and philosophy and other essays.* Trans. Ben Brewster. New York: Monthly Review Press.

Amato, Paul R. 2001. Children of divorce in the 1990s: An update of the Amato and Keith (1991) meta-analysis. *Journal of Family Psychology* 15, no. 3: 355–70.

Amato, Paul R and Bruce Keith. 1991. Parental divorce and the well-being of children: A meta-analysis. *Psychological Bulletin* 110, no.1: 26–46.

Anderson, Jackie. 1994. Separatism, feminism, and the betrayal of reform. *Signs* 19: 437–48.

Andujo, E. 1988. Ethnic identity of transethnically adopted Hispanic adolescents. *Social Work* 33: 531–35.

Ang, Ien. 1995. I'm a feminist but . . . "Other" women and postnational feminism. In *Transitions: New Australian feminisms,* ed. Barbara Caine and Rosemary Pringle, 57–73. Sydney: Allen and Unwin.

Anzaldúa, Gloria. 1987. *Borderlands/la frontera: The new mestiza.* 2nd ed. San Francisco: Aunt Lute Books.

———, ed. 1990. *Making face, making soul, Haciendo Caras: Creative and critical perspectives by feminists of color.* San Francisco: Aunt Lute Books.

————. 1998. Bridge, drawbridge, sandbar or island, Lesbians-of-color *Hacienda Alianzas*. In *Social perspectives in lesbian and gay studies,* ed. Peter M. Nardi and Beth E. Schneider, 527–635. London and New York: Routledge.

Appel, Jacob M. 2009. When infanticide isn't murder. *Huffington Post,* Sept. 8.

Arendt, Hannah. 1958. *The human condition.* Chicago: University of Chicago Press.

Ashe, Marie. 1995. Postmodernism, legal ethics, and representation of "bad mothers." In Fineman and Karpin, 1995, 142–66.

Atwood, Thomas C. Lee A. Allen, Virginia C. Ravenel, and Nicole F. Callahan, eds. 2007. *Adoption Factbook IV.* Sterliing, VA: National Council for Adoption.

Baby business. 1995. Directed by Judy Jackson. Montreal: National Film Board of Canada.

Bachelard, Gaston. 1994. *The poetics of space.* Trans. Maria Jolas. Boston: Beacon Press.

Backus, Margot Gayle. 2001. I am your mother; she was a carrying case. In *Imagining adoption: Essays on literature and culture,* 133–49. Ann Arbor: University of Michigan Press.

Balsamo, Anne. 1996. *Technologies of the gendered body: Reading cyborg women.* Durham, NC: Duke University Press.

Banking on heaven. 2007. Directed by Dot Reidelback. NV: Over the Moon Productions.

Baptists in Haiti could face U.S. kidnapping charges. 2010. *National Public Radio,* Feb. 1.

Barney, Kevin. 2011. Meet the Dargers. *By Common Consent.* October 9. http://bycommonconsent.com/2011/10/09/meet-the-dargers/ [accessed May 2012].

Barry, Ellen. 2006. Parents in prison, children in crisis. In Trenka, Oparah and Shin 2006, 59–74.

Bartholet, Elizabeth. 1991. Where do Black children belong? The politics of race matching in adoption. *University of Pennsylvania Law Review* 139: 1163–256.

————. 1993. *Family bonds.* Boston: Houghton Mifflin.

————. 2007a. International adoption: Thoughts on the human rights issues. *Buffalo Human Rights Law Review* 13: 151–203.

————. 2007b. Slamming the door on adoption: Depriving children of loving homes. *Washington Post,* Nov. 4.

Beizer, Janet. 2002. One's own: Reflections on motherhood, owning, and adoption. *Tulsa Studies in Women's Literature* 21, no. 2: 237–56.

Berg, Barbara. 1995. Listening to the voices of the infertile. In Callahan, 80–108.

Bergquist, Kathleen Ja Sook. 2004. International Asian adoption: In the best interests of the child? *Texas Wesleyan Law Review* 10, no. 2: 343–50.

Berlant, Lauren and Michael Warner. 1998. Sex in public. *Critical Inquiry* 24, no. 2: 547–66.

Bhabha, Homi. 1992. The world and the home. *Signs* 32: 141–53.

Biddick, Kathleen. 1993. Stranded histories: Feminist allegories of artificial life. In *Research in philosophy and technology,* ed. Joan Rothschild and Frederick Ferre, 165–82. Greenwich: JAI Press.

Big love, seasons 1–5. 2011. HBO entertainment. New York: Time Warner. DVD.

Boedecker, Hal. 2009. Casey Anthony: She could face three trials next year. *Orlando Sentinel,* Dec. 19.

Borshay Liem, Deann. 2000. *First person plural.* Center for Asian American Media.

———. 2010. *In the matter of Cha Jung Hee.* Mu films.

Bourne, Jenny. 1987. Homelands of the mind: Jewish feminism and identity politics. *Race and Class* 29, no. 1: 1–24.

Boy's dad has doubts on Madonna's adoption. 2006. *CBS,* Oct. 22.

Braidotti, Rosi. 1994. *Nomadic subjects: Embodiment and sexual difference in contemporary feminist theory.* New York: Columbia University Press.

Brennan, P. A., S. A. Medrick, B. Jacobsen. 1996. Assessing the role of genetics in crime using adoption cohorts. *Ciba foundation symposium* 194: 115–23.

Brennan, Teresa. 1992. *The interpretation of the flesh: Freud and femininity.* London: Routledge.

———. 2004. *The transmission of affect.* Ithaca, NY: Cornell University Press.

Briggs, Laura. 2006. Orphaning the children of welfare: "Crack babies," race, and adoption reform. In Trenka, Oparah and Shin 2006, 75–88.

Brodzinsky, David. M. 2003. *Adoption by lesbians and gays: A national survey of adoption agency policies, practices, and attitudes.* New York: The Evan B. Donaldson Adoption Institute.

Brown, Kody, Meri Brown, Janelle Brown, Christine Brown and Robyn Brown. 2012. *Becoming sister wives: The story of an unconventional marriage.* New York: Gallery.

Brown, Sara A. 1922. Rural child dependency, neglect, and delinquency. In *Rural child welfare,* ed. Edward N. Clopper, 165–237. New York: Macmillan.

Brown, Sheila. 1998. *Understanding youth and crime: Listening to youth?* Buckingham: Open University Press.

Brown v Board of Education. 347 U.S. 483 [1954].

Büskens, Petra. 2004. From perfect housewife to fishnet stockings and not quite back again: One mother's story of leaving home. In *Mother outlaws: Theories and practices of empowered mothering,* ed. Andrea O'Reilly, 105–22. Toronto: Women's Press.

Butler, Judith. 1993. *Bodies that matter: On the discursive limits of "sex."* New York: Routledge.

———. 1997. *The psychic life of power.* Stanford, CA: Stanford University Press.

———. 2004. *Undoing gender.* New York: Routledge.

———. 2005. *Giving an account of oneself.* New York: Fordham University Press.

Calhoun, Cheshire. 1997. Family's outlaws: Rethinking the connections between feminism, lesbianism, and the family. In Lindemann Nelson 1997, 131–50.

——. 2000. *Feminism, the family, and the politics of the closet: Lesbian and gay displacement.* New York: Oxford University Press.

——. 2005. Who's Afraid of polygamous marriage? Lessons for same-sex marriage advocacy from the history of polygamy. *San Diego Law Review* 42: 1023–42.

Call, Eran A. 1997. The home: A refuge and sanctuary. *The Church of Jesus Christ of the Latter-day Saints* 167th semiannual general conference proceedings. October. http://www.lds.org/general-conference/1997/10/the-home-a-refuge-and-sanctuary? [accessed February 2009].

Callahan, Joan C., ed. 1995. *Reproduction, ethics, and the law: Feminist perspectives.* Bloomington: Indiana Press.

Campbell, Angela, et al. 2005. *Polygamy in Canada: Legal and social implications for women and children.* Ottawa: Status of Women Canada.

Campbell, Gwynn, Suzanne Miers and Joseph C. Miller. 2009. *Children in slavery throughout the ages.* Athens: Ohio University Press.

Cannon, Katie G. 1988. *Black womanist ethics.* Oxford: Oxford University Press.

Cannon, Janell. 1993. *Stellaluna.* New York: Scholastic.

Carp, E. Wayne. 1998. *Family matters: Secrecy and disclosure in the history of adoption.* Cambridge: Harvard University Press.

Caulfield, Mina Davis. 1984. Imperialism, the family and cultures of resistance. In *Feminist frameworks: Alternative theoretical accounts of the relations between women and men,* 3rd ed., ed. Allison M. Jaggar and Paula S. Rothenberg, 442–47. New York: McGraw-Hill.

Caulum, Melissa S. 2007. Postadolescent brain development: A disconnect between neuroscience, emerging adults, and the corrections system. *Wisconsin Law Review* 729: 740–43.

Child Welfare Information Gateway. 2004. How many children were adopted in 2000 and 2001? http://www.childwelfare.gov/pubs/s_adopted/index.cfm [accessed September 2007].

City of Richmond v J.A. Croson Company. 488 U.S. 469 [1989].

Clarke, Andy. 2004. *Natural-born cyborgs: Minds, technologies, and the future of human intelligence.* Oxford: Oxford University Press.

Cloud, Dana. 1992. The possibility of a liberating narrative: *Woman on the edge of time* as radical, mythic, moral argument. In *Constructing and reconstructing gender: The links among communication, language, and gender,* ed. Linda A. M. Perry, Lynn H. Turner, and Helen M. Sterk, 5–16. Albany, NY: SUNY Press.

Coats, Carol. 2004. *Looking glasses and Neverlands: Lacan, desire and subjectivity in children's literature.* Iowa City: University of Iowa Press.

Code, Lorraine. 1992. Experience, knowledge, and responsibility. In *Women, knowledge, and reality: Explorations in feminist philosophy,* 157–72. New York: Routledge.

Collier, Rachel Quy. 2006. Performing childhood. In Trenka, Oparah and Shin 2006, 207–19.

Collins, Natalie R. 2010. *Sister wife* (sisters of sin). Ogden, UT: Binary Press.

Collins, Patricia Hill. 1990. *Black feminist thought. Knowledge, consciousness and the politics of empowerment.* Boston: Unwin Hyman.

———. 1994. Shifting the center: Race, class, and feminist theorizing about motherhood. In *Mothering: Ideology, experience, and agency,* ed. Evelyn Nakano Glenn, Grace Chang, and Linda Rennie Forcey, 45–65. New York: Routledge.

Cox, Alexandra. 2011. *Cracked lenses: The visual exploitation of crack mothers. Women and prison: A site for resistance.* Womenandprison.org. [accessed December 2011].

Cvetkovitch, Ann. 1995. Sexual trauma/queer memory: Incest, lesbianism, and therapeutic culture. *GLQ: A Journal of Lesbian and Gay Studies* 2, no. 4: 351–77.

Darger, Joe, Alina Darger, Vicki Darger, Valerie Darger, and Brooke Adams. 2011. *Love times three: Our true story of a polygamous marriage.* New York: HarperOne.

Dean, Jodi. 1996. *Solidarity of strangers: Feminism after identity politics.* Berkeley: University of California Press.

De Landa, Manuel. 2006. *A new philosophy of society: Assemblage theory and social complexity.* London: Continuum.

De Lauretis, Teresa. 1990a. Eccentric subjects: Feminist theory and historical consciousness. *Feminist Studies* 16, no. 1 (Spring): 115–50.

———. 1990b. Sexual indifference and lesbian representation. In *Performing feminisms: Feminist critical theory and theatre,* ed. Sue-Ellen Case, 17–39. Baltimore: Johns Hopkins Press.

Deleuze, Gilles and Félix Guattari. 1987. *A thousand plateaus: capitalism and schizophrenia.* Trans. Brian Massumi. Minneapolis: University of Minnesota Press.

Deutscher, Penelope. 2002. *A politics of impossible difference: The later work of Luce Irigaray.* New York: Cornell University Press.

Dill, B. Thornton. 1988. Our mothers' grief: racial ethnic women and the maintenance of families. *Journal of Family History* 13: 415–31.

Douglas, Susan J. and Meredith W. Michaels. 2004. *The mommy myth: The idealization of motherhood and how it has undermined women.* New York: Free Press.

Dozier, Al. 2005. Smith courtroom drama begins. *Herald,* Rock Hill, S.C., July 19.

Dubinsky, Karen. 2010. *Babies without borders: Adoption and migration across the Americas.* Toronto: University of Toronto Press.

Duggan, Lisa. 2003. *The twilight of equality?: Neoliberalism, cultural politics, and the attack On democracy.* Boston: Beacon Press.

———. 2006. Making it perfectly queer. In *Sex wars: Sexual dissent and political culture,* ed. Lisa Duggan and Nan Hunter, 149–63. New York: Routledge.

Dworkin, Andrea. 1987. Women and war. New York: Basic Books.

———. 1989. *Letters from a war zone.* New York: Penguin.

Eastman, P. D. 1960. *Are you my mother?* New York: Basic Books.

Ebershoff, David. 2008. *The 19th wife*. New York: Random House.

Edelman, Lee. 2004. *No future: Queer theory and the death drive*. Durham, NC: Duke University Press.

Edley, Paige P. 2001. Technology, employed mothers, and corporate colonization of the lifeworld: A gendered paradox of work and family balance. *Women and Language* 24, no. 2: 28–35.

Eng, David. L. 2010. *The feeling of kinship: Queer liberalism and the racialization of intimacy*. Durham, NC: Duke University Press.

Fagan, Patrick F. and Robert E. Rector. 2000. The effects of divorce in America. *The Heritage Foundation Backgrounder*: 1373.

Fanon, Franz. 1967. *Black skin, white masks*. Trans. Charles Lam Markmann. New York: Grove.

———. 1968 *The wretched of the earth*. Trans. Constance Farrington. Harmondsworth: Penguin.

Fardy, Kimberly R. 2006. The finer meaning. In Trenka, Oparah and Shin 2006, 57–58.

Ferguson, Ann. 1989. A feminist aspect theory of the self. In Garry and Pearsall 1989, 93–108.

Fessler, Ann. 2006. *The girls who went away: The hidden history of women who surrendered children for adoption in the decades before* Roe v. Wade. London: Penguin.

Fetzer, Philip L. 1999. Child abuse and neglect: A multicultural perspective. In *Morals, marriage and parenthood: An introduction to family ethics*, ed. Laurence D. Houlgate, 175–83. Belmont: Wadsworth.

Fieweger, Mary Ellen. 1991. Stolen children and international adoptions. *Child Welfare* 7: 285–91.

Fineman, Martha A. 1995a. Images of mothers in poverty discourse. In Fineman and Karpin, 1995, 205–23.

———. 1995b. Preface. In Fineman and Karpin, 1995, ix–xiii.

Fineman, Martha A. and Isabel Karpin, eds. 1995. *Mothers in law: Feminist theory and the legal regulation of motherhood*. New York: Columbia University Press.

Flynn, Dennis. (2004) *Severe emotional disturbances in children and adolescents*. New York: Brunner-Routledge.

Former FLDS teens, plus Kody Brown & "Sister Wives." 2011. *Anderson Live*. September 29.

Foucault, Michel. 1967. *Madness and civilization: A history of insanity in the age of reason*. Trans. R. Howard. New York: Random House.

———. 1978. *The history of sexuality*. Vol 1, *An introduction*. Trans. Robert Hurley. New York: Vintage.

———. 1979. *Discipline and punish: The birth of the prison*. Trans. Alan Sheridan. New York: Vintage.

———. 1980. *Power/knowledge: Selected interviews and other writings, 1972–1977*. Trans. and ed. Colin Gordon. New York: Pantheon.

———. 1996. Friendship as a way of life. In *Foucault live: Collected interviews, 1961–1984*. Ed. S. Lotringer, 304–12. New York: Semiotext(e).

———. 2010. *Government of self and others. Lectures at the Collège de France 1982–1983*. Trans. Graham Burchell. New York: Palgrave MacMillan.

———. 2011. *The Courage of Truth: Lectures at the Collège de France 1983–1984*. Trans. Graham Burchell. New York: Palgrave MacMillan.

Franke, Kathleen. 2004. The domesticated liberty of *Lawrence v. Texas*. *Columbia Law Review* 104: 1399–426.

Freud, Anna. 1936. *Ego and the mechanisms of defense*. Trans. Cecil Baines. London: Hogarth.

Freud, Sigmund. 1953–1964. *The Standard Edition of the Complete Psychological Works*. Ed. J. Strachey with Anna Freud, 24 vols. London: Hogarth Press.

Freudberg, Judy and Tony Geiss. 1986. *Susan and Gordon adopt a baby*. Toronto: Random House.

Freundlich, Madelyn. 2000. *Adoption and ethics: The market forces in adoption*. Washington: Child Welfare League of America Press.

Friedan, Betty. 1963. *The feminine mystique*. New York: Dell.

———. 1992. *Willful virgin: Essays in feminism 1967–1992*. Freedom: Crossing Press.

Frye, Marilyn. 1983. *The politics of reality: Essays in feminist theory*. Freedom, NY: Crossing Press.

Fujiwara, T., C. Barber, J. Schaechter, D. Hemenway. 2009. Characteristics of infant homicides: Findings from a U.S. multisite reporting system. *Pediatrics* 124: 210–17.

Garry, Ann and Marilyn Pearsall, eds. 1989. *Women, knowledge, and reality: Explorations in feminist philosophy*. Boston: Unwin Hyman

Gauthier, D. K., N. K. Chaudoir, and C.J. Forsyth. 2003. A sociological analysis of maternal infanticide in the United States, 1984–1996. *Deviant behavior*, 24, no. 4: 393–404.

Gerald, Amy Spangler. 2003. Teaching pregnant: A case for holistic pedagogy. In *The Teacher's body: Embodiment, authority, and identity in the academy*, eds. Diane P. Freedman and Martha Stoddard Holmes, 179–86. New York: SUNY Press.

Gibson, H.B. 1969. Early delinquency in relation to broken homes. *Journal of Child Psychiatry and Psychology* 10, no. 3: 195–204.

Gilman, Charlotte, Perkins. [1892] 1997. The yellow wallpaper. In *"The yellow wallpaper" and other stories*, ed. Paul Negri, 1–16. Minneola, NY: Dover Publications.

———. 1898. *Women and economics: A study of the economic relation between men and women as a factor in social evolution*. Boston: Small, Maynard & Co.

Goddard, L. L. 1996. Transracial adoption: Unanswered theoretical and conceptual issues. *Journal of Black Psychology* 22: 273–81.

Goodwyn, Wade, Howard Berkes and Amy Walters. 2005. Warren Jeffs and the FLDS. National Public Radio, May 3.

Gray, Chris Hables. 2002. *Cyborg citizen*. New York: Routledge.

Griffin, Penny. 2007. Sexing the economy in a neo-liberal world order: Neo-liberal discourse and the (re)production of heteronormative heterosexuality. *British Journal of Politics and International Relations* 9, no. 2: 220–38.

Grimm, Jacob and Wilhelm Grimm. 1978. *Cinderella*. Trans. Anne Rogers. New York: Larousse.

———. 1996. *Snow white*. Avenel: Park Lane Press.

Gross, Terri. 2007. Mark Olsen and Will Scheffer, feeling the "Big love." *Fresh air*, National Public Radio, August 1.

Grossberg, Michael. 1985. *Governing the hearth*. Chapel Hill: University of North Carolina Press.

Grosz, Elizabeth. 1990. *Jacques Lacan: A feminist introduction*. New York: Routledge.

Gurstein, M. 2001. Community informatics, community networks and strategies for flexible networking,. In L. Keeble and B. Loader, eds. *Community informatics: Shaping computer-mediated social relations*. 263–83. London: Routledge.

Haiti nixes kidnapping charges against Americans. 2010. *CBS News*, Apr. 27.

Halberstam, Judith. 1998. Automating gender: Postmodern feminism in the age of the intelligent machine. In *Sex/Machine: Readings in culture, gender and technology*, ed. Patrick Hopkins, 468–83. Bloomington: Indiana University Press.

———. 2005. *In a queer time and place: Transgender bodies, subcultural lives*. New York: NYU Press.

———. 2005. *Perfect madness: Motherhood in the age of anxiety*. New York: Riverhead.

———. 2011. *The queer art of failure*. Durham, NC: Duke University Press.

Hall, G. Stanley. 1904. *Adolescence: Its psychology and its relations to physiology, anthropology, sociology, sex, crime, religion, and education*. Vols. I and II. New York: D. Appleton & Co.

Haraway, Donna. 1991. *Simians, cyborgs, and women: The reinvention of nature*. New York: Routledge.

Harrison, Kate. 1995. Fresh or frozen: Lesbian mothers, sperm donors, and limited fathers. In Fineman and Karpin, 1995, 167–204.

Haslanger, Sally. 1996. Objective reality, male reality, and social construction. In *Women, knowledge, and reality*, eds. Ann Garry and Marilyn Pearsall, 2nd ed., 84–107. New York: Routledge.

Haslanger, Sally and Charlotte Witt, eds. 2005. *Adoption matters: Philosophical and feminist essays*. Ithaca: Cornell University Press.

Hastings, Patti Belle. 2002. *The cyborg mommy: User's manual*. Excerpted in *Art journal* 59, no. 2: 78–87.

————. 2006a. *Gender machine.* http://pattiebellehastings.net/projects/ gendermachine/gender.htm [accessed June 2009].

————. 2006b. *Cyborg mommy.* http://www.icehousedesign.com/cyborg_mommy/home.html [accessed June 2009].

Hayles, Katherine. 1999. *How we became posthuman: Virtual bodies in cybernetics, literature, and informatics.* Chicago: University of Chicago Press.

Heidegger, Martin. [1927] 1996. *Being and time.* Trans. by Joseph Stambaugh. Albany: SUNY Press.

Herring, Scott. 2010. *Another country: Queer anti-urbanism.* New York: NYU Press.

Hobbes, Thomas. [1651] 1904. *Leviathan.* Cambridge: Cambridge University Press.

Holmes, M. 2004. An equal distance? Individualisation, gender, and intimacy in distance relationships. *Sociological Review* 10: 180–200.

Holt, Marilyn Irvin. 1992. *The orphan train: Placing out in America.* Lincoln: University of Nebraska Press.

Homans, Margaret. 2002. Adoption and essentialism. *Tulsa studies in women's literature* 21, no. 2: 257–74.

Honey, Margaret. 1994. The maternal voice in the technological universe. In *Representations of motherhood,* ed. Donna Bassin, Margaret Honey, and Meryle Mahrer Kaplan, 220–39. New Haven: Yale University Press.

Honig, Bonnie. 1996. Difference, dilemmas, and the politics of home. In *Democracy and difference: Contesting the boundaries of the political,* ed. Seyla Benhabib, 257–77. Princeton: Princeton University Press.

————. 2001. *Democracy and the foreigner.* Princeton: Princeton University Press.

Honneth, Axel. 1996. *The struggle for recognition.* Trans. Joel Anderson. Boston: MIT Press.

hooks, bell. 1984. *Feminist theory: From margin to center.* Boston: South End Press.

————. 1990. *Yearning: Race, gender and cultural politics.* Boston: South End Press.

————. 1998. *Talking back: Thinking feminist, thinking black.* Toronto: Between the Lines.

————. 2000. *All about love: New visions.* New York: William and Morrows.

Hübinette, Tobias. 2006. From Orphan trains to baby lifts. In Trenka, Oparah and Shin 2006, 139–50.

Hughes, Judith. 1996. The philosopher's child. In *Children's rights re-visioned,* ed. Rosalind Ekman Ladd, 15–28. New York: Wadsworth.

Human Rights Campaign. 2011. Parenting laws: Joint adoption. http://www.hrc.org/files/assets/ resources/parenting_laws_maps%281%29.pdf [accessed March 2012].

Hylton, Hilary. 2007. The exiled children of Utah. *Time*, September 24.

In God's country. 2007. Directed by John L'Ecuyer. Montreal, Quebec: Canadian Television.

Jackson, Rosie. 1994. *Mothers who leave: Behind the myth of women without their children*. London: Pandora.

Jessop, Carolyn. 2008. Woman learns to be a mother outside FLDS. *The Arizona Republic*, May 11.

Jessop, Carolyn and Laura Palmer. 2008. *Escape*. New York: Broadway.

Johnson, E. Patrick. 2005. "Quare" studies or (almost) everything I know about queer studies I learned from my grandmother. In Johnson and Henderson, 124–60.

Johnson, E. Patrick and Mae G. Henderson, eds. 2005. *Black queer studies: A critical introduction*. Durham, NC: Duke University Press.

Jonsson, Patrik. 2010. Haitian orphans: Americans fight red tape to hasten adoptions. *Christian Science Monitor*, January 21.

Juffer, Femmie and Marinus H. van Ijzendoorn. 2007. Adoptees do not lack self-esteem: A meta-analysis of studies on transracial, international and domestic adoptees. *Psychological Bulletin* 133, no. 6: 1067–83.

Juno. 2007. Directed by Jason Reitman. Los Angeles, CA: Twentieth Century Fox. DVD.

Kalson, Sally. 2009. International adoptions by Americans get really tough. *Pittsburgh Post Gazette*, Mar. 15.

Kanazawa, Satoshi. 2008. The paradox of polygamy: Why most Americans are polygamous. *Psychology Today*, February 17. http://www.psychologytoday.com/blog/the-scientific-fundamentalist/200802/the-paradox-polygamy-ii-why-most-women-benefit-polygamy-an [accessed May 2012].

Kant, Immanuel. [1855] 1933. *Critique of pure reason*. Trans. Norman Kemp Smith. London: Macmillan.

Karas, Beth. 2010. Casey Anthony pleads guilty in check fraud case. *CNN Justice*, January 25.

Kasza, Keiko. 1992. *A mother for Choco*. New York: G.P. Putnam's Sons.

Katz, Michael B. 2001. *The price of citizenship: Redefining the American welfare state*. New York: Henry Hold and Co.

Keller, Holly. 1991. *Horace*. New York: William Morrow and Co.

Kennedy, Randall. 1994. Orphans of separatism: The painful politics of transracial adoption. *American Prospect* 17 (Spring): 38–45.

Kernberg, Otto. 1984. *Severe personality disorders*. New Haven: Yale University Press.

Khokha, Sasha. 1995. Unfolding the complicated layers of racial and cultural identity: Review of *Miscegenation blues: Voices of mixed race women*, ed. Carol Camper. *Sojourner* 20 (May): 22–29.

Kim, Eleana J. 2010. *Adopted territory: Transnational Korean adoptees and the politics of belonging*. Durham, NC: Duke University Press.

Kim, Jae Ran. 2006. Scattered seeds. In Trenka, Oparah and Shin 2006, 151–64.

King, Shani. 2009. Challenging *monohumanism*: An argument for changing the way we think about intercountry adoption. *Michigan Journal of International Law* 30: 413–70.

Kipnis, Laura. 2003. *Against love: A polemic.* New York: Pantheon.

Kirk, David H. and Susan A. McDaniel. 1984. Adoption policy in Great Britain and North America. *Journal of Social Policy* 13, no. 1: 75–84.

Kittay, Eva Feder. 1999. "Not *my* way, Sesha, *your* way, slowly": "Maternal thinking" in the raising of a child with profound intellectual disabilities. In *Mother troubles: Rethinking contemporary maternal dilemmas,* ed. Julia E. Hanigsberg and Sara Ruddick, 3–30. Boston: Beacon Press.

Kleiman, Devra G. 1977. Monogamy in animals. *Quarterly Review of Biology* 52, no. 1 (Mar.): 39–69.

Kline, Marlee. 1995. Complicating the ideology of motherhood: Child welfare law and First Nation women. In Fineman and Karpin, 1995, 118–41.

Koehler, Phoebe. 1990. *The day we met you.* New York: Simon and Schuster.

Kristeva, Julia.1982. *Powers of horror: An essay on abjection.* Trans. Leon Roudiez. New York: Columbia University Press.

———. 1987. *Tales of love.* Trans. Leon Roudiez. New York: Columbia University Press.

———. 1991. *Strangers to ourselves.* Trans. Leon Roudiez. New York: Columbia University Press.

———. 1997. *New maladies of the soul.* Trans. Ross Guberman. New York: Columbia University Press.

Lacan, Jacques. 1977. *Écrits: A selection.* Trans. Alan Sheridan. New York: Norton.

Lasch, Christopher. 1987. What's wrong with the right? *Tikun* 1: 23–29.

Laufer, Moses and M. Égle Laufer. 1984. *Adolescence and developmental breakdown.* New Haven: Yale University Press.

———. 1990b. Sexual indifference and lesbian representation. In *Performing feminisms: Feminist critical theory and theatre,* ed. Sue-Ellen Case, 17–39. Baltimore: John Hopkins Press.

Lavergne, Chantal, Sarah Dufour, Nico Trocmé, and Marie-Claude Larrivée. 2008. Visible minority, aboriginal, and caucasian children investigated by Canadian protective services. *Child Welfare Journal* 87, no. 2: 59–76.

Lawrence v. Texas. 539 U.S. 558 [2008].

LeBlanc, Adrian Nicole. 2003. *Random family: Love, drugs, trouble, and coming of age in the Bronx.* New York: Scribner.

Lee, Ellen. 2008. *Once they hear my name: Korean adoptees and their journeys toward identity.* Silver Spring, MD: Tamarisk books.

Lehr, Valerie. 1999. *Queer family values: Debunking the myth of the nuclear family.* Philadelphia: Temple University Press.

Leonard, Eileen B. 2002. *Women, technology and the myth of progress.* Upper Saddle River, NJ: Prentice Hall.

Lerman, Nina, Ruth Oldenziel, and Arwan Mohum, eds. 2003. *Gender and technology.* Baltimore: John Hopkins Press.

Levin, I. 2004. Living apart together: A new family form. *Current Sociology* 52: 223–40.

Levin-Epstein, Jodie et al. 2002. *Spending too much, accomplishing too little: An analysis of the family formation provisions of H.R. 4737 and recommendations for change.* Washington D.C.: Center for Law and Social Policy.

Levine, Carole. 1990. AIDS and changing conceptions of family. *Milwaukee Quarterly* 68, supp. 1: 33–58.

Lindsey, Duncan. 1994. *The welfare of children.* New York: Oxford University Press.

Locke, John. [1693] 1964. *Some thoughts concerning education.* Ed. F.W. Garforth. Woodbury, NY: Barron's Educational Series.

Loving v Virginia, 388 U.S. 1 [1967].

Lubin, Nancy. 1998. *Pandora's box: Feminism confronts reproductive technology.* New York: Rowan and Littlefield.

Lugones, Maria. 2003. *Pilgrimages/Peregrinajes: Theorizing coalition against multiple oppressions.* New York: Rowan and Littlefield.

Lugones, Maria C. and Elizabeth V. Spelman. 1983. Have we got a theory for you! Feminist theory, cultural imperialism and the demand for "the woman's voice." In *Feminist theory,* ed. Wendy Kolmar and Frances Bartkowski, 17–27. Mountain View: Mayfield.

Luibhéid, Eithne and Lionel Cantú Jr., eds. 2005. *Queer migrations: Sexuality, U.S. citizenship and border crossings.* Minneapolis, MN: University of Minnesota Press.

MacGruder, Joseph and Terry V. Shaw. 2008. Children ever in care: An examination of cumulative disproportionality. *Child Welfare Journal* 87, no. 2: 169–88.

Madge, Clare and Henrietta O'Connor. 2005. Mothers in the making? Exploring liminality in cyber/space. *Transactions of the British Geographers Institute* 30, no. 1: 83–97.

Mahany, Barbara. 2009. Products and ideas for making your home a refuge from the hard times outside. *Catholic Online Magazine,* Mar. 2. http://www.catholic.org/hf/home/ story.php?id=32362 [accessed January 2010].

Mahmood, Saba. 2005. *Politics of Piety: The Islamic revival and the feminist subject.* Princeton: Princeton University Press.

Mahoney, Joan. 1995. Adoption as a feminist alternative to reproductive technologies. In Callahan 1995, 35–54.

Mann, Barton J., Charles M. Bourdin, Scott W. Henggeler, and David M. Blaske. 1990. An investigation of systemic conceptualizations of parent–child coalitions and symptom change. *Journal of Consulting and Clinical Psychology* 58: 336–44.

Martin, Biddy and Chandra Talpade Mohanty. 1986. Feminist politics: What's home got to do with it?" In *Feminist studies/Critical studies,* ed. Teresa de Lauretis, 191–212. Bloomington: Indiana University Press.

McClintock, Ann, Aamir Mufti, and Ella Shohat, eds. 1997. *Dangerous liasons: Gender, nation, and postcolonial perspectives.* Minneapolis: University of Minnesota Press.

McDermott, Patrick. 2006. Disappeared children and the adoptee as immigrant. In Trenka, Oparah and Shin 2006, 105–16.

McDowell, Linda. 1999. *Gender, identity, place: Understanding feminist geographies.* Minneapolis: University of Minnesota Press.

McNamara, Mary. 2010. Television review: "Sister Wives." *Los Angeles Times,* September 25.

Meyer, C. L., M. Oberman, K. White, M. Rone, P. Batra, and T. C. Proano. 2001. *Mothers who kill their children: Understanding the acts of moms from Susan Smith to the "prom mom."* New York: NYU Press.

Miko, Francis. 2000. *Trafficking in women and children: The U.S. and international response.* Washington: U.S. Department of State.

Miller, Jean Baker. 1976. *Toward a new psychology of women.* Boston: Beacon Press.

Miller, Nancy. 1995. Mothers, daughters, and autobiography: Maternal legacies and cultural criticism. In Fineman and Karpin, 1995, 3–26.

Modell, Judith. 1994. *Kinship with strangers: Adoption and interpretations of kinship in American culture.* Berkeley: University of California Press.

Moffat, Tracey. 1994. *Birth certificate.* Reprinted in Trenka, Oparah, and Shin 2006, 164.

———. 2004. *Early theft, draw a map.* Reprinted in Trenka, Oparah, and Shin 2006, 38.

Moraga, Cherríe L. 1993. Queer Aztlán: The re-formation of Chicano tribe. *The last generation: Prose and poetry.* Cambridge, MA: Southend Press.

———. 2011. *A Xicana code of changing consciousness: Writings 2000–2010.* Durham, NC: Duke University Press.

Morgan, D. 1999. Risk and family practices: Accounting for change and fluidity in family life. In *The new family?,* ed. E.B. Silva and C. Smart, 13–30. London: Sage.

———. 2002. Sociological perspectives on the family. In *Analysing families: Morality and rationality in policy and practice,* ed. A. Carling, S. Duncan, and R. Edwards, 147–64. London, Routledge.

Muñoz, José. 1999. *Disidentifications: Queers of color and the performance of politics.* Minneapolis: University of Minnesota Press.

Munsch, Robert. 1982. *Murmel, murmel, murmel.* Toronto, ON: Annick Press.

Murdoch, Iris. 1971. *The sovereignty of good.* New York Shocken Books.

Nancy S. v. Michele D. 228 Cal. App. 3d 831 [1991].

Narayan, Uma. 1999. Family ties: Rethinking parental claims in the light of surrogacy and custody. In *Having and raising children: Unconventional families, hard choices, and the social good*, ed. Uma Narayan and Julia J. Bartkowiak, 65–86. University Park: Pennsylvania State University Press.

National Association of Black Social Workers. [1972] 1974. Position statement on transracial adoption. In *Children and youth in America: A documentary history, vol. 3, parts 1–4*, ed. Robert H. Bremner, 777–80. Boston: Harvard University Press.

———. 1994. *Preserving African-American families*. Washington: NABSW.

Nelson, Kim Park. 2006. Shopping for children in the international marketplace. In Trenka, Oparah, and Shin 2006, 89–104.

Night cries—A rural tragedy. 1989. Directed by Tracey Moffat. Sydney, Australia: Australian Film Commission.

North American Council on Adoptable Children. 1991. *Barriers to same race placement*. St. Paul: NACAC.

Novy, Marianne. 2001. Introduction: Imagining adoption. In *Imagining adoption: Essays on literature and culture*, ed. Marianne Novy, 1–16. Ann Arbor: University of Michigan Press.

Off and running: An American coming of age story. 2009. Directed by Nicole Opper. New York: Nicole Opper Productions.

Oliver, Kelly. 1997. *Family values: Between culture and nature*. New York: Routledge.

———. 2001. *Witnessing: Beyond recognition*. Minneapolis: University of Minnesota Press.

Oliver, Toni and James Freeman. 2007. Family preservation task force report. http://www.nabsw.org/mserver/KinshipCare.aspx [accessed May 2010].

Olson, Mark and Will Scheffer. 2011. "Faith and family." HBO *Big Love* Website. http://www.hbo.com/big-love/index [accessed November 2011].

Oparah, Julia Chinyere, Sun Yung Shin, and Jane Jeong Trenka. 2006. Introduction. In Trenka, Oparah, and Shin 2006, 1–15.

Orphan. 2009. Directed by Jaume Collet-Serra. Burbank, CA: Warner Bros.

Overall, Christine. 1987. *Ethics and human reproduction: A feminist analysis*. Boston: Allen and Unwin.

Overpeck, Mary D. et al. 1998. Risk factors for infant homicide in the United States. *New England Journal of Medicine* 139: 1211.

Pafunda, Danielle. 2010. Occult motherhood, queer time, the oracular orifice: Excursions and bullets. *Montevidayo*. Oct. 12. http://www.montevidayo.com/?p=415 [accessed May 2012].

Palmore v Sidori. 466 U.S. 429 [1984].

Park, Shelley. 1996. Mothering across racial and cultural boundaries. In *Everyday acts against racism: Raising children in a multiracial world*, ed. Maureen T. Reddy, 223–37. Seattle: Seal Press.

———. 2005. Real (m)othering: The metaphysics of maternity in children's literature. In *Adoption matters: Philosophical and feminist essays*, eds.

Sally Haslanger and Charlotte Witt, 171–94. Ithaca, NY: Cornell University Press.

———. 2006. The adoptive maternal body: A queer paradigm for rethinking mothering? *Hypatia* 21 (Winter): 201–26.

———. 2009. Is queer parenting possible? In *Who's your daddy? And other writings on queer parenting*, ed. Rachel Epstein, 316–27. Toronto: Sumach Press.

———. 2010. Cyborg mothering. In *Mothers who deliver: Feminist interventions in public and interpersonal discourse*, eds., Jocelyn Stitt and Pegeen Powell, 57–76. Albany, NY: SUNY Press.

Park, Shelley M. and Cheryl Evans Green. 2000. Is transracial adoption in the best interest of ethnic minority children?: Questions concerning legal and scientific interpretations of a child's best interests. *Adoption Quarterly* 3, no. 4: 5–34.

Pateman, Carole. 1998. *The sexual contract*. Stanford: Stanford University Press.

Pêcheux, Michel. 1982. *Language, semantics and ideology*. New York: St. Martin's.

Peck, Jamie. 2001. *Workfare states*. New York: Guilford Press.

Petrella, Serena. 2005. A geneology of serial monogamy. In *Geneologies of identity: Interdisciplinary readings on sex and sexuality*, eds. Margaret Sönser Breen and Fiona Peters, 169–82. Amsterdam: Rodopi.

Phillips, Randa. 1995. Closed adoption is child abuse. *Sojourner* 20 (May): 1–7.

Pierson, Paul. 1994. *Dismantling the welfare state? Reagan, Thatcher and the politics of retrenchment*. Cambridge: Cambridge University Press.

Polygamists share their faith and family lives. 2011. *Faith matters*. National Public Radio, April 19.

Posner, Richard A. 1992. *Sex and reason*. Boston: Harvard University Press.

Poster, Mark. 2001. *What's the matter with the internet?* Minneapolis: University of Minnesota Press.

Potter, Claire. 2011. The problem that has no name: Or, if computers are a labor saving device, then why am I working a double shift? *The tenured radical*. Chronicle of higher education blog network, Sept 17. http://chronicle.com/blognetwork/tenuredradical/2011/09/the-problem-that-has-no-name-or-if-computers-are-a-labor-saving-device-why-am-i-working-a-double-shift/ [accessed November 2011].

Pratt, Minnie Bruce. 1984. Identity: skin, blood, heart. In *Yours in struggle: Three feminist perspectives on anti-Semitism and racism*, ed. Elly Bulkin, Minnie Bruce Pratt and Barbara Smith, 9–43. Brooklyn: Long Haul Press.

Puar, Jasbir. 2007. *Terrorist assemblages: Homonationalism in queer times*. Durham, NC: Duke University Press.

———. 2011. I would rather be a cyborg than a goddess: Intersectionality, assemblage, and affective politics. *European institute for collective public policies* (January). http://eipcp.net/transversal/0811/puar/en (accessed January 2012).

Quiroz, Pamela Ann. 2007. *Adoption in a color-blind society*. New York: Rowan and Littlefield.

Rakow, Lana & Vija Navarro. 1993. Remote mothering and the parallel shift: Women meet the cellular telephone. *Critical Studies in Mass Communication* 10, no. 2: 144–57.

Rapaport, Elizabeth. 2006. Mad women and desperate girls: Infanticide and child murder in law and myth. *Fordham Urban Law Journal* 33: 527–69.

Rapp, Rayna. 2000. *Testing women, testing the fetus: The social impact of amniocentesis in America*. New York: Routledge.

Reagon, Bernice Johnson. 1983. Coalition politics: Turning the century. In *Home girls: A black feminist anthology*, ed. Barbara Smith, 356–68. New York: Kitchen Table Press.

Reference re: Section 293 of the Criminal Code of Canada, 2011 BCSC 1588 (CanLII), http://canlii.ca/t/fnzqf [accessed June 2012].

Resnick, Phillip J. 1969. Child murder by parents: A psychiatric review of filicide. *American Journal of Psychiatry* 126: 328–30.

Rich, Adrienne. 1986. *Of woman born: Motherhood as experience and institution*. New York: Norton.

Richman, Kimberly D. 2009. *Courting change: Queer parents, judges, and the transformation of American family law*. New York: NYU Press.

Rio, Cecelia. 2008. A treadmill life: Class and African-American women's paid domestic service in the postbellum South, 1863–1920. *Rethinking Marxism* 20, no. 1: 91–106.

Rivaux, Stephanie L., Joyce James, Kim Wittenstrom, Donald Baumann, Janice Sheets, Judith Henry, and Victoria Jeffries. 2008. The intersection of race, poverty, and risk: Understanding the decision to provide services to clients and to remove children. *Child Welfare Journal* 87, no. 2: 151–68.

Robinson, Elise L. E., Hilde Lindemann Nelson, and James Lindemann Nelson. 1997. Fluid families: The role of children in custody arrangements. In Lindemann Nelson 1997, 90–101.

Rodriguez, Juana Maria. 2003. *Queer Latinidad: Identity practices, discursive spaces*. New York: NYU Press.

Rodriguez, Richard T. 2009. *Next of kin: The family in Chicano/A cultural politics*. Durham, NC: Duke University Press.

Rose, Nancy Ellen. 1995. *Workfare or fair work: Women, welfare, government work programs*. New Brunswick, NJ: Rutgers University Press.

Rosenau, Pauline Marie. 1992. *Postmodernism and the social sciences: Insights, inroads, and intrusions*. Princeton: Princeton University Press.

Ruddick, Sara. 1995. *Maternal thinking: Toward a politics of peace*. Boston: Beacon Press.

———. 1997. The idea of fatherhood. In Lindemann Nelson 1997, 205–20.

Rushdie, Salman. 2008. *The wizard of Oz*. BFI film classics. London: British Film Institute.

Rushkin, John. 1867. *Sesame and lilies: Two lectures delivered at Manchester in 1864*. New York: John Wiley and Sons.

Sabra, Samah. 2008. Re-imagining home and belonging: Feminism, nostalgia, and critical memory. *Resources for Feminist Research* 33, no. 1/2: 79–102.

Saunders, Debra J. 2006. Could same-sex marriage lead to legalized polygamy? *Real clear politics,* January 19. http://www.realclearpolitics.com/Commentary/com-1_19_06_DS.html [accessed May 2011].

———. 2010. Polygamy debate evokes familiar rights argument. *San Francisco Gate,* November 28.

Scarr, S. and R.A.Weinberg. 1976. IQ test performance of black children adopted by White families. *American Psychologist* 31, 726–39.

Secomb, Linell. 2007. *Philosophy and love: From Plato to popular culture.* Bloomington: University of Indiana Press.

Sedgwick, Eve. 1990. *The epistemology of the closet.* Berkeley: University of California Press.

Senna, Danzy. To be real. In *To be real: Telling the truth and changing the face of feminism,* ed. Rebecca Walker, 5–10. New York: Anchor Books.

Sepinwall, Alan. 2010. "Big Love" season 4 review. *The Star Ledger,* January 26.

Seuss. 1940. *Horton hatches the egg.* New York: Random House.

Schmidt, Susan Ray. 2009. *Favorite wife: Escape from polygamy.* Guilford, CT: Lyons Press.

Shanley, Mary L. 2001. *Making babies, making families: What matters most in an age of reproductive technologies, surrogacy, adoption, same-sex and unwed parents.* Boston: Beacon Press.

Shaw v Reno. 113 U.S. 2816 [1993].

Simon, R., H. Alstein, and M. Melli. 1994. *The case for transracial adoption.* Washington: The American University Press.

Simon R. and H. Altstein. 2000. *Adoption across borders: Serving the children in transracial and intercountry adoptions.* New York: Rowan & Littlefield.

Simone, Samira J. Harris Whitbeck, and Verjee Zain. 2008. Halted foreign adoptions leave would-be parents in limbo. *CNN News,* May 28.

Smith, Andrea. 2009. *Indigenous peoples and boarding schools: A comparative study.* United Nations permanent forum on indigenous issues. Eighth Session. January 26. http://www.un.org/esa/socdev/unpfii/documents/E_C_19_2009_crp1.pdf [accessed September 2009].

Smith, Stacy Jenel. 2009. Adoption fever among celebrities: Good or bad? *Netscape celebrity.* http://webcenters.netscape.compuserve.com/celebrity/becksmith.jsp?p=bsf_celebadoption [accessed January 2010].

Smithey, Martha. 2001. Maternal infanticide and modern motherhood. *Women and Criminal Justice* 13, no. 1: 65–83.

Spar, Debora L. 2006. *The baby business: How money, science and politics drive the commerce of conception.* Boston: Harvard Business School Press.

Spears, Shandra. 2007. If I pull away. In Trenka, Oparah, and Shin 2006, 117–24.

Spelman, Elizabeth. 1988. *Inessential woman: Problems of exclusion in feminist thought.* Boston: Beacon.

Stanworth, Michelle, ed. 1990. *Reproductive technologies: Gender, motherhood, and medicine.* Minneapolis: University of Minnesota Press.

————. 2000. Birth pangs: Conceptive technologies and the threat to motherhood. In *Feminist theory*, eds. Wendy Kolman and Francis Barkowski, 449–64. Mountainview: Mayfield.

Stasiulis, Daiva and Abigail Bakan. 1997. Negotiating citizenship: The case of foreign domestic workers in Canada. *Feminist Review* 57: 112–139.

Stern, Danielle, Nadia Bruschweiler-Stern, and Alison Freeland. 1998. *The birth of a mother*. Bloomsbury: Basic Books.

Stockton, Kathryn Bond. 2009. *The queer child, or growing sideways in the twentieth century*. Durham, NC: Duke University Press.

Stoler, Laura Ann. 2002. *Carnal knowledge and imperial power: Race and the intimate in colonial rule*. Berkeley: University of California Press.

Stone, Allucquère Rosanne. 2001. *The war of desire and technology at the close of the mechanical age*. Cambridge: MIT Press.

Stone, Linda. 2000. *New directions in anthopological kinship*. New York: Rowan and Littlefield.

Sullivan, H. 1940. *Conceptions of modern psychiatry*. New York: Norton.

————. 1953. *The interpersonal theory of psychiatry*. New York: Norton.

Syfers, Judy. 1971. Why I want a wife. *Ms. Magazine*. December 31.

Tan, Amy. 1989. *The joy luck club*. New York: Putnam

————. 1991. *The kitchen god's wife*. New York: Putnam

Taylor, Charles. 1989. *Sources of the self*. Cambridge: Harvard University Press.

Taylor, Kim. 2010. *Daughter of Zion: My family's conversion to polygamy*. Grants Pass, OR: Rogue Hill.

The moth chase. 2010. Is the grand gesture enough? *Elevating the art of procrastanalysis: Two academics waste time on popular culture.* February 22. http://themothchase.com/2010/02/22/is-the-grand-gesture-enough/ [accessed May 2011].

The 19th wife: A Lifetime movie. 2010. Directed by Rod Holcomb. New York: A&E Networks.

The Omen. 1976. Directed by Richard Donner. Twentieth Century Fox, 1976.

The Orphan Society of America. 2007. On the state of parentless children and youth in the U.S. (August) http://www.theorphansociety.org/pdf/OSAReport_Final%20High%20Res.pdf [accessed February 2009].

Thomson, Judith Jarvis. 1971. A defense of abortion. *Philosophy and Public Affairs* 1, no. 1 (Fall): 47–66.

Turley, Jonathan. 2012. Sister wives: Prosecutors drop investigation of Brown family and promise not to prosecute for polygamy. May 31. http://jonathanturley.org/2012/05/31/ prosecutors-drop-investigation-of-brown-family-and-promise-not-to-prosecute-for-polygamy/ [accessed June 2012].

Trenka, Jane Jeong. 2009. *Fugitive visions: An adoptee's return to Korea*. St. Paul, MN: Graywolf Press.

Trenka, Jane Jeong, Julia Chinyere Oparah and Sun Yung Shin, eds. 2006. *Outsiders within: writing on transracial adoption*. Cambridge: South End Press.

Turner, Ann. 1990. *Through moon and stars and night skies.* New York: HarperCollins.

Udall, Brady. 2010. *The lonely polygamist.* New York: Norton.

Unger, Steven, ed. 1977. *The destruction of American Indian families.* New York: Association on American Indian Affairs.

United Nations. 1987. *The family: Strengthening the family, guidelines for the design of relevant programmes.* New York: United Nations University.

———. 1993. *Hague convention on the protection of children and co-operation in respect of inter-country adoption* (Hague Convention on international adoption). Ser.UN Treaty 31922.

United Nations Children's Fund (UNICEF). 2007. Position on inter-country adoption. http://www.unicef.org/media/media_41118.html [accessed February 2009].

———. 2010. Position on inter-country adoption. http://www.unicef.org/media/media_41918.html [accessed January 2011].

U.S. Bureau of Justice Statistics. 2010. Homocide trends in the U.S.: Infanticide. http://bjs.ojp.usdoj.gov/content/homicide/children.cfm (accessed on October 2010).

U.S. Census Bureau. 2009. *America's families and living arrangements: 2007.* Washington: U.S. Department of Commerce.

U.S. Congress. 1994. *Multiethnic placement act of 1994.* Public Law 103–382.

———. 1996. Personal responsibility and work opportunity reconciliation Act, Public Law 104–193, 110 Stat. 2105.

U. S. Department of Children and Family Services. 1996. Compliance with the multiethnic placement Act. *Policy Guide* 96. 12, 1–3. Washington: U.S. Government Printing Office.

U. S. Department of Health and Human Services, Administration on Children, Youth and Families. 2009. *Child maltreatment 2007.* Washington: U.S. Government Printing Office.

U.S. Department of Health and Human Services, Administration for Children and Families. 2011a. *African American healthy marriage initiative.* http://www.aahmi.net/ [accessed January 2012].

———. 2011b. *Healthy marriage initiative.* http://www.acf.hhs.gov/healthymarriage/index.html [accessed January 2012]

———. 2011c. *Promoting responsible fatherhood:* Federal research site. http://fatherhood.hhs.gov/ [accessed January 2012].

———. 2012. Stepparent adoption. http://www.childwelfare.gov/pubs/f_step.cfm [accessed June 2012].

U.S. Department of Health and Human Services, Administration for Children and Families, U.S. Administration for Native Americans, and the Healthy Marriage Initiative Program. 2011. *Reference guide for Native American family preservation programs.* http://www.acf.hhs.gov/programs/ana/relevant/Documents/ReferenceGuidePres.pdf [accessed January 2012].

U.S. Department of Justice, Office of Juvenile Justice and Delinquency Preven-
accessed June 2012].

Valentine, Gill. 2006. Globalizing intimacy: The role of information and com-
munication technologies in maintaining and creating relationships. *Women's Studies Quarterly* 34, no. 1/2: 365–93.

Virilio, Paul. 1986. *Speed and politics: An essay on dromology*. Trans. Patrick Camiller. New York: Verso.

———. 1995. *La vitess de liberation*. Paris: Galilee.

Wajcman, Judy. 1991. *Feminism confronts technology*. University Park: Penn State University Press.

———. 2004. *Technofeminism*. Cambridge: Polity

Walker, Kristin. 1996. The importance of being out: Sexuality and refugee status. *Sydney Law Review* 18: 568–592.

Waller, Elissa and Lisa Pulitzer. 2009. *Stolen innocence: My story of growing up in a polygamous sect, becoming a teenage bride, and breaking free of Warren Jeffs*. New York: Harper.

Wallerstein, Judith S., Julia M. Lewis, and Sandra Blakeslee. 2000. *The unexpected legacy of divorce: The 25 year landmark study*. New York: Hyperion.

Warner, Michael. 1991. Introduction: Fear of a queer planet. *Social Text* 29: 3–17.

———. 1999. *The trouble with normal: Sex, politics, and the ethics of queer life*. Boston: Harvard University Press.

Weinberg, R. A., S. Scarr and I.D.Waldman. 1992. The Minnesota Transracial Adoption Study: A follow-up of IQ test performance at adolescence. *Intelligence* 16, 117–35.

Weir, Allison. 2008a. Home and identity: In memory of Iris Young. *Hypatia* 23, no. 3 (Sept.–Oct.): 4–21.

———. 2008b. Global feminism and transformative identity politics. *Hypatia* 23, no. 4 (Oct.–Dec.): 110–33.

Weston, Kath. 1991. *Families we choose: Lesbians, gays, kinship*. New York: Columbia University Press.

Whitbeck, Caroline. 1989. A different reality: Feminist ontology. In Garry and Pearsall 1989, 51–76.

Wilkinson, Karen. (1974). The broken family and juvenile delinquency: Scientific explanation or ideology? *Social Problems* 21, no. 5: 726–39.

Williams, Margery. [1922] 1995. *The velveteen rabbit or how toys become real*. New York: Smithmark.

Williams, Patricia. 2009. Eight is enough. *The Nation*, Mar 2.

Wilson, Natalie. 2001. Butler's corporeal politics: Matters of politicized abjection. *International Journal of Sexuality and Gender Studies* 6, no. 1–2 (Apr.): 109–21.

Winnicott, D.W. 1963. Adolescence: Struggling through the doldrums. In *The family and individual development*. 79–87. London: Tavistock.

———. 1986. *Home is where we start from. Essays by a psychoanalyst*. New York: W.W. Norton.

Winnubst, Shannon. 2006. *Queering freedom*. Bloomington: Indiana University Press.

Woliver, Laura R. 1995. Reproductive technologies, surrogacy arrangements, and the politics of motherhood. In Fineman and Karpin, 1995, 346–60.

Woodhouse, Barbara Bennett. 1993. Hatching the egg: A child-centered perspective on parents' rights. *Cardoza law review* 14: 1814–20.

———. 1995. Are you my mother? Conceptualizing children's identity rights in transracial adoptions. *Duke Journal of Gender, Law, and Policy*, 2: 1–21.

Young, Iris Marion. [1984] 1995. In *Feminism and philosophy: Essential readings in theory, reinterpretation, and application*, ed. Nancy Tuana and Rosemary Tong, 407–19. Boulder: Westview Press.

———. 1997. *Intersecting voices: Dilemmas of gender, political philosophy, and policy*. Princeton: Princeton University Press.

Young, Larry J., Wang, Zuoxin. 2004. The neurobiology of pair bonding. *Nature Neuroscience* 7, no. 10: 1048–54.

Ziv, Amalia. 2011. What's queer about queer breeders? Queer Sexualities conference. Lecture, Warsaw, Poland. May 15.

Index

14105065R00187

Printed in Great Britain
by Amazon.co.uk, Ltd.,
Marston Gate.